VISIBLE AT DUSK
Selected Essays

VISIBLE AT DUSK

Selected Essays

BURT KIMMELMAN

With an introduction by Edward Foster

DOS MADRES

2021

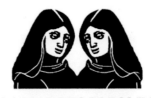

DOS MADRES PRESS INC.

P.O. Box 294, Loveland, Ohio 45140

www.dosmadres.com   editor@dosmadres.com

Dos Madres is dedicated to the belief that the small press is essential to the vitality of contemporary literature as a carrier of the new voice, as well as the older, sometimes forgotten voices of the past. And in an ever more virtual world, to the creation of fine books pleasing to the eye and hand.

Dos Madres is named in honor of Vera Murphy and Libbie Hughes, the "Dos Madres" whose contributions have made this press possible.

Dos Madres Press, Inc. is an Ohio Not For Profit Corporation and a 501 (c) (3) qualified public charity. Contributions are tax deductible.

Executive Editor: Robert J. Murphy

Illustration & Book Design: Elizabeth H. Murphy
www.illusionstudios.net

Cover image: "Mostecká ulice" ("Bridge Street"), Prague
1940, by Karel Plicka
Typeset in Adobe Garamond Pro & Warnock Pro
ISBN 978-1-953252-12-8
Library of Congress Control Number: 2021937235

First Edition

ACKNOWLEDGEMENTS

Earlier versions of these essays appeared in the following publications, revised here with gratitude to their editors.

"The Blues, Tom Weatherly, and the American Canon," *Jacket2*

"Code and Substrate: Reconceiving the Actual," *Humanities*

"The Dead and the Living: Hugh Seidman's Late Poetry," *Jacket2*

"The End of Language: Art, Poetry, and the Materiality of Writing in the Nineties," *Dispatches from the Poetry Wars*

"Enid Dame's Householdry," *Rain Taxi Review of Books*

"Film Noir," *Dichtung Yammer*

"George Oppen, Martin Heidegger, and the Poetry of *Gelassenheit*," *Jacket/Jacket2*

"Letter from Antwerp," *Hyperallergic*

"Lorine Niedecker's Subjective Objects," *Talisman: A Journal of Contemporary Poetry and Poetics*

"Oppen→Schwerner→Heller→Finkelstein (Tracking the Word)," *Shofar: An Interdisciplinary Journal of Jewish Studies*

"Painting, Poetry, Basil King," *Light Abstracts the Smallest Things: The Aesthetics of Basil King* (Talisman House, Publishers)

"Prague and Memory," *B O D Y: A Journal of Literature and the Arts*

"Stephanie Strickland's Universe," *American Book Review*

"Susan Howe, William Bronk, Henry David Thoreau, and the New New England Mind," *Talisman: A Journal of Contemporary Poetry and Poetics*

"Vanessa Place, Kenneth Goldsmith and the Disenchantment of Art," *Dispatches from the Poetry Wars*

Heartfelt thanks to Charles Borkhuis, Jon Curley, Johanna Drucker, Thomas Fink, Michael Heller, Eric Hoffman, Sherry Kearns and Andrew Levy for their suggestions on revising essays for this collection.

Grateful acknowledgement is also being made to the following persons and institutions for use of their respective materials.
Courtesy of Robert Archambeau. Courtesy of the Estate of John Baldessari. Courtesy of Susan Bee. Courtesy of Charles Bernstein. Courtesy of the Estate of William Bronk and Talisman House,

Publishers. Courtesy of the Estate of Robert Creeley and the University of California Press; "A Piece," p. 352, Collected Poems, U of California P, 2006. Courtesey of the Estate of Enid Dame. Courtesy of Johanna Drucker. Courtesy of Norman Finkelstein. Courtesy of Robert Fitterman. Courtesy of Kenneth Goldsmith. Courtesy of Samantha Gorman. Courtesy of Michael Heller. Courtesy of the Estate of Billie Holiday, Commodore Records, and Refried Vinyl. Courtesy of Jenny Holzer, Oren Slor, and the Public Art Fund. Courtesy of Susan Howe. Courtesy of the Estate of On Kawara and the Guggenheim Museum, New York City. Courtesy of Basil and Martha King. Courtesy of the Estate of Barbara Kruger and the Guggenheim Museum, New York City. Courtesy of the Estate of Joseph Kosuth and the Artists Rights Society. Courtesy of the Estate of Ronald Johnson and Flood Editions. Courtesy of the Estate of Donald Lev. Courtesy of the Estate of Sherrie Levine and the Metropolitan Museum of Art, New York City. Courtesy of Tan Lin. Courtesy of James Little. Courtesy of Harryette Mullen. Courtesy of the Estate of Lorine Niedecker. Courtesy of the Estate of George Oppen and New Directions Publishing. Courtesy of M. NourbeSe Philip. Courtesy of Vanessa Place. Courtesy of the Estate of Karel Plicka. Courtesy of The Rubens House, Antwerp. Courtesy of the Estate of Fred Sandback and the David Zwirner Gallery, New York City. Courtesy the Estate of Armand Schwerner. Courtesy of Hugh Seidman. Courtesy of Ron Silliman and The University of Alabama Press. Courtesy of Stephanie Strickland. Courtesy of the Estate of Cy Twombly and the Chicago Art Institute. Courtesy of the Estate of Kara Walker. Courtesy of the Estate of Thomas Weatherly, Jr. Courtesy of the Estate of William Carlos Williams and New Directions Publishing. Courtesy of the Estate of Louis Zukofsky and Musical Observations, Inc.

Author photo: Jane Kimmelman, © 2021.
Cover and book design, Elizabeth Murphy, © 2021.

For Diane and Jane

Tot iorn meillur et esmeri
—Arnaut Daniel

"I got off the subway and climbed the stairs to the street, looking up between buildings at the blue incandescence of dusk."

—William Benton, *Madly*

TABLE OF CONTENTS

INTRODUCTION

Burt Kimmelman possesses an enviable ability to unravel a range of complex subjects. He speaks with equal authority on the diamond district in Antwerp, conceptualism in poetry, Czech culture, film noir and much more. An established and admired poet, he is particularly concerned with how the arts can represent or express the actual, a challenge which he traces from Henry David Thoreau to Ezra Pound and the Imagists through Louis Zukofsky and the Objectivists to contemporary poets such as Michael Heller and Susan Howe. George Oppen plays an especially prominent role in this thinking, with notions about language that Kimmelman effectively compares to Heidegger's.

In so doing, Kimmelman leads his readers through questions involving the materiality of words, their ontological foundations, and problems that follow when a poem is guided by subjectivism. In an essay focused on the New England mind, he draws attention to Howe and William Bronk, not as imitating Henry David Thoreau but as learning from him the importance of sustaining an independent vision. They are, he says, effectively kindred spirits, rejecting academia, which both knew well (Howe's father was a professor at Harvard, where Bronk studied long enough to know he had no desire to continue). Like Thoreau, they knew well the problems "names" might have in seeming to identify what they named. For Thoreau, why should a certain pond be named Flint's, merely because it was on Flint's farm. Thoreau, Howe, and Bronk are drawn to the specificity of things and words rather than what can be made from them.

Kimmelman draws readers into meditations on words and how they come to replace the actual. For example, his essay on Prague compares it to Berlin and Vienna, two places that cultivated an identity linguistically and culturally radically different from Prague's. Language and naming can promote radically different worlds, much as the pond expresses cycles of nature far beyond the farmer's control. Kimmelman quotes Oppen, "[W]ords are the constant enemy: the thing seems to exist because the word does." Taken to an extreme, words become the malleable means with which a culture invents itself.

Kimmelman repeatedly cites Duchamp, whose readymades insist that they be seen for what they are, rather than the means toward some further end. They are the polar opposites of, say, William Wordsworth's "splendor in the grass, . . . glory in the flower" or similar romantic leanings that sought to replace religion with art.

Using words to invent an imagined reality undercuts poetry itself, as Kimmelman argues in his analysis of the work of Lorine Neidecker. Zukofsky claimed that poetry was essentially subjective: that, as Kimmelman puts it, "any hope of arriving at truth, in poetry, appear[s] to depend on a pure subjectivism—that is, on an ideal."

In a world dependent on science and engineering (not incidentally, Kimmelman teaches at a technical university), poetry fails in any thrust toward the actual if it depends on subjectivism—all Wordsworth and no Niels Bohr. But as Kimmelman explains, Niedecker moved from naming to syntactical constructions such that the constructions themselves constituted a poetic act, not simply naming but constituting verbal presentations to be understood like readymades.

Transforming poetry into visual things is itself problematical, however, as he illustrates in "The End of Language," specifically On Kawara's *One Million Years*, which lists, year by year, the million years that preceded the creation of his book. But has Kawara pushed the notion too far? Kimmelman asks, "Do we really read the numbers in Kawara's book?" At what point indeed does a book cease to be a book and become a very different kind of work?

Kimmelman's essay on Enid Dane takes readers in the opposite direction. She is, one might say, a poet of day-to-day life, concerned with her vexed relations with her mother and ways in which these are played out in her relations with her husband as reflected in her poems. Another essay focuses on Tom Weatherly and the embodiment of his Southern culture in his poems and lyrics.

Kimmelman, in short, moves fluidly from one concern to another, and although his mind returns again and again to difficulties inherent in the representation or presentation of the actual, he refuses to be trapped by any single issue. In an essay on Stephanie Strickland, he remarks, "Perhaps poetry is, or is meant to be, about never arriving." Arguments themselves are Kimmelman's ground. He embraces skepticism. Always questioning, never quite at rest, Kimmelman is a Talmudic critic, and his brilliance depends on his restless mind that will not settle for this solution or that. The argument itself is what matters. For the rest, he quotes a very un-Wordsworthian poem by Bronk, "Flowers, the World and My Friend, Thoreau": "It no longer matters what the names of flowers are. / Some I remember; others forget . . . . " It is not the name but the thing itself that matters.

—Edward Foster

LETTER FROM ANTWERP

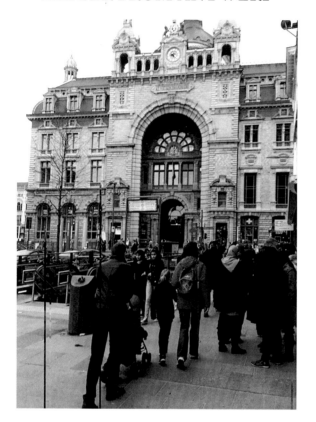

Part I: Trains and Diamonds

The *Rubenshuis* is not a long walk from the *Station Antwerpen-Centraal* (the *Gare Anvers Centrale*, if you like). Antwerp's central train station rises above a wide promenade that can get you there. This marvelously sculpted stone terminal is defined by its gilded domes and clock that keeps accurate time. Its tall paneled windows sit atop graceful arches that frame passage in or out of high doors. The station looks out on the promenade and announces to arriving passengers the phantasmagoria arrayed before it, which is Antwerp.

Leaving the grand station, you enter into the flow of life. Beyond the main entrance, steps lead belowground to the metro. Further on, trams of various designs and sizes glide on street-level tracks heading in a number of directions, drop off or pick up passengers at a number of stops. Thousands of people walk about, on a gray and chilly Friday.

The promenade is quite broad, most of it meant for mingling. A single lane to one side is dedicated to automobiles, another to motorbikes and bicycles—so what is actually a boulevard stretching on and on feels and looks like a huge plaza filled by people who seem mostly to be at leisure, who are casually eating, talking, strolling about, dressed in many fashions and speaking in a number of languages, who are alive to everyone else, who are alive in the moment—as might be expected of a large port city. Some people are entering or exiting fast food joints (like a *Quik* for hamburgers) grouped along one side of the wide concourse. On the other side people sit in *brasseries* indoors or at *plein aire* tables with electric-coil heaters overhead for late winter evenings, drinking coffee, beer or wine, perhaps eating a pastry. Waiters thread themselves among them. Across a slender lane from there are shops selling mobile phones and the like. The lane leads to lesser streets of small stores and restaurants.

If you were on your way to the *Rubenshuis* (the Rubens House), coming from the magnificent station, you would enter into this sea of humanity, head up the promenade and, in a multitude, traverse an equally wide thoroughfare reserved solely for the purpose of getting cars, trucks and motorcycles from one side of the city to the other. Hundreds of us form to get to the other side at a single traffic light, where we'll enter a new portion of our boulevard, set up for more serious shopping—an out-and-out, no-apologies, open-air wide walkway framed by fancy and faux-fancy department stores—some of which are in older buildings decorated with stone filigree and on upper stories gentle statuary. There are also newer structures of glass and steel, the curse of the International Style's afterglow, rising up before our eyes. We have to pick our way around some construction sites as we realize that those lovely statues will soon tumble into oblivion.

Behind us, in the distance, is the train station. To be amazed by it from afar, especially once having sighted the department stores ahead of us, was to savor how this historic structure made of stone, glass, iron and gold remains as a paean to another era. In its utter grandeur, its delicate yet massive beauty, the station commands the vista so very comfortably. My American-tourist's too-quick, casual glance backward nearly tricked me into thinking that a soaring gothic cathedral was what had inaugurated the bustling plaza we'd just left behind. In reality the vibrant sections of the immense terminal—the building articulated, vivid, in its splendidly tall domed towers—are a unique blend of classical Roman and Italian Renaissance styles. One might imagine the onlooker's sense of anticipation as the building's design became ever more palpable, more real, once construction began over the course of a decade starting in 1895.

In its entirety the station includes a long train shed built later, which communicates with the ticketing area in the stately stone edifice that now anchors this even more massive structure when seen from a distance. The hugely tubular shed, its design and feel of a more recent time, is nevertheless quite graceful. It contains multiple levels of track and pedestrian platforms and walkways taking people past rows of cafés and jewelry shops, some selling expensive diamonds. This long conduit, as it were, extends about a quarter mile. Attachment is not really the appropriate word to describe how it coexists with the magnificently old-world lofty structure at one end of it—the older building is what holds everything in place. The much more extensive train shed (here, too, the term belies the experience of it) is truly complementary. Inside it a steel-and-glass dragon's tail gently undulates under its elongated dome; its passages gradually weave up or down, with stairways composing both horizontal and vertical events.

Yet it's the grandeur of the original creation—its self-consciously beautiful stone- and ironwork, its own huge scale outside and in where there are high vaulted, decorated ceilings—which nowadays decrees the promenade and beyond that the shoppers boulevard. In ambition it must have been meant to be comprehended as one of the world's great landmarks, a historic architectural site, and in fact it is. I can't help but think that Sebald missed the point of it in his novel *Austerlitz*, seeing it as a monument to Belgium's colonial triumph. It might be understood as that (even if Leopold II's Congo was his own private operation—to say nothing of how profoundly duplicitous, ruthless, and morally criminal it was). The sheer splendor of the station exudes its turn of the twentieth-century, giddy sense of confidence and expectation. The sensuous domed towers intend upward, as do Europe's great cathedrals. Yet this heartbreakingly beautiful old building, which is perhaps sui generis, does not derive from the Middle Ages. Hart Crane's notion of a hymn might come to mind (in *Brooklyn Bridge* the "immaculate sigh," the "prayer") except that this "cathedral" means to mark time instead of eternity. I suspect that the present boulevard, for all its sense of holiday, was not much anticipated, however. Was it merely careless civic planning that the station, this great work of art, really, sends newly arrived passengers out onto a most worldly pilgrimage culminating in the tawdry, twenty-first-century urbanity of shopping within voids formed by glass-and-steel boxes ("Ik shop, dus ik ben," "Je fais du shopping, donc je suis")?

Diane and I had come to Antwerp particularly to explore the city's famous Diamond Quarter. So before setting out to see some art, having disembarked at the breathtaking station, we exited through the great main entrance, then veered sharply left. The diamond district is just there. The perimeter of the Jewish Quarter, of which the diamond district is a part, extends past the train shed, the station's side entrances pacing the street alongside. We followed Pelikaanstraat (Pelican Street)—delineating one of the station's long edges beyond the train shed—as we peered, along the way, into a neighborhood whose streets were populated mostly by Hasidim, and whose architecture contrasted sharply with the nearby station.

This area's collage of workaday plate glassed shops, and older stone facades, would be pretty much replicated in the diamond district, once we turned back to enter it. The urbanscape in both Quarters was an abrupt change.

From the luxurious terminal, we had merely to cross the narrow street to experience the difference. In fact, the Diamond Quarter is slightly ramshackle in appearance. And the juxtaposition of tasteful and drab was not merely a visual dramatization of the struggle between older and newer societies—the train station's entrance, the Jewish Quarter's dowdy structures, the Diamond Quarter's unprepossessing diamond exchanges and other buildings (to call them unremarkable would be kind), later the promenade that leads to the garish shoppers walk, finally the stunningly beautiful and lavish Rubens House. In what is actually a tiny area, whose buildings and streets reveal a studied plainness, the largest and most important diamond business in all the world is being conducted— the trading of diamonds, also their selection, classification, cleaving, cutting and polishing—all within a few city blocks. While, in Antwerp, the people who work in either industrial or precious diamonds are not exclusively Jewish, furthermore, the business is dominated by Hasidic and, to a lesser extent, other Jews. (In recent years this is no longer quite the case—a sizable number of Indians having joined in, yet nearly all of Antwerp's Jews run a business whose annual worth is about forty billion dollars.) Most transactions are conducted in Yiddish.

As we strolled the Diamond Quarter's streets, which looked quite mundane, we came to realize we were inside a *cordon sanitaire* whose demarcation was invisible (we didn't notice the eruv circling the two Quarters together —a six foot-high wire meant to indicate to Jewish inhabitants the limits of their zone—a reminder not to neglect their daily religious duties).

Hints of security procedures were noticeable throughout. What we construed (later to read about it) made me think of how different the atmosphere in Manhattan is. My memories of walking along 47th Street, going back to the days of the wonderful Gotham Book Mart, include the prominent diamond shops 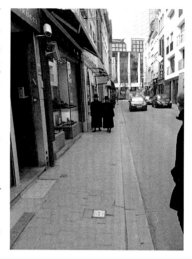 there, the jewelry trade's outsized presence while sharing pedestrians' attention with other commercial activities on the street and in shops. Today, that's pretty much the same state of affairs. Not so Antwerp's Diamond Quarter, which is euphemistically referred to as "the square mile."

We took some photos of one another in front of a diminutive, narrow synagogue wedged between two unremarkable, squat buildings. Ambling up the street afterward, my phone in hand, snapping the occasional picture, I noticed a large, clean shaven man heading toward me, wearing a yarmulke and thin headset with a microphone wire extending along his jaw; he was carrying a small bag. He missed a step in his deliberate gait once he fixed upon my phone, then pivoted to enter an office building nearby. Further on, a Hasidic man stepped briskly out of a doorway and saw me just as I saw him. Our eyes met—

sort of. I looked into his; he looked at me but his eyes were without expression. There was an invisible wall between us, as he surveyed the scene with me in it. If he knew I was a Jew it would not have mattered. (I confess to my voyeuristic delight at seeing another man in full religious black garb, riding a bicycle up to one of the diamond exchanges. If there had not been a

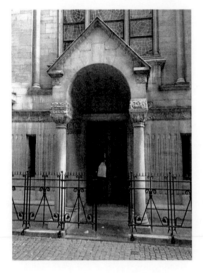

modest sign to indicate what it was, you'd never have realized the gravity of the place. Admission to the exchanges requires a full background check, surrender of passport, and passing through a metal detector.) We were definitely no longer on 47th Street, or in Borough Park for that matter.

We entered a gallery of shops and eateries, putting ourselves down at a *brasserie* whose tables and chairs spilled into the corridor. A diamond polisher with dirty apron and hands came by on his break, indulging himself in friendly banter with the staff of our lunch place where we were now having soup (served with warm pita!) that could have come from my grandmother's kitchen in Brownsville, Brooklyn a long time ago. The menu was comprised entirely of Hebrew. Signage on the walls was in Dutch and French. More people eating lunch with us were Jewish than were not. The language mostly spoken was Yiddish. Many other people, representing all continents, but especially from south Asia, were eating there too, conversing over their meals. People came and went after their meal, maybe sauntering up to someone at another table, to shake hands and chat with what we thought, given what we'd observed on the street, was a surprising ease. Some of these conversations might have been a prelude for a future deal.

It was Friday midafternoon. The rather late, and leisurely, lunch-taking by a good deal more men than women, came at the end of the work week; the diamond trading had ceased in preparation for the sabbath to begin at sundown. At a kosher sushi place next door, no one was ordering the "Titanic" bowl (a slightly-off, cultural translation, not quite on a par with the infamous Ginza department store that had displayed a crucified Santa Claus at Christmas time). The humongous "boat" of fish rolls could be had for the everyday price of a hundred twenty-five euros. Who would have the time to digest such a meal on a stop after work, before heading home for Friday evening's boiled chicken (the fewer women in the gallery were home cooking, with the kids)?

Part II: More Diamonds, & the Jewish Diaspora

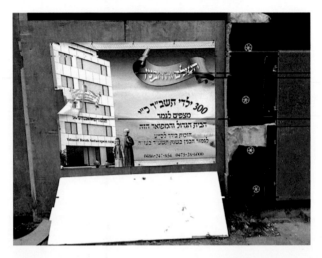

The Jewish Diaspora, and the diamond trade, are not synonymous. Their stories don't merely intertwine, either. Together, they've given rise to two cultural and literary archetypes, the Wandering Jew and the Court Jew. Is it just coincidence that the historic world routes of the diamond trade line up, on a map showing Jewish settlements? The reason why diamonds have been brokered, bought and sold as well as cloven, cut and polished by Jews, it's said, lies in the nature of the Diaspora itself.

Far greater in value than their actual size suggests, diamonds can easily be hidden for transport. Diamonds have been highly valued by Jews for at least as long as they've had to leave their homes on short notice. Once resettled somewhere, newly arrived, those not involved in diamonds have often found the processing of the stones to be conducive to their lifestyle, so the work gets readily taken up. Two other, basic, reasons account for the many Jews involved in the business. Some of the tasks involved in processing diamonds can be learned quickly, and they can be completed at home. The piece work has allowed the religiously observant to forgo toil on a non-Christian Sabbath or religious holiday. There is also, perhaps needless to say, the fact that, in times past, Jews were usually banned from most professions.

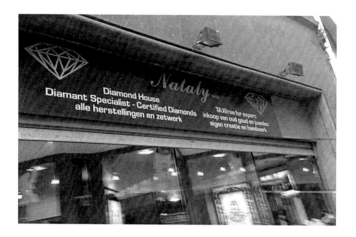

There is one more, crucial, element still to be considered when thinking about diamonds and Jews. The typical practice of trading diamonds has always necessitated the diamonds' actual changing of hands many times. In this situation, *trust* is of the utmost importance. Extensions of credit—not by banks insisting on a lot of oversight as well as onerous interest rates—required trust.

Diamonds not only need to be held in the hand. They also must be scrutinized by the human eye. They come in sixteen thousand varieties. No technology exists for evaluating or sorting them. Diamond deals involve the hand-to-hand sale of batches of stones, numerous varieties in each batch. A community of trust is of absolute necessity to conduct these deals. One characteristic of an orthodox Jewish community is that it's closed. The nature of this kind of group, moreover, is that it needs trust, and so the group nurtures trust among its members, faithful people. A good number of Jainists have emigrated to Antwerp, mostly from Gujarat. They, too, live closely bound to each other. Thus the Jews, and these Indian members of the Jain sect, make up the core of the city's diamond activity.

Eighty-five percent of the world's diamonds changes hands on a single, small street, *Hoveniersstraat*, in the Antwerp Diamond Quarter. This was where we enjoyed our afternoon soup. It's said that the Gujaratis also conduct their transactions in Yiddish. The flavor of that soup, and its consistency, were to me like the *mama loschen* I listened to when I was being fed as a small child. (I almost hear that language in the Flemish-Dutch spoken all over Flanders, occasionally in Brussels.) This was soup prepared by my mother, or her eastern European Ashkenazi mother. Surely this recipe was brought to Antwerp well more than a 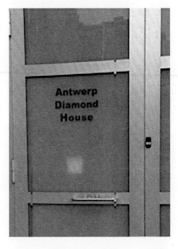 century ago, by Poles and their erstwhile neighbors, who were on their way across the Atlantic—yet they never departed, staying to work in the diamond trade. Some shops sell Polish food in the Jewish Quarter.

Records show Jews living in Antwerp at least as early as the thirteenth century, possibly due to their having been thrown out of France and England. The city would come to be the European heart of commerce, over the course of several periods, and once many of the Iberian Peninsula's Jews had settled in Antwerp and Amsterdam, after their expulsion. (Until the silting of its waterways, Bruge was most prominent, and it was there that a breakthrough method for polishing diamonds caused a great increase in the trade.) Following the mid fourteenth-century's Black Death, the Jews were kicked out of the city, yet these "Portuguese New Christians" were welcomed back, a little more than a century later. The Sephardic community in Antwerp, involved in diamonds at that time, raised diamond polishing to a fine art, the stones' inherent beauty much more apparent. The alluring jewels stimulated greater trade.

Eventually, Antwerp's Jewish population and diamond industry would shift to Amsterdam. Yet there were also *Sephardim* in London (later, Ashkenazi Jews lived in both London and Amsterdam, as well as Antwerp). The extent of the Jewish presence in the diamond trade was made dramatically plain to all in the mid seventeenth century, when Jewish resettlement in England caused a serious depression in the Low Countries' trade—at a point in time when England, through its British East India Company that permitted individuals to operate, was enjoying greater access to the Indian diamond supply. The majority of the English diamond importers were Jews, as were the exporters in India.

The diamonds were sent from England to Amsterdam for cutting. After the French Revolution, though, Jews were once again able to get a toehold in Antwerp. The formation of the Belgian nation state, in 1830, and a newly relaxed regulatory climate, attracted larger numbers of Jewish diamond workers and traders to the city, who were Amsterdam migrants. The Belgian diamond community

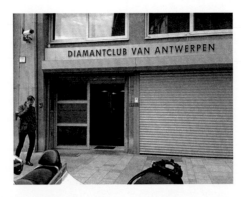

swelled dramatically in the late nineteenth century when the eastern European Jews, bent upon relocating to the Americas or Australia by way of Antwerp, settled there instead. It wasn't long before a newly increased demand for diamonds, around the world, was met by supplies of the raw stones now from South Africa rather than India or Brazil.

Decades later, with the help of Flanders' Nazi sympathizers, Antwerp's Jews met their fate in Auschwitz, the Germans having all but eradicated them—but not right away, due to the diamond trade. Out of this debacle arose Israel's diamond industry—a fit rejoinder. Yet Antwerp's charisma would prove irresistible. After the war, with concerted efforts, the Antwerp diamond juggernaut was back to its former prowess and then some.

Part III: Rubens

As for the rise of modern Antwerp, the story of its art and architecture—are they merely tangential to the histories of diamonds and the Diaspora? How amazing that diamonds tell so much of Antwerp's story, the story of an uniquely urban dynamic—an admixture of businesses, peoples, languages, thrilling and scary energy, graceful and gorgeous architecture, as well as garish and tawdry architecture, art and artlessness, possibly thoughtlessness, verve. I understand now how the poet Armand Schwerner, who migrated to America (his ancestors were rabbis), could have been imbued with, like the city itself, an astonishing energy to be found in his psychologically deep, riotous epic *The Tablets*—almost an outlandishness, certainly a daring originality. The fact that he came from here is obvious to me. It's not merely a matter of his multilingualism or unique and far-reaching imagination. There's also his supple regard for beauty, which is not without its perils, and there's his irony.

Diamonds are cut and polished to a perfection. Their designs bring into being paradigms of exquisite expression. And then there's a diamond's obduracy in and of itself, its unforgiving tangibility, also responsible for its huge value. Diamonds are our aesthetic and material facticity like nothing else, for better or worse. Ephemeral beauty is caught in the diamond jewel, held there.

The Central Station is a work of perfect beauty. The boulevard proceeding from it seems to have emerged from this city's superlative edifice, which is a perfection not merely in the etymological sense of *completion* but

15

rather in the sense of *consummation*, in any case an acme of beauty. The station sits flush against the Diamond Quarter—whose buildings, outdoor walks, passageways indoors, are without glory or grace. Yet the station and the Quarter each bless human industry and ingenuity, as was epitomized by the industrial age's railroads and, more prophetically, the agrarian past that unwittingly led to postmodernity's magical ride into insubstantiality—up through the point of our digital revolution that values ephemera such as the glow of light, color, emitted from mobile phones and from polished, smartly cut diamonds, yet in another way the haunting coloring and sense of light in Rubens' still lifes (in still another, the products on display, their saturated colors, to be purchased from the equally throw-away box stores on the shopping boulevard so near to the grand train station).

The humble, undersized synagogue we photographed in the Diamond Quarter (shall we compare it with the newly restored, opulent, magisterial synagogue lavishly feted in Berlin some years ago?) is nevertheless the evidence of Jews living openly as Jews (not *conversos*, "Portuguese New Christians"). The diminutive synagogue stands just a single street over from the great, towering, majestic, decorative, utterly lush and otherwise gorgeous, central station—the city's jewel. These two buildings were erected at the same time. Can this coincidence, too, be simply a paradox?

This fundamental juxtaposition of a stone-built, eventually a religiously built, graceful world being celebrated by the station, and an unrelentingly, programmatically, boring and seemingly self-diminished, world being portrayed assiduously through the architecture and mannerisms in the Diamond Quarter (perhaps equally religious), serves as a corollary to the cacophony of spoken and written languages, dress codes, skin colors, body languages, and buying habits to be found on the promenade and shopper's boulevard. This is where the Rubens House survives, within this international city. The juxtaposition of the crowded shopping district and the quietude of the Rubens' home is in itself the stark contrast progress always presents us.

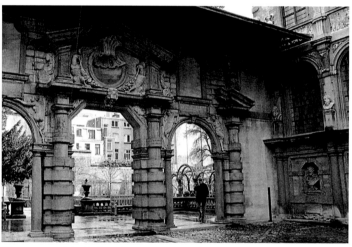

The portico of the Rubens House, Antwerp (Courtesy Ramón, @Wikimedia)

Had you not the street address for the *Rubenshuis* you could miss it, except for a glass rectangular box set dead in the middle of the walk in front it, off from the stores. Cafés have been placed on either side of it. To enter what was actually the Rubens' house, you must purchase admission across the way, in this see-through container. Inside it, the gift shop is transparently partitioned in *trompe l'oeil* fashion. Then you step back outside to enter the artist's early seventeenth-century, sumptuous world, which is a world of another order. The rooms of the house, all the spaces inside and out, are a sanctuary.

Rubens lived and worked here most of his adult life. He and Isabella Brandt, his first wife, bought the house in 1610. Some land came with it. They added extensions and

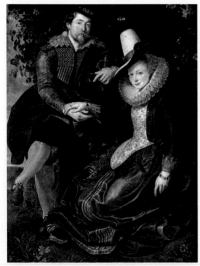

a garden pavilion, all of which he designed. The enlargement, and accompanying outdoor arrangements, combine the aesthetics of Roman antiquity and the Italian Renaissance (as would happen later in the train station). He was a very wealthy man. You might wonder if his self-centered immodesty in life—not in his art—helped him to accrue the many paintings,

Double Portrait of Rubens & Isabella Brandt, 1609-10 (Wikimedia)

sculptures, fine furniture and trappings he and Isabella came to own. He was a collector who filled the spaces with widely esteemed, increasingly valuable art, until his death three decades after they moved in. Their collection has been replaced with his own creations.

This old-world home of equally sublime paintings, drawings, sculptures and furniture has been protected against its neighborhood's detritus of temporaneity, which consists of our new First World. We figured out, in the late afternoon, how to get to what was their house (a diamond in the rough, so to speak) where the Rubens raised their children and collected art whose imagery was of another consequence than what had held our attention along the way. I don't wish to credit him for the flourishing of Antwerp. Instead, it seems to me that Rubens was its beneficiary. (Nor do I credit the mostly Jewish world-wandering diamond workers who insisted on a life in Antwerp, over the course of several historical periods, for all the city's outsized financial presence.) Yet, like diamond jewels,

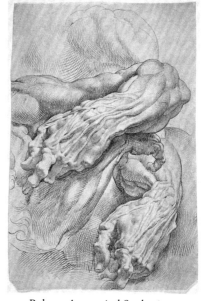

Rubens, Anatomical Study *circa.* 1600-1605 (courtesy Met Museum)

Rubens' pictures are *present*, have a *presence*. And it can be subtly disturbing. Especially viewing his still lifes, their carefulness and delicacy, I wondered if he had wished to demonstrate a painterly perfection—no easy feat, since the images of the various objects in these paintings (a dead rabbit or pheasant, fruit, bowls and cups) must somehow have needed to be assembled so they'd not look arranged. At the same time, in his paintings each of them seems to exist on its own, apart from the ensemble. This paradox is immediately striking, as palpable as the things themselves. Or perhaps in them there's not so much a disturbance as that visual conundrum. On the other hand, in maybe the least likely or explicit way, another of his paintings unnerves in a manner not dissimilar to, finally, the juxtapositions of the Antwerp cityscape, thus intentionally telling a story, at first not to be detected, about the costs of civilization.

One of his sprawling oils is a large tableau tilted at an angle toward the visitors below from its room's high ceiling. (The picture plays its part in one of the grander rooms all now stuffed with his art.) The disturbance in this picture is quite calculated. The painting's narrative consists of some purebred beagles, presumably from an estate situated outside the frame, who are attacking two large bears, one male and one female, just at the edge of some woods. The bodies of the upright bears, even their faces, in some way express the moment of recognition that they've found themselves in a life-and-death struggle. Before they know it, they're besieged. The dogs are all over them. A few have been flung to the side, bleeding, wounded. Others have blood in their mouths, in their fangs.

For all the dramatic violence in the story, the subtleness of the imagery does not go unnoticed. Like the contrasting dark browns and bright cerulean, red or other attention-getting hues in many of Rubens' still lifes—a spot of bright blood at the mouth of a dead rabbit hanging upside down, or in the festive plumage of a wild bird pierced by an arrow, now lying upon a kitchen table—the compelling, comfortable, ordered world of Antwerp comes into relief. We're reminded that the artist has done this. Indeed, we've been led to him in our journey from the train station—just as much as through our appreciation of his quiet flamboyance.

Domesticated dogs—soft and cuddly to the touch, who in their look express the greatest empathy, in Rubens' depiction, marked by the bright blood of the bears (as well as their own)—have been drawn out from the estate to lose all sense of everything around them. They are aware of nothing else, can think of nothing else, other than the slaying of these great beasts—their prey. Surely he wanted us to wonder how these dogs, bred for domesticity, the most obedient of all creatures, can kill, still do possess such ferocity, such bestiality, within them. This Rubens brings off with the greatest aplomb.

What one realizes about living in Brussels for a while (as we are, or in Ghent where I'm teaching, or in Antwerp) is that everything here works. There is a calmness. Many people in Brussels keep pet dogs they take everywhere, frequently on the metro. These dogs are invariably well behaved, totally quiet. I have thought of how dogs at home behave too often, barking at passersby, sometimes snarling at other dogs or even at us. A dog's empathy involves absorbing, inhabiting its human's emotional state and point of view. Do we Americans wear our savagery openly, undisguised?

I write this as Europe, particularly Belgium, makes ready for the centennial of what in America is still called "The Great War," more usually "World War I," yet referred to here by the possibly sanitized "14-18." The brevity alone of this name, its casualness, seems to me so incongruous to the enormity of Belgium's suffering in that war (the title of *the* great Belgian novel is *The Sorrow of Belgium*). The Belgians' agony in that conflagration is obvious to anyone who visits the Royal Museum of Military History in Brussels, or tours Iepers (Ypres), which was totally razed. The war in 1914 quickly spread throughout Flanders and elsewhere—the Germans never imagined the Belgians would not give way to their request to march through the country, to attack France. This rare act of principled bravery—the Belgian's government's communique the morning following the German request—was to garner its terrible result. In the centennial exhibits, the war erupts out of a European dormancy, overnight, seemingly all at once, horrible and senseless, and everyone knew it was pointless yet ineluctable, a drama played to its awful end.

Anyway, here the trains usually run on time.

February, Train to Ghent

Strand of empty
trees in a green
field, muddy ditch
near – passing my

window – they are
there and I am
here, the warm car
rocking gently,

the muffled pitch
of wheels on steel
tracks, civilized
travelers reading

their books or phones,

out of the rain,
a gray day like
the day before.

PAINTING, POETRY, BASIL KING

after Kim Lyons

Basil King and I were talking about art, over lunch in a Park Slope café some decades ago. "Everything comes from the circle," he said. He then drew a circle on a napkin—effortlessly, all in one go. The circle he drew was perfect. I don't mean to say merely that it was *complete* (*perfect* from the classical Latin *perfectus*) or just that it was immaculately even. There was the sheer ease of his circle. There was, I felt, its *presence*. It seemed as if, simply, he was making evident something he knew was there.

Is an invisible circle any less present? Is the circle, even if invisible, nevertheless the source of, let's say, an abstract image? Could King have been thinking of this? I later would wonder, after our lunch, about that.

Does the circle make possible one of Jackson Pollock's drip paintings, for instance? Pollock must have wanted to create something that existed in only two dimensions. And in the drip paintings he avoided even the trace of perspective. There is no point of attention in them—as in the phrase "all-over painting." Is there an *absent* point of attention, though?

Would King say that the circle underlies the painting's aura, its manifestation of an immanence? If we sense a painting's immanence—if we are aware of, *in* the painting, an immanence—is that the unseen circle? I could ask King about this. But that day, in that café, he'd drawn the circle on a napkin. And he'd said what he said. The circle *was* complete.

A tautology is circular. A circle need not be tautological. I have begun to consider if King also meant to say that the circle underlies his poems as well. His work as a poet came after he had arrived at both a visual and tactile language.

When he was still a young man, not yet writing consistently or truly seriously—that is, before writing had become a vocation for him—King found himself in the throes of a crisis. He was no longer able to paint in the abstract. So many artists around him, including the Abstract Expressionists he hung around with (Pollock one of them), had abjured the figure.

More than a year later, the crisis had run its course, as King's archetypal figure emerged. It had come into view. Its presence was not unlike that circle on the napkin over lunch. King's figure had coalesced.

It sponsored a range of uniquely provocative images. At times they were classically beautiful or they were, otherwise, equally arousing, or disturbing in their subliminally intriguing as well as searching qualities.

Yet, oddly—in thinking about the immanent circle—I would say that the ground in his post-abstract paintings is what became vital. Sometimes his figures are quasi-abstract; these tease us with the possible disappearance of the figure. The figure is there, actually. We are always being drawn into a ground, though—the ground in which the figure, with all its manifest certainty, resides.

The circle calls us—obviously so in his paintings of birds or baseball players or in his portraits; the people there in the painting await our attention. The ground holds them, however, in their utter presence. If we look we might take notice. We are called to that. Surely any artist is aware of the ground. Pollock's abstractions lack it, but the lack was intentional, strategic. We might consider it to have been what we are

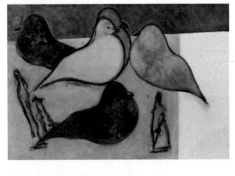

Basil King, *Birds & Company (Cousin Green)*, 2018 (mixed media on canvas)

meant to realize when viewing them, even if we do not. All the same, the figure-ground relationship, in one of King's mature paintings, is singularly dynamic. It can, sometimes, threaten to dominate the painting's narrative.

We need not bother to think about how his foray into abstraction might have prepared him for what came after. King's paintings stand forth uniquely. And, at least for me, their narratives are the least of the experience of them. Nonetheless, the narratives in King's paintings are an element—a peculiar one—within a larger, especially dynamic, gestalt.

How this is so may be explained when taking his poems into account. King became a serious, practicing—in the sense of the work that was entailed every day—writer. This was after his mature figurative painting had already started to emerge. So, where is the ground and what does it do in one of his poems? And how might his poems help us to comprehend that peculiar ground-figure energy in his paintings?

I venture to say that readers might see his poems as unique among the writings of poets—as well as among the poems of those artists or art critics who attempt to write poetry— indeed, whose poems I find compelling particularly for reasons having to do with their awareness of the spatial plane (timelessness and silence are elements of that plane).

A Basil King poem continually digresses from a center line that is most often not actually stated. There is a kind of narrative in the poem, yet it is one we may sense could in itself invent, or reinvent, the center line we have begun to hold onto in our minds. We can reimagine that center line.

In this, let us call it, non-structure, there is overall a constant reconjuring of the direction we believe the narrative is about to take. This reconjuring, or we could call it perhaps a refiguring, undermines our otherwise sense of a coherence. And we sense that, moreover, as a threat to the coherence.

Thus a structure/non-structure is held in place—by what? It is held by the work of art's immanence. The immanence, furthermore, seems to be the essence of digression.

Is this a circle? Is the circle *there*, undetected, unseen? Does the visual form of the circle imply departure from *form*, as might be derived out of some Platonic sense of form?

The coherence, a coherence not really manifest on the page, partakes of an immanence we come to apprehend. It is not

27

that King's poem starts over and over *in medeas res* (which, in a way, it does). Rather, it is that the poem has turned out to be something a reader might have thought of but did not—the poem wending on, in a kind of dalliance, not at all lost somewhere although not at all interested in heading toward some destination possibly to be imagined.

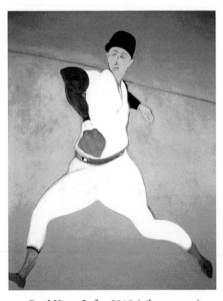

Basil King, *Lefty*, 2018 (oil on canvas)

In this manner, the poem always heads for home. However, like the destabilized figure King's painting contains, there is no home. There is a ground in the King poem, just like the ground in the King painting. The ground is unmentioned, while it holds the world—precariously, we may feel—in an unlikely stasis. Is what is most disturbing, in King's paintings, the profound yet delicate sense that our condition is homelessness? And is this how we somehow continue on, perhaps with a subtly unnerving, and at the same time engrossing, restlessness? And, in King's invitation to enter into the subliminal, perhaps to contemplate it, do we also detect a yearning for a home?

Or, just the opposite, is there a radically determined undermining of order, the order of the psyche ultimately, which may be most disturbing in a number of the paintings? I am not sure I find this undermining of some posited order in his poems. Even so, like the paintings, a King poem is not quite amusing. Neither is it a meditation. Nor is it a story. While it tolerates a reader finding a comfort in the assumption that the poem has a story to tell, not only is the story never to be told; the story is not the point. To be sure, the reader may likely conclude that there is no story at all, no story available.

Is it as if the reader is falling through time, groundless? There is an unseen—there is an unknown—ground in a Basil King poem. We might as well ask, in a comparison, if the ground in a King poem is finally nothing but an illusion. Or we can ask if there is the promise of a story but the story dissolves, so to speak, before our eyes. It would be too easy to say that that an immanence welling up in his poem derives from, emerges out of—is—the circle ("the ever-essential circle that brings me back to where," as King writes in *Learning to Draw / A History*).[1]

And, no doubt, his pretense at times of a story, either in his poems or paintings—his poem's seduction, not unlike that of one of his paintings—unfolds neither in a circle nor in a spiral. The unexpected turns of mind, the percepts, in his poems—we might say something like this as regards his paintings' figurative narratives—will never make quite enough narratological sense. But they delight, insofar as his pseudo-narratives reside within an unobserved ground.

Only a painter could write like this. I am reminded that

poetry should, at least ideally, aspire to the condition of art. Usually that attempt is not to be made by poets. And visual artists may never know the burden of words. Their involvement lies, instead, in something else already-free of them, of thoughts.

King's figurative paintings possess a kind of narrative arc, yet when we succumb to it we miss the *real*, as it were, in them, which is not a story at all. His art is not even, ultimately, the attention to, the love of paint, light, figure. Rather, his visual art is how the ground, unremarked, unremarkable, nevertheless threatens to loom up—while it never does.

We sense the threat. Can the same be said for his poems? The poems, like the paintings, are all the most informed and elegantly turned digressions. And it is what is unspoken in the poems that suggests the immanence his paintings contain, as if the text's digressions, the canvas' destabilized figures, can only be sustained by some function in the service of the circle.

1. *Learning to Draw / A History* (Skylight P: Cheltenham, Gloucestershire, UK, 2011), 13. Cf. Kim Lyons, "Here Is Another Somewhere," *Dispatches from the Poetry Wars* (5 July 2017).

LORINE NIEDECKER'S
SUBJECTIVE OBJECTS

*I used to feel that I was goofing off unless I held only to the
hard, clear image, the thing you could put your hand on but
now I dare do this reflection.*
- Lorine Niedecker[1]

*The thing things. In thinging, it stays earth and sky, divinities
and mortals [. . .]. As we preserve the thing qua thing we
inhabit nearness.*
- Martin Heidegger "The Thing"[2]

When Louis Zukofsky coined the term "Objectivist" for
his 1931 special issue of *Poetry Magazine*, he was making
a distinction (whether he meant to or not) between
philosophic and poetic articulations of truth. Philosophy
and poetry each posit an ideal world, and yet the world they
each conceive of may not be identical. If I were to imagine
an ideal world in which language is free of inertia, would
the truth philosophy and poetry each promise, in such a
world, be the same? It strikes me that Zukofsky sensed
language was the source of our inertia, and that philosophy
and poetry were cognitively opposed to one another. His
assumption was, though, that each questions language's
capacity to provide a full and accurate description of the
world. Zukofsky's distinction reflected this questioning
and sought to align the ideal with what he envisioned as an
authentic world, while his distinction threw into relief the
paradoxical recognition that any hope of arriving at truth,
in poetry, appeared to depend on a pure subjectivism—
that is, on an ideal.

Lorine Niedecker, among others including Zukofsky, who came to be known as the Objectivists, was caught up in trying to achieve this subjectivism. Poetry's potential to render an authentic, thus a true, world had been intuited by the Objectivists in the Imagism of Pound, H.D. et al. Imagism's regime, which was to present the imagery of a visual field without extraneous comment, was an attempt to achieve a kind of pure expression—yet it precluded either the speaker of the poem or its author. At least, this was how the Imagist poem was *meant* to be, in principle. Zukofsky's special issue of *Poetry* may have been an attempt to emend the Imagists' precepts.

In a letter Niedecker sent to Kenneth Cox, thirty-five years later, she looks back upon that issue of *Poetry* as critical to her "[development] as a poet" (10 December 1966 [Penberthy *Niedecker* 20]). What's remarkable is how, in embracing the Objectivist procedure, Niedecker transforms it, taking it beyond Zukofsky's reach, thereby fully realizing a potential he may or may not have glimpsed. Again, much later in life, she ruminates upon this, in a letter to Clayton Eshelman: "I went to school to Objectivism but now I often say *There is something more*" (18 November 1967 [in DuPlessis and Quartermain 11]). To her friend Gail Roub, at about this same time, she describes herself as "[m]uch taken up with how to define a way of writing poetry which is not Imagist nor Objectivist fundamentally nor Surrealism alone . . . I loosely [call] it 'reflections' [...]" (20 June 1967 [in DuPlessis and Quartermain 12]).

Pound had been concerned with the nature and effects of metaphor. He wanted poetry to fulfill its primary function of *namin*g the world landscape (as implied in the dual function of the ancient Greek word *noma: name* and *noun*). In a letter to Harriet Monroe, *Poetry's* editor, he describes the poetry of his fellow Imagist, H. D., as "laconic speech," "Objective," without "slither—direct," and containing *"No metaphors that won't permit examination.—It's* straight talk." H. D. had lived with the things she wrote of; she "knew them before she had any book-knowledge of them" (October 1912 [*Selected Letters* 11]). Nearly four decades hence, a letter of Niedecker's, to Zukofsky, remarks that H.D. "never seems directly now, living in the present whirl" (9 November 1949 [in "Knee Deck Her Daisies" 119]). Pound's use, in his letter, of the term *objective* turns out to be prescient.

Pound's prescription for attaining simplicity—that a reader might experience a greater degree of associative power when the poetic image stood by itself and for itself—just as simply fell short of the goal (when the poet merely *names* it). As Michael Heller has commented, in T. E. Hulme's poem "Autumn," for instance, the moon is likened to "a ruddy-faced farmer" standing under a sky full of "wistful" stars (Heller 4). Hulme's images are mere ornaments; the farmer and moon are brought together on an extrinsic and therefore arbitrary basis, their coincidence a matter of physical, perhaps sensual proximity, but with no phenomenological grounding. The poem demonstrates nothing *essential* about these things. No kinship among them is revealed. Hulme's metaphors didn't "permit examination" (to cite Pound again, who may have been thinking of Aristotle's *Poetics* in which metaphor is defined as an analogy engendering a new semantic element, a third term). Ungrounded, Hulme's metaphors didn't give rise to third terms; no insights into analogical relationships had come into being.

The Objectivist poets, on the other hand, paid close attention to what Pound seemed to be struggling toward, coming to view words as "real . . . because they instate an existence beyond the words" (Heller, 4). This claim, for the reality of words, marks a change in the concept of metaphor. The Objectivists understood that the moon in Hulme's poem, as well as the farmer, had been rendered as objects rather than as "things"—to borrow Martin Heidegger's distinction. Heidegger thought of the term *thing* as it resonates in the German *Ding* or the Latin *res*, in other words as a dynamic agent or event, as an ontological gathering.[3]

Heidegger's contemporaneous ideas make their way into Objectivist poetry, obviously in the case of George Oppen, who echoes him—yet all the Objectivists were searching for the "thingly" qualities of objects, generally speaking for an engaged world to be recreated in poems. In Objectivist poetics, then, there are no objects—yet no "ideas" either, as William Carlos Williams would say ("No ideas / but in things"). There should be no perceptions except as they're conveyed by "things." *Objectivist* could mean, according to Rachel Blau DuPlessis and Peter Quartermain, "a non-symbolist, post-imagist poetics, characterized by a historical, realist, antimythological worldview, one in which 'the detail, not mirage' [quoting Zukofsky] calls attention to the materiality of both the world and the word" (3). Well, that's a mouthful. Yet it boils down to what Zukofsky called "sincerity" in his seminal essay "An Objective," written for the *Poetry* issue (cf. Zukofsky's *Prepositions* 13). "Sincerity" becomes an elegant way through to something like a ground, one supporting an essentially philosophical stance predicated on faith in a language that would have an inherent, albeit difficult, relationship to reality.

The subjective nature of Zukofsky's position, in comparison with Pound's or Hulme's, is aptly suggested in Burton Hatlen's comment on the Objectivists who were "generally less concerned with the thing seen than with the way we see," and, while this emphasis became "in their poetry profoundly problematic," it resulted in our understanding of the Objectivists as having taken

> a significant step beyond the work of their modernist models. Pound and Williams were still haunted by the dream of a "natural" language, the word that will be "true" because it gives us, in effect, the thing itself. But the Objectivists […] discovered that there is no natural language: and with this discovery they passed beyond modernism into postmodernism. All languages are, the Objectivists realized, codes, "made up." The signifier cannot […] touch the signified. No code can claim to be "truer" than any other code. [….] Their sense of the arbitrary character of all codes leads the Objectivists to look at words with the same "objectivity" that they bring to the perception of other "historic and contemporary particulars" [quoting Zukofsky]. (49)[4]

Zukofsky's notion of sincerity is grounded in a phenomenological understanding of experience. Is there, then, a correlation between "sincerity" and "metaphor"? Pound realized that one of the problems with analogical expressions is they tend toward opacity and privacy. Such had been the case for early poetic innovators like Mallarmé,

Baudelaire, even the Romantics. A symbol is especially powerful. It signifies a system of associated meanings in a synthetic instant, and its imagistic values will dominate an entire poem. A symbol affects the texture of its poem's discourse by configuring the poem's dialectic in relation to that symbol. Readers read a symbolical poem and feel it to be pregnant with meaning; they sense the poem's symbols to be important or weighty.

What symbols do *not* do, however, is convey the sense of *nearness* Heidegger writes of. Rather, a symbol appropriates nearness for itself, removing readers from the world— as all language potentially does. So to allow language to describe the world through analogical expressions, such as symbols, or metaphors, is to distance the language user, paradoxically, the reader or writer. Zukofsky realized that, because of the opportunity only poetry affords, language may be used as a vehicle by which to come to terms with experience or, let's say, reality. What, though, is meant by "reality"? Both he and Pound believed that language might accurately reflect the sensual world—but such reflection should not be tied to the physical realm, for then there would be description, which could lead to symbolizing. Just the opposite, the Objectivist needed to construct a language as a speech that might simply stand for the world, so that a heuristic process could bring the reader to a truth beyond the poem; the words of such a language, Zukofsky proclaimed, are "metaphor enough" (*Prepositions* 14). Such a language would, in most instances, include metonyms as opposed to metaphors or symbols.

Niedecker went further. For her, objectness resided not

merely in words—not merely in nouns, metonymic or otherwise but also in their overall statements, in the very syntax of expression, in that which makes expression what it is. The first of several letters she writes to Monroe indicates that this view of poetry, and of language generally, is psychologically rooted: "In my own experience sentences have appeared full-blown in the first moments of waking from sleep" (31 January 1933 [Penberthy *Niedecker* 21-22]). The fabric of dreams may be comprised of, say, Jungian symbols, or simply of words, or of sentences.

For Niedecker, what's important is that her inner, private self as well as her public life—a life shaped by formal poetic statements as well as informal, everyday talk—can be brought together in a single language. Does she believe that reality is comprised of language? The very context of Niedecker's statement implies an effort to bring into agreement various aspects of her life—those life-events marked by time as well as her states of consciousness—which, in order that they be conceived, must be viewed as transcending temporal bounds, such as occurs in a dream state.

Charles Olson wryly comments: "The trouble / with symbol, / it does not trouble" ("The Post Virginal" 1-3). If there's a symbol to be found in Niedecker's arrangement, that symbol must be the statement itself—the utterance, indeed the poem per se—not the symbol within the poem. By redirecting discourse unto itself, a symbol forecloses on poetic statement. Pound substituted the Chinese translator Ernest Fenollosa's ideogrammic method for the symbols, both in Pound's theorizing and practice, from which comes the terse poem "In a Station of the Metro": "The apparition of these faces in the crowd; / Petals on a wet, black bough." Pound's percept of the station is presented as if it were an engram lifted out of the brain and simply placed on the blank page. His association is uncannily visual; hence it's "real" in the sense that it's vivid. Ironically, though, Pound finally can't avoid the annunciation of self-import, that calling attention to itself of the symbol, in a way not unlike how language tends to talk about itself rather than about the world it must signify. Thus the subjective is missing, in a sense, the human being removed from the linguistic equation.

Pound's poem correlates natural or rural, and industrial or urban worlds. Yet even as the poem is vivid, its connection leads away from the fundamental, underlying relationship between these worlds and, instead, dwells upon the rich visuality of their very images. One of Niedecker's verses (from *In Exchange for Haiku*) furnishes an instructive contrast; it's like Pound's poem in its approach, but its lasting effect is quite different:

> Popcorn-can cover
>
> screwed to the wall
>
> over a hole
>
>   so the cold
>
> can't mouse in

(*My Life by Water* 76)

This brief statement never allows the reader to pause until what becomes clear is the poem's narrative involved in the effort to keep out the cold. The poem invites the reader to contemplate the cover fastened to the wall. The image of the cover lingers after the reading. The poem is not finally about the cover, however, or its relation to the hole in the wall, but instead about protecting oneself from harsh weather and rodents. The image of the cover occurs forcefully, with great clarity. Pound's poem is about crowds, social cohesion, dissonance or alienation, the similarity between landscape and human beings—but what his poem is about, finally, is the petals on that black bough.

One of Zukofsky's short lyrics (the first section of "All of December toward New Year's") strikes a balance between Niedecker and Pound:

> Not the branches
> half in shadow
>
> But the length
> of each branch
>
> Half in shadow
>
> As if it had snowed
> on each upper half
>
> (*Anew* 150)

In this poem, individual nouns and individual images are vivid and pleasurable. Additionally, the poem conveys the notion of shadows and, overall, visual contrast—which is what this verse is about. The reader doesn't retain the percept of a branch either bare or half covered with snow, in either light or shadow. The objects have receded, replaced by an emphasis on the idea of contrast—which is quite the opposite from Pound, but like Niedecker insofar as the poem goes beyond or rather undercuts the full potential impact of its images, in order to make a statement.

Pound's poetic aspiration toward "the image," typified by "In a Station of the Metro," does provide a world that's objectified, but only in terms of its otherness from the perceiver: there's the "crowd," the "apparition," the unseen looker. The poetic landscape is made up of objects, the "faces" in the crowd, and the "petals." In terms of its images, the poem's world suggests these images seek to indicate a totality far beyond their particular instantiations. In this way, the images take on a sense of importance. They convey a feeling of promise. Yet to Zukofsky Pound's images implied that there were symbols in the world, rather than that the world was in the poem—for ultimately one's mind does the symbolizing of experience. This phenomenology is most fully developed in Niedecker's writing; in her work, the world comes into being through the symbolizing work of the poet-perceiver—which is what Niedecker explains to Gail Roub:

> The visual form is there in the background and the words convey what the visual form gives off after it's felt in the mind. A heat that is generated and takes in the whole world of the poem. A light, a motion, inherent in the whole. (qtd in Roub, "Getting to Know Lorine Niedecker" 86).

Late in her life, Niedecker was casting about for the proper terminology to describe the urge she felt to develop what

40

was essential in the Objectivist impulse. Rather clumsily, perhaps, she writes to Zukofsky as follows.

> I'm trembling on the verge of something, a form of poetic thinking that depends maybe too much on readers' imagination, but we'll see. I don't know if it's called metaphysical or not, not necessarily, I guess, but anyhow this has been in me from the beginning and somehow it's got to come out. (7 February 1964 [Penberthy *Niedecker* 343])

The struggle to articulate this poetics, to explain it at least to herself, on an intellectual basis, continued for some time. Four months later, she writes to Cid Corman (about a book of his, *in no time*):

> I feel this keenly—you're going into a conversational —metaphysical?? (You won't like that word metaphysical anymore than I do) but you know what I mean—and going into it faster than I am. All our lives we steer away from it but when we do attain it we know there's nothing like it. (5 June 1964 [Faranda, *Between Your House and Mine*, 46; cf. 47, n. 4])

By the following October, in another letter to Corman, Niedecker wishes to take back the term *metaphysical* though she clearly desires to continue pursuing whatever it was she meant to express by it: 'Please don't mind my 'metaphysical' in my last letter. I meant it but evidently didn't use the right word" (October 1964 [Faranda, *Between Your House and Mine*, 48]). Even to be worked into the poem were her characteristic habits of writing and thinking:

41

Cleaned all surfaces
and behind all solids
and righted leaning things

Considered, then, becurtained
the metaphysics
of flight from housecleanings

(*From this Condensery* 179)

Diction and emotional registers aside, this poetry is a far cry from Pound's cool visuality. It's also a distant aftershock of Niedecker's early infatuation with Surrealism.[5] DuPlessis and Quartermain take note of her "aim to privilege the subjective and her desire to create a new psychosocial subjectivity [...] in her remark, 'I conceive poetry as the folk-tales of the mind and us creating our own remembering'" ("Lorine Niedecker: Local Letters" 88 [DuPlessis and Quartermain, "Introduction" 11]). Reflection, metaphysics, Surrealism—Niedecker is making, Peter Middleton contends, "the choice [...] between mere perceptual clarity and the complexities of reflective consciousness" (167). He quotes Niedecker in order to pronounce "Good poetry [as being] the 'outcome of experimentation with [the] subconscious'" (173 [Penberthy *Niedecker* 60]).

The world is imagined by the poet from within her interior. Peter Nicholls explains that "[f]or Niedecker [...] the 'subconscious' seems to make itself felt as a kind of trace or sedimentation within language [...]" (204). This language, in turn, resides within syntax. She writes to Monroe to observe that "certain words of a sentence,—

prepositions, connectives, pronouns—belong up toward full consciousness, while strange and unused words [such as nouns] appear only in subconscious" (in Nicholls 202-03). In another letter to Monroe (31 January 1933, some of which is quoted above), Niedecker opines that for poetry "the greatest reason for existing must be illogical." Why is this? It's because an "idea, a rumination such as more or less constantly roams the mind, meets external object or situation with quite illogical association." In her

> experience sentences have appeared full-blown in the first moments of waking from sleep. It is a system of thought replacements, the most remote the most significant or irrational; a thousand variations of the basic tension; an attempt at hard clear images but absorption of these. (In Nicholls 205)

How are these images "absorbed"? What does a poet's language look like when "absorption" of images occurs? Pound, Zukofsky and Niedecker—regardless of the psychological wellspring all three poets might variously have tapped—share an interest in metonymy. Pound had seen the possibility of both a more accurate and more authentic poetry. His Imagist poetry tended toward, if not always actual metonymic language, than what metonymy produces: a sense of sparsity and a feeling of space conditioned by the clarity of detail. Indeed, he'd said that "the natural object is always the adequate symbol" and he warned: "Go in fear of abstractions" ("A Retrospect" 9). These are important theoretical moves. But his advice is to be weighed against Zukofsky's idea of writing as "the detail, not the mirage, of seeing, of thinking with the things as they exist" (*Prepositions* 12). Here, once again, Niedecker goes further. Having completed her reading of Zukofsky's poem "Non Ti Fidar," she writes to him: "I love it because I feel that I think this way, not *thought* but everything in a movement of words" (27 February 1949 [Penberthy *Niedecker* 157; cf. 84-85]).

In their essays and letters, Zukofsky and Niedecker are striving for a kind of mimetic realism metonymy affords (as discussed and analyzed by the linguist Roman Jacobson, years later [92]). This possibility of a true, or rather real, version of a world is most fully accomplished in Niedecker's verse. Consider, in this regard, her poem "Violin Debut." The fact that this poem remained unpublished until after her death might demonstrate her struggle to reconcile what she at times called the "metaphysical" with both the Imagist and Objectivist enterprises. The poem is one of the "For Paul" group, from the 1950s. That it was not destroyed is significant. It possesses a severity and it's strangely powerful—and violent, in its consideration of the relationship between inert objects and dynamic human intention—which might suggest the difficulty Niedecker must have experienced with it:

Violin Debut
Carnegie Hall, the great musicbox –
lift the lid on the hard-working parts
of the boy whose smooth power
is saved –

his tone and more: what he's done with his life
– those two who sent the flow thru him have done
he's been true to himself, a knife
behaved.

(*From This Condensery* 107)

The "musicbox" here, in its associative reach, can represent, in terms of function and shape, a piano that accompanies the young violinist, or maybe the auditorium in which the musical performance takes place, or even the boy. More interesting is the knife image, which enjoys a minimally proximal or causal relationship to the actual violinist whose appearance is suggested by the analogy of knife and boy— although, admittedly, seen from a distance, the shape of the boy on stage does vaguely resemble that of the knife. In fact we never, imagistically, *see* the violinist except *through* the instantiation of the knife, a knife that otherwise more accurately portrays the boy's energy. To be sure, we only essentially know him through the knife—but, significantly, that's within the phrases "he's been true to himself, a knife / behaved." Is the knife, then, a metaphor or symbol, not a metonym? The short answer is yes.

The purpose and some of the attributes of a knife suggest the musician's once raw power now honed into a brilliant, still powerful, instrument—just as the boy "hones" the violin and thereby produces fine music. This poem is, finally, about such a honing—what the intelligent and driven application of human energies can accomplish. Hence in one sense the knife image is metaphoric, even symbolic, since it exists as part of a fully drawn analogy, or rather a number of analogies. The knife figure transports us to a new and substantially different place. Aristotle would say that the figure teaches something, perhaps many things. In other words, the knife is an active agent, a subject. A knife is an unlikely emblem for a violinist, but this poem conveys the oxymoronic message that refined music is the product of brute force; we learn that, like the violinist, all great musicians were once raw potential, and that the beauty of music comes only by way of possibly bloody sacrifice, the music maker's energy and precision. Visually alone—especially if the young violinist were being viewed from the back of the concert hall—the boy can be associated with the violin bow, just as he might distantly resemble the knife.

Niedecker's poem has breadth. At the same time it's terse. It has a sense of space, and of talk. If the knife is a symbol, then we must also acknowledge it as deeply an aspect of the poem itself, as a part of the poem's architecture (not unlike the architecture of the mechanical "musicbox"). To put this another way, we can say that the knife enjoys a structural rather than topical significance. For one thing, the image is accessible, significantly within the surrealist phrase "a knife / behaved," and so it's the phrase that stands out as a decidedly illogical, surreal proposition. Whatever other private meanings this possible symbol may contain, it signifies the boy, his energy, his parents' and his own determination, or, as an alternative instrument, the violin now tamed by the boy.

In any case, "Violin Debut" provides spaciousness, in part because its figures stand for both subliminal and structural arrangements—as well as physical coincidence. The poem's spaciousness and clarity, usually a function of metonymic language, is due to the precision of images like "knife" and "musicbox." Perhaps Niedecker's bald insistence that the knife stand for the boy—no matter how abnormal such an association may seem—is an effort to forge a monovalent, metonymic relationship. Still, the presence of metaphoric-like constructions in language is evident here—the knife provides a wealth of meanings. The trick for the poet, then, may be to avoid being overwhelmed by the force of metaphor.

Wallace Stevens' poetry, to employ a stark and ready-to-hand contrast to Niedecker's, often removes readers from an immediate realm in which the poem's imagery is abstracted. His images are sensuous and rich; they speak of another spiritual or possibly intellectual world. Niedecker, however, presents a world of things. Both worlds are conversant in phenomenology. In Stevens' case his discourse is pointedly entrenched in the thinking of Husserl and Heidegger (Hines 145-46). In Niedecker's case, we may find these philosophers to be of some assistance in plumbing the depths of her usually casual and, therefore, in philosophical terms, disarming talk. According to Heidegger, in order that things appear as things, one must become "vigilant"; a poet must "step back from the thinking that merely represents—that is, merely explains—to the thinking that responds and recalls" (Heidegger in Hofstadter 181). Symbols do represent. In the sense that meaning and conception coincide in prose writing (Levin "Allegorical" 33)—if such a response is actually possible when we mean the real world as that which includes the metaphysical and transcendent—we can say that symbols explain the real world in what appears to be an attempt to forego prosaic response to that world. Yet symbols tend to explain the world in terms other than what we see: a world, as Heidegger would say, which would otherwise be "recalled." Nevertheless, the symbolical terms are imaginative.

Niedecker's comprehension of presence, or immanence, her use of language, is merely the symptom of a vitality residing in how she renders the world filtered through— reinvented by—her imagination. She's a poet emptied out of subjectivity, however. If there's finally an object in her Objectivist equation, that object is herself rather than what she as a poet sees and records. In Niedecker's work there's never the private ideation of a typical Stevensian trope such as "green phrases" (really not unlike Hulme's "wistful" stars). For Niedecker, the element of objectivity has to do with her capacity for *sincerity*, as Zukofsky would say, necessary in order to achieve a complete appreciation of the perceptible world. At such a point there occurs a "rested totality [that] may be called objectification" (*Prepositions* 13). Niedecker's poems show their author's stance vis-à-vis the world.

In 1968, Niedecker writes to Corman about the turn her poetry has taken, describing it as a "strange and new thing" (in Nicholls 213). Nicholls rightly sees this turn as

a return to that mobility of mind which she had sought in the early forms of Surrealist automatic writing. But now, since she could not so easily "goof off" from the hard clear image,"[7] Niedecker was seeking more expanded structures in which perceptions could be coordinated according to "the vertical more than the simple straight line." (213 [Letter to Corman 30 January 1968, in Faranda, *Between Your House and Mine*, 149])[8]

Paradoxically, the Objectivist reifies the world's objects into things by undertaking, conceivably through the power of imaginative sympathy, the element of a thing that causes it to be perceived as near. This nearness has nothing at all to do with physicality—it's not Hulme's nearness. It's not the nearness of a trope that partakes of a Cartesian dualism. The poet might stay clear of a dynamic she erects between the seer and the thing seen—which is the operative dynamic in Pound's two-line vignette—and between reader and image in the poem. After Imagism, Objectivist poetics, especially as we see it elaborated in the powerful poetry of Niedecker, implies the interaction with the world-things that proclaim the very universe supporting them. The fabric of that relationship is the language itself. Here poetry is an epistemological method by which the world might be discovered, because only in poetry can these things of the world be at once celebrated and examined.

Notes

1. Letter to Gail Roub of 20 June 1967; Faranda, *Between Your House and Mine* 9-10.

2. Das Ding dingt. Dingend verweilt es Erde und Himmel, die Göttlichen und die Sterblichen. . . . Insofern wir das Ding als das Ding schonen, bewohnen wir die Nähe (142-43, 146). (Trans. Hofstadter 177, 181). Note the double entendre in ""verweilt" meaning "to make to linger" as well as "to hold back" (my trans.).

3. I take note of Tatyana Lyaskovets' article "From Imagisme to Postmodern Poetics" that states, "Among the main imagistic peculiarities of [Niedecker's] verse we can note 'thingness' [*sic*] of images [...]" (20). In comparison with the present discussion, this essay uses the term "thingness" loosely, with no reference to Heidegger's concept.

4. Once again I must take issue with Lyaskovets' argument that states in part: "Though this poetic influence [i.e., Imagism] remained important and noticeable throughout Niedecker's creative life, she was too independent a thinker and artist to fit a frame of a style or a direction. Resistant to any tradition that takes the shape of a code, Niedecker develops her independent voice, the idiosyncrasy of which is in questioning and rejecting of all the codes" (20). While Lyaskovets quotes a portion of Hatlen's comment (above), she seems to be confusing the issue Hatlen is raising regarding the nature of language itself, by using *code* as a synonym for, say, *tradition*, such as when she writes that "Niedecker exposes, questions, and doubts traditional, set usages of words, traditional modes of speaking" (16). The development of an "independent voice," as Lyaskovets puts it, is what I am aiming to anatomize in this essay; to do so, I must qualify the respective idea of *thingness* and *code*, and must define as well as plot the course of Niedecker's arrival at a subjectivity. Lyaskovets is perhaps further from my argument, and closer to Hatlen's observation that "a poetic sense of language, conjoined with a Marxian materialism, leads all the objectivists to treat words not merely as symbols that stand in for things, but as things in their own right, 'historic and contemporary particulars' [quoting Zukofsky] among all the other such particulars that, collectively, make up the world" (43).

5. This proclivity has been thoroughly documented and commented upon. See, for instance, Roub, "Getting to Know Lorine Niedecker"; Niedecker, "Letters to Poetry Magazine, 1931-1937"; Jeffrey Peterson, "Lorine Niecker: 'Before Machines'"; Lisa Pater Faranda, "Composing a Place"; DuPlessis and Quartermain, "Introduction"; Peter Middleton, "Lorine Niedecker's 'Folk Base'"; "Jenny Penberthy's review of Robert J. Bertholf's edition of Niedecker's verse, *From This Condensery*; and see especially Peter Nicholls, "Lorine Niedecker: Rural Surreal." On Zukofsky's rejection of Surrealism see, e.g., Hatlen, "A Poetics of Marginality," and DuPlessis and Quartermain, "Introduction."

6. This is a misquote of a letter to Cid Corman 30 January 1968; cf. the note below.

7. Nicholls attributes these phrases to Niedecker's 1968 letter to Corman quoted above and which he finds quoted in Faranda, *Between Your House and Mine*, 149, but cf. her 1967 letter to Roub quoted at the start of this essay and in Faranda 9-10.

8. "If I don't get over into the new and strange thing I feel I'll bust! . . . It's a feeling of the vertical more than the simple straight line—shades of *Transition* [i.e., the early-century magazine that featured Surrealist work] (ever see those copies?—of forty years ago). It's probably only that old *dream* thing that threatens to mess things up but never really does—still, this time when it comes, it might" (Letter to Cid Corman 30 January 1968, *Letters* 149, qtd in Peterson 268).

Works Cited

DuPlessis, Rachel Blau, and Peter Quartermain. "Introduction." *The Objectivist Nexus: Essays in Cultural Poetics*. Eds. Rachel Blau DuPlessis and Peter Quartermain. Tuscaloosa and London: U of Alabama P, 1999. 1-24.

Faranda, Lisa Pater. Ed. and Intr. *"Between Your House and Mine": The Letters of Lorine Niedecker to Cid Corman, 1960 to 1979*. Durham: Duke UP, 1986.

_____. "Composing a Place: Two Versions of Lorine Niedecker's 'Lake Superior'." *North Dakota Quarterly* 55.4 (Fall 1987): 348-64.

Hatlen, Burton. "A Poetics of Marginality and Resistance: The Objectivist Poets in Context." *The Objectivist Nexus: Essays in Cultural Poetics*. Eds. Rachel Blau DuPlessis and Peter Quartermain. Tuscaloosa and London: U of Alabama P, 1999. 37-55.

Heidegger, Martin. *Poetry, Language, Thought* Tr. Albert Hofstadter. New York: Harper & Row, 1971.

Heller, Michael. *Conviction's Net of Branches: Essays on the Objectivist Poets and Poetry*. Carbondale, Ill.: Southern Illinois U Press, 1985; hereafter cited as Heller.

Hines, Thomas J. *The Later Poetry of Wallace Stevens: Phenomenological Parallels with Husserl and Heidegger*. Lewisburg: Bucknell U Press, London: Associated U Presses, 1976.

Hofstadter, Albert. Trans. *Poetry, Language, Thought* by Martin Heidegger. New York: Harper & Row, 1971.

Jakobson, Roman and Morris Halle. *Fundamentals of Language*. The Hague and Paris: Mouton and Co., 1971.

Levin, Samuel. "Allegorical Language." *Allegory, Myth, and Symbol*. Ed. Morton W. Bloomfield. *Harvard English Studies* 9. Cambridge, Mass.: Harvard U P, 1981.

Lyaskovets, Tatyana. "Lorine Niedecker: From Imagisme to Postmodern Poetics." *Journal of Imagism* (Fall 2000): 10-22.

Middleton, Peter. "Lorine Niedecker's 'Folk Base' and Her Challenge to the American Avant-Garde." *The Objectivist Nexus: Essays in Cultural Poetics*. Eds. Rachel Blau DuPlessis and Peter Quartermain. Tuscaloosa and London: U of Alabama P, 1999. 160-90.

Nicholls, Peter. "Lorine Niedecker: Rural Surreal." *Lorine Niedecker: Woman and Poet*. Ed. and Intr. Jenny Penberthy. Orono: National Poetry Foundation, 1996. 193-218.

Niedecker, Lorine. *From This Condensery: The Complete Writing of Lorine Niedecker*. Ed. Robert J. Bertholf. The Jargon Society, 1985.

____. "'Knee Deck Her Daisies': Selections from Her Letters to Louis Zukofsky." *Sulfur* 18 (Winter 1987): 110.

____. "Letters to Poetry Magazine, 1931-1937." Ed. Jenny Penberthy. *Lorine Niedecker: Woman and Poet.* Ed. and Intr. Jenny Penberthy. Orono: National Poetry Foundation, 1996. 49-64.

____. *My Life by Water: Collected Poems 1936-1968.* Fulcrum Press, 1970.

Olson, Charles. "The Post Virginal." *The Collected Poems of Charles Olson (Excluding the Maximus Poems).* Berkeley / Los Angeles / London: U of California P, 1997. 354-55.

Penberthy, Jenny. Ed. *Niedecker and the Correspondence with Zukofsky 1931-1970.* Cambridge: Cambridge UP, 1993.

____. Review of *From This Condensery* Ed. Robert Bertholf. *Sagetrieb: A Journal Devoted to Poets in the Imagist / Objectivist Tradition* 5.2 (Fall 1986): 139-51.

Peterson, Jeffrey. "Lorine Niedecker: 'Before Machines'." *Lorine Niedecker: Woman and Poet.* Ed. and Intr. Jenny Penberthy. Orono: National Poetry Foundation, 1996. 245-80.

Pound, Ezra. "A Retrospect." *Literary Essays of Ezra Pound.* Ed.T. S. Eliot. New York: New Directions, 1968.

____. *Selected Letters.* Ed. D. D. Paige. New York: New Directions, 1971.

Roub, Gail. "Getting to Know Lorine Niedecker." *Lorine Niedecker: Woman and Poet.* Ed. and Intr. Jenny Penberthy. Orono: National Poetry Foundation, 1996. 79-86.

Zukofsky, Louis. *Anew: Complete Shorter Poetry*. New York: New Directions, 2011.

____. *Prepositions: The Collected Critical Essays of Louis Zukofsky*. Expanded Edition. Berkeley: U of California Press, 1981.

THE END OF LANGUAGE: ART, POETRY, & THE MATERIALITY OF WRITING IN THE NINETIES

Art-trolling in Chelsea, I stepped into a gallery to look at some sculptures and installations by Fred Sandback. These included skeins of yarn held taut between ceiling and floor. His work had a purity. The designs demarcated space.

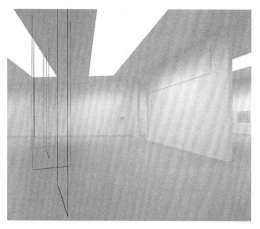

Fred Sandback, Yarn Sculptures, David Zwirner
Gallery, New York City, 2009

In the other half of that gallery, a man and woman stood at a podium, reading a series of numbers aloud from a book created by On Kawara. The book, titled *One Million Years*, listed in order the million years before the artwork's conception, and the million after it. The installations were not *expressions* of space. The book of numbers did not quite demarcate time.

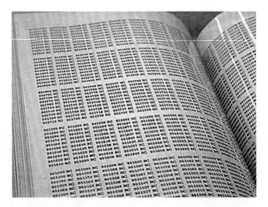

On Kawara, *One Million Years*, David Zwirner Gallery,
New York City, 2009 (courtesy Artists' Processes,
Mazime Chanson)

Kawara is best known for his date paintings, but I feel
more affection for his postcards. These postcards are the
artifacts of his *I Got Up* series. Starting in 1968, for
eleven years, he mailed his friends and others two
postcards a day, each containing his "name, address, the
date, the name and address of his recipient, and the
phrase I GOT UP AT," which was "followed by the time
he rose from bed" (*Post Cards: I Got Up*, Guggenheim
Museum).

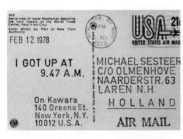

On Kawara, *I Got Up at 9.47 A.M.*,
Feb. 12 1978) (courtesy WikiArt)

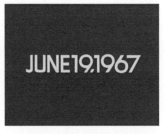

On Kawara, date painting from
Today series (courtesy Andrew
Russeth)

56

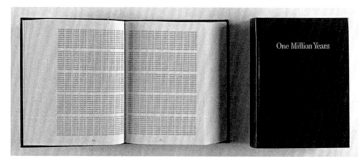

On Kawara, *One Million Years*,
Editions Micheline Swacjer & Michèle Didier-uitgever, 1999

Written numbers are different from written speech. A number is not a noun. A series of numbers as printed, like in Kawara's book, has a certain force. I wonder if Kawara had read Stéphane Mallarmé's 1897 poem, *Un Coup de dés jamais n'abolira le hasard*, before he began making *One Million Years*. Kawara's book implicitly asks about the nature of reading. For me, it renews the question of how *to read* a poem.

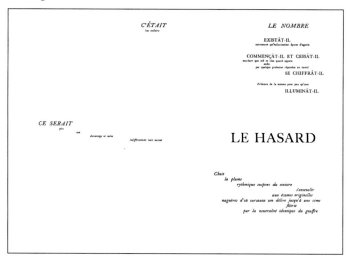

Stéphane Mallarmé's, *Un Coup de dés jamais n'abolira le hazard*, 1897

The styles and font sizes of Mallarmé's text migrate across the page and its book's gutter.

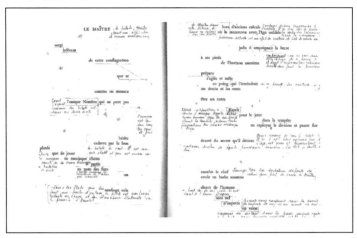

Stéphane Mallarmé's, *Un Coup de dés jamais n'abolira le hazard*, 1897

After Mallarmé, three Modernist poets take me through time to Kawara: Gertrude Stein, William Carlos Williams, and George Oppen. We can add Robert Creeley (if we want to think about avant-garde poetry in the 1990s, and art). Younger than these Modernists, his poems having appeared in Donald Allen's 1960 anthology *The New American Poetry*, he became a transitional figure and influence upon even younger poets. The generation of experimentalists, which followed the poets in the Allen book, could not have missed Creeley's early poetry in its newness and elegance.

The next milestone in the story of the North American poetry avant garde, after *The New American Poetry*, is *This* magazine, edited by Robert Grenier and Barrett Watten, starting in 1972. What was the resonance, then, of a deictic, of a pronoun?

> A CARAFE, THAT IS A BLIND GLASS.
>
> A kind in glass and a cousin, a spectacle and nothing strange a single hurt color and an arrangement in a system to pointing. All this and not ordinary, not unordered in not resembling. The difference is spreading.

Gertrude Stein, A Carafe, that is a Blind Glass

Not unlike her friend Picasso's Cubist paintings, Stein put syntax under such strain that words themselves came to the fore. Williams was "intrigued" by Picasso, writes Herbert Leibowitz. Nevertheless, the common critical view of Williams' poetics, as having been indebted to a Cubist "defamiliarization," falls short. More accurate might be something like Jan-Louis Kruger's comment that, in a Williams poem, "[t]he experience of the moment is defamiliarized as each word acquires an almost tactile quality" (107). Leibowitz describes Picasso, as if from the poet's viewpoint, as an artist busy "subverting received ideas coolly and authoritatively" (38).

Williams invested the accidentals of language with a status equal to that of its substantives. For him, a poem was what he called a "machine made of words" (echoing Mallarmé's quip—*"But my dear Degas, poems are made of words, not ideas"*). In "The Red Wheelbarrow" a preposition—"upon"—occupies a line by itself.

so much depends

upon

a red wheel
barrow

glazed with rain
water

beside the white
chickens

William Carlos Williams,
"The Red Wheelbarrow"

59

Oppen came to see the written word as opaque.

> Possible
> To use
> Words provided one treat them
> As enemies.

George Oppen, from "A Language of New York"

In his daybook he wrote that "words are a constant enemy: the thing seems to exist because the word does" (*Selected Prose* 53). What did Oppen make of Williams' mantra, "no ideas but in things"? A portion of "A Language of New York" (above), in Oppen's 1965 collection titled *This in Which* (notice the pronouns in this title), is a caution about language.

500202 AD	500203 AD	500204 AD	500205 AD	500206 AD	500207 AD	500208 AD
500212 AD	500213 AD	500214 AD	500215 AD	500216 AD	500217 AD	500218 AD
500222 AD	500223 AD	500224 AD	500225 AD	500226 AD	500227 AD	500228 AD
500232 AD	500233 AD	500234 AD	500235 AD	500236 AD	500237 AD	500238 AD
500242 AD	500243 AD	500244 AD	500245 AD	500246 AD	500247 AD	500248 AD
500252 AD	500253 AD	500254 AD	500255 AD	500256 AD	500257 AD	500258 AD
500262 AD	500263 AD	500264 AD	500265 AD	500266 AD	500267 AD	500268 AD
500272 AD	500273 AD	500274 AD	500275 AD	500276 AD	500277 AD	500278 AD
500282 AD	500283 AD	500284 AD	500285 AD	500286 AD	500287 AD	500288 AD
500292 AD	500293 AD	500294 AD	500295 AD	500296 AD	500297 AD	500298 AD
500302 AD	500303 AD	500304 AD	500305 AD	500306 AD	500307 AD	500308 AD
500312 AD	500313 AD	500314 AD	500315 AD	500316 AD	500317 AD	500318 AD
500322 AD	500323 AD	500324 AD	500325 AD	500326 AD	500327 AD	500328 AD
500332 AD	500333 AD	500334 AD	500335 AD	500336 AD	500337 AD	500338 AD
500342 AD	500343 AD	500344 AD	500345 AD	500346 AD	500347 AD	500348 AD
500352 AD	500353 AD	500354 AD	500355 AD	500356 AD	500357 AD	500358 AD
500362 AD	500363 AD	500364 AD	500365 AD	500366 AD	500367 AD	500368 AD
500372 AD	500373 AD	500374 AD	500375 AD	500376 AD	500377 AD	500378 AD
500382 AD	500383 AD	500384 AD	500385 AD	500386 AD	500387 AD	500388 AD
500392 AD	500393 AD	500394 AD	500395 AD	500396 AD	500397 AD	500398 AD

On Kawara, *One Million Years*
(courtesy Fluent Collaborative)

For Stein, Williams and Oppen words resided over against the writer. Williams watches them appear as entities on the page in his typewriter, when composing a poem between seeing patients. Do we really *read* the numbers in Kawara's book?

Creeley's 1966 poem, "A Piece," "reads" as a whole which uses numbers:

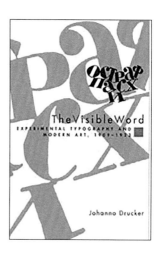

One and one, two, three.

"A Piece" by
Robert Creeley

Creeley once remarked: "I knew that for me ["A Piece"] was central to all possibilities of statement"(in Edelberg 140). What, in 1966, was a *statement*?

Johanna Drucker points out, in *The Visible Word: Experimental Typography and Modern Art, 1909-1923*, that the very presence of the typography in Modernist graphics insisted "upon the autonomous status of the work of art (visual or literary) which veritably defines the founding premise of modernism"; that firmness rested "upon the capacity of words to claim the status of *being* rather than *representing*" (10). Stein and Williams precede the typographical experiments.

What was this very early period like—anticipated, in some respect signaled, by Mallarmé? Allan Bullock's essay "The Double Image" contrasts two images—a 1904 photograph of the street in front of the

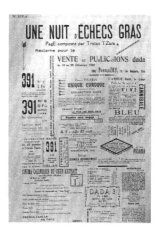

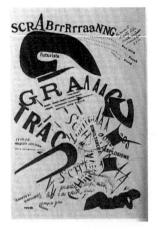

London Exchange, and Picasso's 1907 painting *Les Demoiselles d'Avignon* (58-59). Bullock sketches Modernism's profound changes, not merely in art and poetry. Nevertheless, he doesn't discuss photography, which had burgeoned decades before then (fueling Impressionism). He might have mentioned early cinema. The first time a film was shown to an audience in 1896, in France, the year before *Un Coup de des* was published,

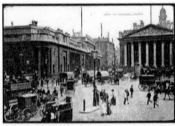

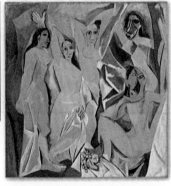

London Royal Exchange, circa 1904
(above; tinted photo, photographer unknown)
Les Demoiselles D'Avignon, 1907
(right, Picasso)

patrons left the movie house transformed. Psychologically, writes Stephen Bottomore, "the very fact of seeing one's own society and, indeed, oneself reflected on the screen was in itself amazing. The cinema enabled a person to 'stand outside of himself' and see again an event he had already experienced" (179). Film also imparted the fundamental sense of motion. People gained a new self-locus. Photography, cinema, made a difference.

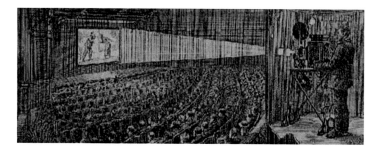

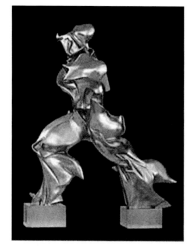

Umberto Boccioni, *Forme uniche
della continuità nello spatio* (*Unique
form of continuity in space*), 1913

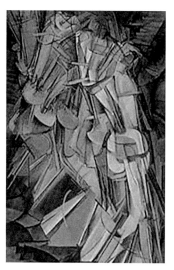

Marcel Duchamp, *Nude
Descending a Staircase*, 1912

Einstein's first paper on Relativity was published in 1905.
Motion, in an intuited space-time, was inherent in a 1913
sculpture by Umberto Boccioni, the principle painter of the

Futurist movement. Boccioni's figure appears to be walking forward as if in *phases* of motion. Marcel Duchamp had painted *Nude Descending a Staircase* the year before. His concept was borrowed from Edward Muybridge's still sequence of motion, such as the famous galloping horse that was captured on film (Malamud 68). Duchamp's nude *descends* the staircase, as depicted in visual stages. His painting was included in New York's 1913 Armory show that mesmerized Williams. I find it difficult to ignore his triadic structure, in this regard,

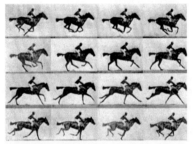

Muybridge's Galloping Horse Sequence, *circa* 1886

which was to be fully developed later as in "Asphodel, That Greeny Flower." Perhaps "The Red Wheelbarrow" discloses that structure still to come, its lineation. The nude's body of Duchamp's painting resonated a new stage of industrialism.

Body parts resemble steel girders of a skyscraper, or parts of an erector set. The Erector Set was first sold the year of the Armory show (1913). The Woolworth Building, rivaled in height only by New York's recently

BOOK I
Of asphodel, that greeny flower,
    I come, my sweet,
        to sing to you!
My heart rouses
    thinking to bring you news
        of something
that concerns you
    and concerns many men. Look at
        what passes for the new.
You will not find it there but in
    despised poems.
        It is difficult
to get the news from poems
    yet men die miserably every day
        for lack
of what is found there.

constructed Metropolitan Life Tower (1909), was also completed in 1913. That year, Duchamp "creates" the first of his *readymades*, the bicycle wheel. His conceptual object celebrates a *machine aesthetic*.

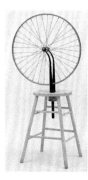

A century on, the sense of motion was an element in the layout of *Silence*, the 2015 Kawara retrospective at New York's Guggenheim Museum—the viewer doing the moving, from one painting of a written date to another, the paintings hung along the museum's descending, circular ramp. The building was completed in 1959. Frank Lloyd Wright proposed it in 1943. Williams' "Asphodel," with its stair-step structure, was published in 1955.

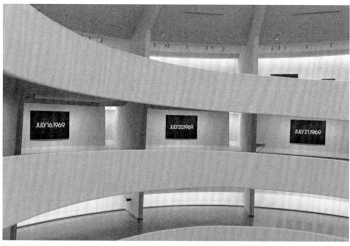

Silence, a Retrospective of On Kawara's work, 2015
(courtesy Guggenheim Museum, NYC)

The *Silence* show at the Guggenheim included a number of the date paintings that themselves made up a series titled *Today*. Kawara began making word art in the mid sixties. Three younger artists would do similar things. About the time when

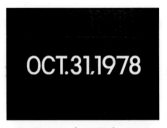

On Kawara, from *Today* series
(courtesy Creative Commons)

he starts his *Today* series, Joseph Kosuth began to create his own verbal statements on canvases.

In the later seventies, Jenny Holzer creates a words series she titles *Truisms*. At first her "Truisms" were simple, italicized inscriptions on white paper, which she affixed to telephone booths. Later, she set her statements in ever

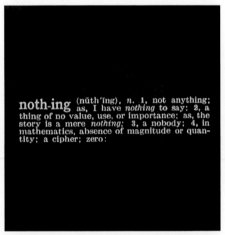

Joseph Kosuth, *Art as Idea as Idea (Nothing)*,
1966-68 (courtesy Creative Commons)

more durable substances: aluminum, bronze, and stone.

In the eighties, Barbara Kruger takes found photographs and adds texts to them. The words are not merely incorporated within the image in these works. Rather, the words are appropriated by the photo's dynamically visual, material values. Any aesthetic, cerebral, ideological potential of the words' syntax is subsumed within the tensions of the photo-image, c o n t r i b u t i n g to a subliminal experience free of formal wording.

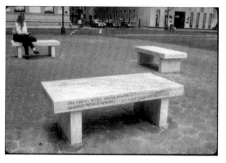

Jenny Holzer: Benches (photo by Oren Slor; courtesy Public Art Fund)

Do Kruger's photos tell us something about conceptual poetry that begins to bloom in the nineties? Our reception of photography has involved what Drucker terms "myths of temporality" ("Temporal Photography" 23). Conditioned by the photo's visual field, the words, the writing as such, contribute to a "radical incompleteness," as Drucker says of the archetypal snapshot (23). The words in a Kruger photo, although vividly presented, have been subordinated to the image's greater, overwhelmingly visual impact of which the words are a part, within the viewer's aesthetic response. As typical of the snapshot, Drucker notes, there's the sense that the photo's "moment of exposure provides instant repleteness." Similarly, "the

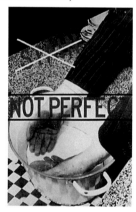

Barbara Kruger, *Untitled (Not Perfect)*, 1980, (courtesy Guggenheim Museum, NYC

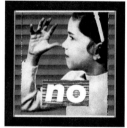

Untitled (No), 1985 (courtesy Smithsonian American Art Museum)

67

static photograph often deceived us into thinking it was a complete image of a bounded moment […]" ("Temporal Photography" 24, 25). Even so, the photo is a "temporal image"; in other words, the photo, "necessarily an event, with duration," is imbued with "uncertain boundaries, arbitrary beginnings and endings" (24).

The semantics of statements are inherently temporal. The snapshot most of all invites a false presumption. Kruger's work challenges this deception, and brings forward the photographic image's integral tensions by, to borrow from Drucker, "introducing a temporal axis into the image" so that an instability is created; hence the photo's "capacity to reify dissolves. The image will not compose, will not stand still […]" (Drucker 24).

caresses cuticle of index finger. Fingers lay atop one another, rubbing repeatedly. Ring finger attempts to cross middle finger. Right pinkie attempts to cross cuticle of right ring finger. Pinkie shifts back. Three middle fingers on right hand join. Bend at middle. Overlap. Thumb bends. Pinkie attempts to cross three bent fingers to meet thumb. Fingers strain. Return to normal position. Arm drops. Grasp. Arm drops. Grasp. Right hand rests. Fingers bend. Fingers outstretch. Arc backwards. Fingers relax. Bend concavely. Right hand forms fist. Thumb bends. Settles perpendicularly across fore and middle fingers. Step up. Body weight rests on balls of feet. Deep breaths. Exhale. Tongue extends and touches cleft on lip. Right arm raises. Elbow juts. Wrist rubs mouth. Sucks mucus. Swallows. Butts tongue against forefingers. Chest swells. Right

Kenneth Goldsmith, from *Fidget* (1994), p. 61

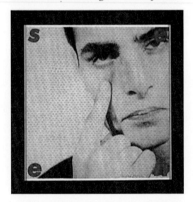

Untitled (Seen), 1985 (courtesy Smithsonian American Art Museum)

It's also true that "[p]hotography has become one of the principal devices for experiencing something, for giving an appearance of participation," as Susan Sontag realized in the early seventies (*On Photography* 177)—and as I believe Kruger has known. Her understanding of the pivotal role of photography in our society lies at the heart of her project. Drucker explains how "[m]uch of our sense of self as a bounded entity [now] comes from photographic processes"; these processes

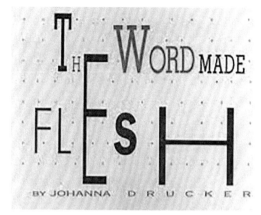

Johanna Drucker,
front cover of *The Word Made Flesh*

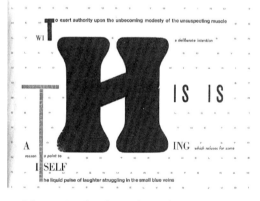

Johanna Drucker, from *The Word Made Flesh*

"transform the fragmented phenomenological sensorium of the embodied, distributed perceiving self into a fragmented, reified image" (24, 25). In thinking about Kruger's work, I wonder if, intrinsically, text is not a force of disaggregation.

I wonder if there's a principle, in this analysis of Kruger particularly, which reveals something about the vanguard conceptual poetry of the nineties. When I think about conceptualist works, in that decade, by Tan Lin, Harryette Mullen, Kenneth Goldsmith, and Rob Fitterman—all pivotal then—I think about how they used print. Then I look forward to the experimental work in our present time.

I also think about the cusp of the nineties. That was when artistic work like Drucker's own *The Word Made Flesh* (1989, 1996) removed the photograph as a presence yet kept the image; in her case 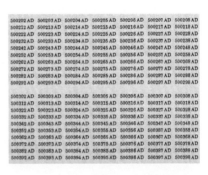 the image is front and center yet it's made of words, of typefaces. At one and the same time, *The Word Made Flesh* fulfills the potential in Mallarmé's *Un Coup de Des* of nearly a century earlier, in wordage and syntax bringing forward inscription that, in hindsight, certainly by the very end of the twentieth century, could be taken (mistakenly) as conceptual, yet which is fully the visual object.

Is the force of text what conceptual poems question? A book like *One Million Years* simply won't accommodate thinking about art in the mode of Adorno's *Aesthetic Theory*—his pronouncement that "all artworks are writing, not just those that are obviously such; they are hieroglyphs for which the code has been lost" (124). Literary people fall into a quandary over what's happening when artists use words.

What about an artist like Cy Twombly? There are images of Twombly's, of course, which invite a "reading" of them. Even their titles bracket any engagement of his images in terms of literacy, such as his *Letter of Resignation* series; these images may seem, in large, in a distant

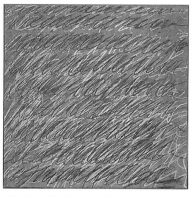

Cy Twombly, *Unknown, from On the Bowery*, 1971 (courtesy Chicago Art Institute)

glance, to resemble the format of a handwritten letter (a good example of which is *Letter of Resignation XXV*, 1967).

While these drawings can be comprehended as examples of asemic writing, his *drawings* need not be. "To read asemic writing," Peter Schwenger notes, "means to resist the pull of words" (146). The question is where Twombly started as an artist. As we see in a Kawara image, while it's an extension of writing,

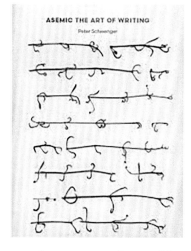

the instrument of "writing" was no longer a prosthesis of the hand, or, as Heidegger would say, it's no longer *vorhanden*. Kawara's *Silence* series evokes print. (The printing press is not immediately *at* hand, not *before* one's hand, such as a

71

pencil would be.) In *Asemic: The Art of Writing*, Schwenger contrasts such "writing" to the chirography we might normally take to be inscribed coding, which "translates into words something that is different from words" (147).

What's our visual and tactile experience of Kawara's printed numbers? We derive a sense of the whole, a totality, when we take his book *One Million Years* as an art object, the inscriptions within it. "The idea of the book," Derrida asserted in 1967, "is the idea of a totality [....] which always refers to a natural totality, [and it] is profoundly alien to the sense of writing" (*Of Grammatology* 30). At the gallery, the day I witnessed Kawara's book being read/recited—a "reading" in time, a work of performance art or conceptual art (take your pick?)—the numbers were not the point. The curators

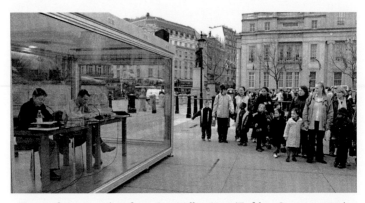

Two performers reading from *One Million Years*, Trafalgar Square in 2004.

of that Chelsea gallery, which I visited, saw an opportunity. The installations there brought forth pure space. In both halves of the gallery, something approaching pure abstraction was being elicited, most of all if I was just *looking* at the art objects. Mimesis, as a literary force, was all but absent.

Kawara's book (first shown in 1999 at New York's MoMA) precedes a book by the conceptual poet Matthew Timmons, which is made up of credit card offerings and dunnings. He titled the book *Credit* (it was published in 2009, the year of the Chelsea gallery show). The book's physical presence is unavoidable. It's materially beautiful. The fact that its purchase price is a bit steep is another element in the work's *conceptualization*—not only might you not need to read the book; you also need not purchase it.

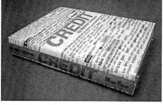

Matthew Timmons, *Credit*, 2009

Credit is thought of as *literary* art. The numbers in Kawara's book elude the notion that inscription can signify speech. In *Of Grammatology*, Derrida's pronouncement stands out: "the problem of language has never been simply one problem among others" (6). A conceptual artist like Kawara flirts with the catastrophe of words. History is record keeping that relies on language's capacity to communicate. (Verse as we know it now, developed from preliterate linguistic techniques used to hold past events in memory.)

The expectation that language communicates is a ruse that was subverted by Language writing. Yet the Language project undermined its very impulse, through its striving to *not* say something in strings of words. These strings—these series?—recall a phantom syntactical order. The syntax has been stretched or disrupted to the point of disclosing a once-hidden recognition. This is not to say that such subversion cannot be accomplished in subtle ways that both celebrate and question tradition—as in *The Nude Formalism* (1989) by Susan Bee and Charles Bernstein, at the cusp of the nineties. Their 1989 collaboration invites into the Language poem classic beauty and élan even as they're destabilized.

Bernstein and Bee collaborated on six published books between 1981 and 1998. Here's *Little Orphan Anagram* (1997):

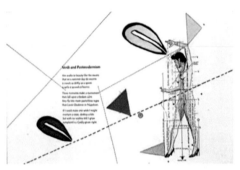

Little Orphan Anagram, 1997 (poems by Charles Bernstein, pictures and typography by Susan Bee)

Bernstein's text in *The Nude Formalism*—while more readable than in this 1997 work, similar to the earlier *Fool's Gold* in 1991—is nonetheless engulfed by Bee's artwork. Bee's presence also comes through, from within other elements of the work, simply in her choice of font. These three

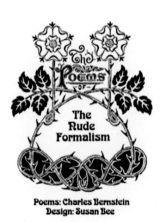

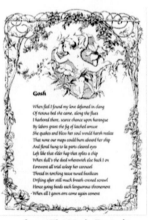

from *The Nude Formalism*

74

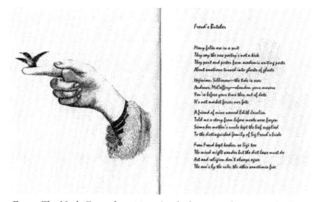

From *The Nude Formalism* 1989 (with design and typography by
Susan Bee and poems by Charles Bernstein)

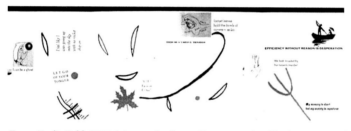

From *Fool's Gold*, 1991 (pictures by Susan Bee, poems by Charles Bernstein)

books are first works of art (even though Bernstein wrote the
poems that appear in *The Nude Formalism* sometime before
Bee took them as her starting point).

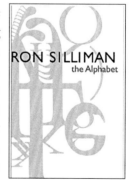

Language poetry, however, is more
often thought of as the kind of thing
Ron Silliman did, for example in
The Alphabet, published in 2008.
Certainly now, in hindsight, it does
seem to me that *The Alphabet*'s
various sections were prototypes for
the conceptualism of the nineties.
Silliman published the sections

beforehand, not necessarily written in alphabetical order (in the book, each section starts with the consecutive letter of the English alphabet), yet they were always projected to be part of an eventual book that would possess a sense of coherence. The eventual book *per se* stands as a monument to that development.

The tome's material heft added to the sense of Silliman's proceduralism. The long poems, which would make up the collection's various sections, foreground inscription. Inscription is also an explicit theme in the collection. *The Alphabet* possesses unusual value in its materialist poetics. The book

> offend no one. End lines precisely
> where it makes least sense, until
> a new order emerges – then examine
> that. Even the one syllable word,
> the simple morpheme (the letter "A")
> contains a caesura. Brush your tongue

The Alphabet (p.754) by Ron Silliman

is literally metatextual. "It is not that / there is no narrative / here (each sentence is a / narrative, / each line *moves*)," Silliman writes, adding "but / that there is no hierarchy / of narratives (not even / the story of the poem), no /sentence / to which the others [. . .] defer and are / ranked" (p. 835).

The book begins and ends with a focus on the physical act of writing. The very first line of *The Alphabet* asks "If the function of writing is to 'express the world'"—the question balanced by the book's final line: "The angle of my pen as it brushes this page[.]" For Silliman, time is constrained in the act of writing, while, akin to the pattern/randomness paradigm that marks his proceduralist method of composition, he calls attention to the actuality of writing, celebrating its material ontology.

76

Kenneth Goldsmith's mid-nineties book *Fidget* (January 1994) has a similar effect upon us. *Fidget* is the third of a triad, along with *One Million Years* and *The Alphabet*. These are three distinct Platonic emanations of a book filled with obdurate text whose paper and design ultimately tell the real story. Timmons' *Credit* makes a fourth.

KENNETH
FIDGET
GOLDSMITH

Aside from the conceptual prank of recording successive moments on a certain day (not necessarily a lift from Kawara), Goldsmith's *Fidget* is a materialist-conceptualist *objet d'art* that must have been an influence on Timmons. Each author's aesthetic choice was hardly capricious. The notion that we should actually be reading a book like *Fidget* is, to my mind (Marjorie Perloff might disagree), essentially absurd, although it's quite unlikely that making

eleven hours walking body moves arm swinging contraunison leg movements deep breath inside salivation nine pm left finger index finger rubs eye counterclockwise one two three times tip of finger moist from eye fluids deep breath mucus expulsion via spit deep breath yawn eyes view sky getting darker upper teeth bite outside of lower lip little finger of right hand itches above eyebrows walking fingers curl on right hand particularly pinkie nestled in flesh of palm thumbs leads out burp left leg crosses over right walk left right left right moon rises deep breath might fist moving in out one two three four he no he right hand reaches into back pocket knees bend in tripod five after nine licks lips licks lick

Fidget by Kenneth Goldsmith

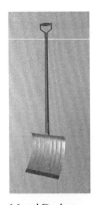

Marcel Duchamp, *Prelude to a Broken Arm* (*En prévision du bras cassé*), 1915

an absurd gesture on the part of any of these authors was an intention, at least in the sense of what goes on in, let's say, the Theatre of the Absurd. Rather, the book itself stands forth as being *there*—just as a *readymade* is *there*.

Reading Kawara's *One Million Years*, aloud, represents a separate set of expectations. I realize that in my saying this I've stepped into my own trap. I don't see the point in distinguishing here between conceptual poetry and conceptual art.

What these books share is the foregrounding of a material substrate. In his study, *No Medium*, Craig Dworkin discusses Ronald Johnson's *RADI OS* (1977)—Johnson's erasure of the first four books of Milton's *Paradise Lost* (just to use *erasure* as an emblem for the aesthetics of all kinds of poetry and art).

Erasure is neither a disappearance nor a dissolution. It's not an end of something. We can, Dworkin says, look

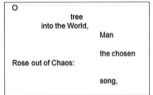

from *Radi Os* by Ronald Johnson

at the opaque material remainder, at the inescapable *residuum of recalcitrant physical matter* left behind when certain inscriptions do not occur as expected. [T]he *substrate* can be seen not as a transparent signifier but as an object in its own right, replete with its own material properties, histories, and signifying potential. (9, my emphases)

78

Dworkin sees art as a presence-absence phenomenon, which comprehends avant-garde poetry, its material "substrate" as being there to be *read*—yet also to be read almost after the fact.

Since the start of the twentieth-century, the materiality of the work is what increasingly occupies our engagement of it. Peter Quartermain describes Stein's writing, in his study *Stubborn Poetries*, as the "sheer presence of [. . .] words, the obduracy of [a] language and its refusal to explain" (8). There is no need to look for "alternative strategies," he points out—whereas Dworkin furnishes them with great aplomb. As for Drucker, she talks about "the basic conflict"—yet it "disappears if the concept of materiality is understood as a process of interpretation rather than a positing of the characteristics of an object" (*The Visible Word* 43); the latter would be to overlook the point of Modernist typography.

The Duchampian *readymade* (with its Dadaist gesture, its dissolving of a distinction between high and low art, etc.), like that typography, stands apart from art criticism or more largely cultural criticism insofar as it represents Duchamp's response, perhaps a subconscious one, to technological transformation, a transformation that has given rise to an industrial machine aesthetic.

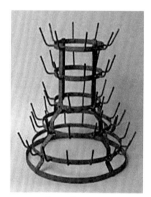

Marcel Duchamp, *Bottle Dryer*, 1914

In hindsight, this machine aesthetic, subject to related forces, heralded the end of art or rather its merging into design and technology, such as, later, we see in the iPhone—which is about the time when Conceptual "poetry" becomes prevalent, the distant consequence of a process R. L. Rutsky describes, echoing Heidegger, as "modern instrumental rationality [turning] on itself, and in the process turning into something else" (*High Technē* 106).

In its "abstraction of form from function," Modernist art was complicit in the eventual dominance of this relentless version of the rational, given "the rise of technological reproducibility" (Rutsky106). Duchamp's bicycle wheel is a case in point. It exemplified, as had come to be true, "the reproduction, alteration, and reassembly of elements removed from their previous contexts," which occurred as part of a process, and which "[became] an end in itself. Stripped of

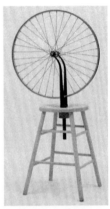

Duchamp, *Bicycle Wheel*, 1913

both aura and instrumentality, these elements [were to] become 'purely' stylistic or 'aesthetic', empty signifiers [. . .] recombined in virtually any way" (106).

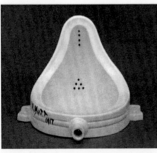

Marcel Duchamp, *Fountain*, 1917

Duchamp intuited the technological shift that underlies cultural codes. (In this respect, we can think about Walter Benjamin's essay, "The Work of Art in the Age of Mechanical Reproduction," which struggles to find a balance as he faced the onslaught of machinic reproducibility.) "Technological reproduction becomes increasingly similar to artistic production," Rutsky writes. This is the case, at least within the avant garde, as the making of art and poetry relies progressively on "technological reproducibility" leading ultimately, she argues, to style supplanting art: "because the process or logic of technological reproducibility itself comes increasingly to be seen as 'aesthetic', as a matter of style," and because "the function of high-tech devices has become increasingly a matter of reproduction." This is to say that high tech becomes "a matter of reproducing and multiplying cultural styles" (106-07).

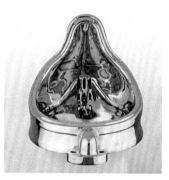

Sherrie Levine,
Fountain (Madonna),1991
(courtesy wikiart.org)

In the cultural moment when the iPhone began to influence art-world productions, "'high-tech' style" was about to be "defined by its 'imitation' of functionalism"—certainly fulfilling Lyotard's conceptualization of *postmodernity* in this way (Rutsky 113).

Modernism in the nineties, nevertheless, still is the force it was originally, at least in some organizing sense. We can call Conceptual poetry, even Language poetry, *Postmodern* if we like, although the very term *Postmodern* pays backhanded homage to Modernism, much what Sherrie Levine pays to Duchamp with her gleaming urinal.

Of course if she merely lifts, in its entirety, a Walker Evans photo (the apt comparison here would be a Goldsmith poem such as *Day*, 2003), then the question of the Poundian "new" takes on an unscripted resonance.

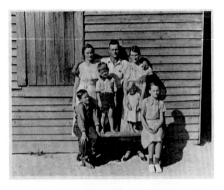

Sherrie Levine, *After Walker Evans: 2* (courtesy Metropolitan Museum of Art, New York City

"All the News that's Fit to Print"
The New York Times
Late Edition
New York: Today, mostly cloudy, high 83. Tonight, warm and muggy, low 73. Tomorrow, cloudy with a few showers, high 80. Yesterday, high 83, low 72. Weather map is on Page A20.
VOL. CXLIX . . . No. 51, 498
Copyright © 2000 The New York Times
NEW YORK, FRIDAY, SEPTEMBER 1, 2000
$1 beyond the greater New York metropolitan area.
75 CENTS
PENTAGON LIKELY TO DELAY NEW TEST FOR MISSILE SHIELD
JANUARY DATE EXPECTED
Deployment Decision Would Fall to Next President — Treaty Issue Remains
By ERIC SCHMITT
WASHINGTON, Aug. 31 — The Pentagon will probably postpone the next test of a national missile defense system until January, administration officials said yesterday. Any decision to deploy the antimissile shield now seems certain to pass out of President Clinton's hands to his successor's.
Administration officials had previously said Mr. Clinton would decide this

11 / A1 Day

from *Day* by Kenneth Goldsmith, 2003

Duchamp, realizing the common root of craft and art, played off it. *Fidget* resonates Goldsmith's instinctive understanding not merely of art or poetry. *Fidget* as well as later work of Goldsmith's are products of digital technology and information overload. The spirit of *The Alphabet*, Silliman's long poem, is inscription as both idea and practice, which anticipated the complete shift from language to material text. *The Alphabet* as a book—during its planned creation only to be imagined—sponsors the Conceptualism that signals Language poetry's obsolescence.

Words, more so visible words (i.e., the technologies of writing and print), create cultural codes. Other conceptual poets share this premise. Mullen, Fitterman, and Lin establish themselves within a lineage extending back to Mallarmé who used the physical structure of the codex for poetic, artistic reasons.

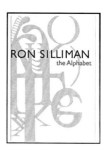

Mullen is explicit in making her understanding of this lineage apparent in *S*PeRM**K*T*. Here is its first page (notice the justified margins either side, and the line breaks):

> Lines assemble gutter and margin. Outside and in, they straighten a place. Organize a stand. Shelve space. Square footage. Align your list or listlessness. Pushing oddly evening aisle catches the tale of an eye. Displays the cherished share. Individually wrapped singles, frozen divorced compartments, six-pack widows all express themselves while women wait in family ways, all bulging baskets, squirming young. More on line incites the eyes. Bold names label familiar type faces. Her hand scanning throwaway lines.

from *S*PeRM**K*T* by Harryette Mullen

S*PeRM**K*T views material and cultural conditions within a hypercapitalist, consumerist society that operates under the aegis of the Baudrillardan *simulacrum*. Mullen's stance, shared by Fitterman and Lin, distinguishes them from older poets like Silliman. That the margins are justified left and right in Mullen's poem is important, especially in her metatextual opening sentence: "Lines assemble gutter and margin."

The book becomes the organization of the *supermarket* (the poem's title—alternately *sperm kit*). A modern day supermarket is a bright and sterile source of what should be, but is not, spiritual sustenance to go along with nutritional sustenance (as such, it's a perversion of fecundity). Mullen's writerly self can,

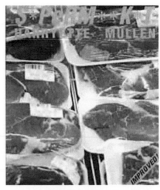

S*PeRM**K*T
by Harryette Mullen

hopefully, find authenticity in the sense of loss through sanitization. The store's Muzak becomes, in her second poem, "the sublime subliminal mobius soundtrack." She shops, making her way in a sexist society, moving through the "radiant stations of the crass" (*Recyclopedia* 66).

Fitterman is less vocal about the absence of the originary *real* and the alienation of consumerism in his *Metropolis* series. Yet his page design, for instance in "Metropolis 16," conveys the spiritual silence in the negative space of a mall's directory, whose visual figuration is that of a list,

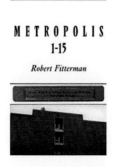
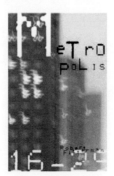
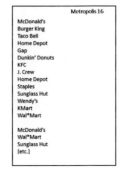

from "Metropolis 16" by Rob Fitterman

the names of corporate retailers, ironically bringing forth the sense of being lost, the opposite of *real*. Years later "Metropolis 16" (1998) is retitled "Directory" (2009), now a stand-alone poem (with a few updated names of stores).

What has disappeared from the vacuous, hypercapitalist world is history (tangibility as well). Tan Lin's 1996 book, *Lotion Bullwhip Giraffe*, comments on this. The book's opening poem, "The Imitations of History," indicates the transformation of language into something that signifies secondarily. The condition of the simulacrum, à la Baudrillard, is imagined as "a coupon facing a mirror."

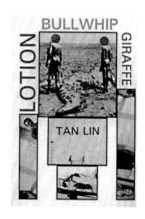

Digital code, nevertheless a simulacrum, is evoked in Lin's cynical line, "the computer enters the moon's tendencies." A shopping coupon's reflection in a mirror is the unreal reflection of the shopper (not even the sun's light reflected to earth by the moon). Products on the supermarket shelves are a lack of authentic connection.

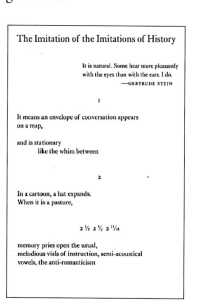

The Imitation of the Imitations of History

It is natural. Some hear more pleasantly
with the eyes than with the ears. I do.
—GERTRUDE STEIN

I

It means an envelope of conversation appears
on a map,

and is stationary
like the whim between

2

In a cartoon, a hat expands.
When it is a pasture,

2 ½ 2 ⅗ 2 ¹¹/₁₆

memory pries open the usual,
melodious vials of instruction, semi-acoustical
vowels, the anti-romanticism

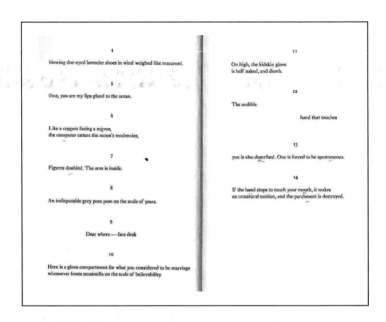

His book discloses a shifting technological as well as cultural paradigm; language in poetry, as signifying, gives way to the material plenitude of art, sheer mark-making. Yet the "real" of "parchment" ("If the hand stops to touch your mouth, it makes / an unnatural motion, and the parchment is destroyed") is to be superseded by the electronic screen's phantasm.

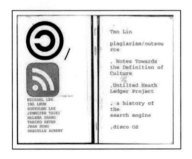

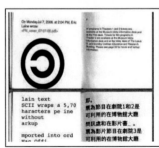

Lin's 2007 poem "plagiarism/outsource" serves as his later counterpoint. Best known in the present time as a digital poet/artist, Lin reprises "The Imitations of the Imitations of History" in this later volume that shows how the mediation of signs in digital code, within a more robust media

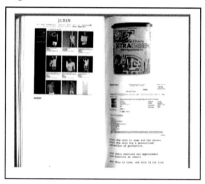

environment, undermines a physical substrate. The many transmutations of design, text or medium in this book demonstrate the material "substance" of an inscription as equivocal. Within Lin's compass, this is exhilarating. And it seems to be taking us back to the paradox of writing as embodied in Kawara's date paintings.

If the numbers are simulacra, then our attempts to express them are futile. Kawara's Guggenheim show was named *Silence*. The material remains of Kawara's works and life are liberating, extant as the traces of a life he conceptualized.

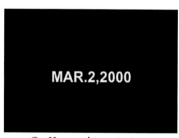

On Kawara date painting
(from Wikimedia, courtesy Espyyyy)

Works Cited

Adorno, Theodor W. *Aesthetic Theory*. Ed. and Trans. Robert Hullot-Kenter. New York / London: Continuum Books, 1997.

Allen, Donald M. Ed. *The New American Poetry: 1945 – 1960*. New York / London: Grove Press / Evergreen Books, 1960.

Baudrillard, Jean. *Simulacra and Simulation*, Ann Arbor: U of Michigan P, 1994.

_____. *Simulations*, New York: Semiotext(e), 1983.

Bee, Susan, with poems by Charles Bernstein. *Fool's Gold*. Tucson: Chax P, 1991.

_____, with poems by Charles Bernstein. *Little Orphan Anagram*. (New York: Granary Books, 1997.

_____, with poems by Charles Bernstein. *The Nude Formalism*. Los Angeles: Sun and Moon, 1989.

Bottomore, Stephen. "The Panicking Audience? Early Cinema and the 'Train Effect'." *Historical Journal of Film, Radio and Television* 19.2 (1999): 177-216.

Bullock, Alan. "The Double Image." *Modernism, 1890-1930*. Ed. Malcolm Bradbury and James McFarlane. New York: Penguin, 1976; 58-70.

Creeley, Robert. "A Piece." *Pieces*. New York: Scribner, 1969.

Drucker, Johanna. "Temporal Photography." *Philosophy of Photography* Vol.1 (2010): 23-29.

_____. *The Visible Word: Experimental Typography and Modern Art, 1909-1923*. Chicago: U of Chicago P, 1994.

Edelberg, Cynthia Dubin. *Robert Creeley's Poetry: A Critical Introduction*. Albuquerque: U of New Mexico P; 1978.

Fitterman, Rob. *Metropolis 15.* Los Angeles: Sun and Moon P, 2000.
_____. *Metropolis 16-29.* Toronto: Coach House Books, 1998.

Goldsmith, Kenneth. *Fidget.* Toronto: Coach House Books, 1994.

Johnson, Ronald. *RADI OS.* Chicago: Flood Editions, 2005.

Kawara, On. *One Million Years.* David Zwirner Gallery, New York
    City. January 9—February 14, 2009.

_____. *On Kawara—Silence.* Guggenheim Museum. New York City. 6
    February – 3 May, 2015.

_____. *Postcards: I Got Up.* 1968-1979. New York: Guggenheim

    Museum. Online. Accessed 14December 2017.
_____. *Today Series / Date Paintings.* Begun 4 January 1966, ending
    five decades later.

Kruger, Jan-Louis. "William Carlos Williams' Cubism: The Sensory
    Dimension." *Literator* 16.2 (August 1995): 195-213.
Leibowitz, Herbert. "Halfway to Hell: William Carlos Williams'
    'Kora in Hell'." *Literary Review* (1 June 2007): 34-56.

Lin, Tan. *Lotion Bullwhip Giraffe.* Los AngelesL: Sun and Moon P, 1996.

_____. *Heath (Plagiarism/Outsource).* La Laguna - Canary Islands, 2007.

Lyotard, Jean-François. *La condition postmoderne: rapport sur le savoir.*
    Paris: Minuit. 1979.

_____. *The Postmodern Condition: A Report on Knowledge.* Tr. Geoff
    Bennington and Brian Massumi. For. Fredric Jameson.
    Minneapolis: U of Minnesota P, 1984.

Mallarmé, Stéphane. *Un Coup de des jamais n'abolira le* hasard.
    Cosmopolis (May 1897): 8 ff.; Bruges: Imprimerie Sainte
    Catherine, 1914.

Malamud, Randy. *An Introduction to Animals and Visual Culture*. New York: Palgrave Macmillan, 2012.

Mullen, Harryette. *Recyclopedia: Trimmings, S*PeRM**K*T, and Muse & Drudge*. Saint Paul: Graywolf P, 2006.

_____. *S*PeRM**K*T*. Philadelphia: Singing Horse P, 1992.

Oppen, George. *New Collected Poems*. Ed. Michael Davidson. Pref. Eliot Weinberger. New York: New Directions, 2002.

_____. *Selected Prose, Daybooks and Papers*. Ed. and Intr. Stephen Cope. Berkeley: U of California P, 2007.

Quartermain, Peter. *Stubborn Poetries: Poetic Facticity and the Avant-Garde*. Tuscaloosa, U of Alabama P, 2013.

Rutsky, R. L. *High Technē: Art and Technology from the Machine Aesthetic to the Posthuman*. Minneapolos and London: U of Minnesota P, 1999.

Sandback, Fred. [Installations and Sculptures.] David Zwirner Gallery, New York City. January 9—February 14, 2009.

Schewenger, Peter. Asemic: *The Art of Writing*. Minneapolis / London: University of Minnesota Press, 2019.

Silliman, Ron. *The Alphabet*. Tuscaloosa, U of Alabama P, 2008.

Sontag, Susan. *On Photography*. 1973. New York: Farrar, Straus & Giroux / Rosetta Books, 2005.

Stein, Gertrude. "A Carafe that is a Blind Glass." *Tender Buttons*. New York: C. Marie, 1914.

Timmons, Matthew. *Credit*. Los Angeles: Blanc P, 2009.

Williams, William Carlos. "The Red Wheelbarrow." *Spring and All*. Paris: Contact Publishing Co., 1923.

THE BLUES, TOM WEATHERLY,
AND THE AMERICAN CANON

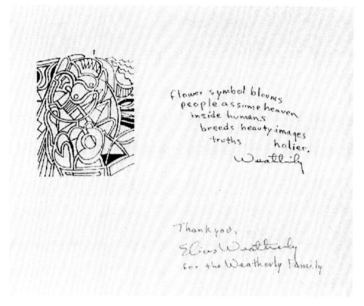

Flower symbol blooms
people assume heaven
inside humans
breeds beauty images
truths holier.
Weatherly

Thank you,
EC..s Weatherly
for the Weatherly family.

Letter to the author, August 26, 1991.

In 1964, as I was about to leave for college, I attended James Baldwin's new play *Blues for Mr. Charlie*. By then, Everett LeRoi Jones (a.k.a. LeRoi Jones, subsequently Amiri Baraka) had moved to Greenwich Village, though I would not discover him till the following year. Jones's equally brilliant and even more searing play, *Dutchman*, was also first produced that year. Baldwin had published *Notes of a Native Son* in 1955, which helped to create a Harlem of nearly mythic stature as he delved into its sorrows, complexities, and triumphs. *Nobody Knows My Name* (his title essay first appearing in 1959) was published three years before his play. The two books would find me much later in life. Not so *Preface to a Twenty Volume Suicide Note*, LeRoi Jones's first poetry collection, which also appeared three years before *Blues for Mr. Charlie* and *Dutchman*. The poems in that book seized me and would not let me go in the mid-sixties— which was when I met Tom Weatherly.

If you read Weatherly's sixties and early seventies poetry in something more than a cursory way, you'll see *Preface* in them. Jones's book seized him too—although I won't say that it was seminal for him. *Preface to a Twenty Volume Suicide Note*, *Dutchman*, and *Blues People* (appearing in 1960) were written by someone hailing from Newark, New Jersey, who had made a life in Greenwich Village. *Notes of a Native Son*, *The Fire Next Time* (1963), *Blues for Mr. Charlie*, and *Nobody Knows My Name*, which contained the great essay "Nobody Knows My Name: A Letter from the South," were written by someone born and raised in New York City. I wonder now if all these canonical works, already being seen by some in the sixties as just that, constituted a basic premise Weatherly—who was born and raised, and who died, in Alabama, after living most of his adult life in New York— would transform into his own overwhelmingly powerful and beautiful language, style, and point of view. What did he bring to the discussion, not only in New York, which neither Baldwin nor Jones (who becomes Amiri Baraka) could? The terribly moving and profoundly insightful "Nobody Knows My Name" was the observations of someone, Baldwin, who was seeing something for the first time, having just discovered the South. This great achievement of investigative journalism was a profoundly poetical meditation on just that:

It was on the outskirts of Atlanta that I first felt
how the Southern landscape—the trees, the silence,
the liquid heat, and the fact that one always seems
to be traveling great distances—seems designed for
violence, seems, almost, to demand it. What passions
cannot be unleashed on a dark road in a Southern
night! Everything seems so sensual, so languid, and
so private. Desire can be acted out here; over this
fence, behind that tree, in the darkness, there; and no
one will see, no one will ever know. Only the night
is watching and the night was made for desire. […]
In the Southern night everything seems possible, the
most private, unspeakable longings; but then arrives
the Southern day, as hard and brazen as the night was
soft and dark. It brings what was done in the dark to
light.

What Baldwin discloses to his northern readership (he was
on assignment from *Partisan Review*) was the very hot,
languid air Weatherly breathed from his first day on earth.

I met Tom Weatherly (a.k.a. Thomas Elias Weatherly Jr., a.k.a.
Elias Weatherly, a.k.a. Weatherly, a.k.a. eliyahu ben Avraham
in later life after he converted to and devoutly practiced
orthodox Judaism) in 1966–67, when both he and I were
setting ourselves down in the Village (East and West) to be
poets in some serious way. I tried to emulate the then-Jones
(as well as other poets mostly of what were considered to be
the Black Mountain School, such as Joel Oppenheimer). In
Weatherly's 1970 collection of poems, *Maumau American
Cantos*, references to—and otherwise the calling out of—

Jones abound. I didn't know it then like I know it now, but Weatherly's arrival in downtown Manhattan was momentous in ways mostly forgotten. It's time to remember.

Weatherly marks his arrival with a poem he names "a proper song, entitled: coonbitch, to polly green":

Traveln salesmen pump my joint
collective farm wife, make this
killn floor stern, killn deck
aft   document:
                    roi jones
                    in the year of our lady
                    did you not write
                    on page 17
                    "old envious   blues feeling"
the hound diggings where
ole bean dug up a pewter raccoon
our roots too deep to go down

or own to bunny
                    who'll buy my violets
                    I can't get started.

the peckers ride off
lookout mountain to some pass.
cut them off at possibly

possibly mosby is the posse
the marshal clan &
chases the treed muse, the flower of
backdoor.[1]

Get outta town, Roi!

By the time Weatherly came on the scene, Jones had
already married Hettie Cohen, and they'd had children
together. Here's Weatherly's poem "roi rogers and the
warlocks of space" (the third in a "roi rogers" series):

hadassah leavenburg
baby you're selected
marry me in my pre
fascist period. Why
because i
dig yo fat
thighs
rumped ass
bald domed tits
cunt that's a live
home to huge beasts.
we be fuckn kosher
'til I find what
shine means.[2]

Weatherly also married a Jewish woman, Carolyn Samuels,
and they had a son, Thomas Weatherly III ("Lil' Tomcat,"
back when). Here's a poem, "east corinthian" (the eleventh
and final canto in his 1970 volume), telling some of that story:

village period piece hettie
cohen got her jones, wiped th colostrum
off th mouf of his first poems
days down wif it.

east fifth street kikes have retreated to
maw of long-guyland, few ulanower cong.
a saturday holdn act from soap opera kahn.

lissen mama   right-handed-wingd
i'm head tomcat round this spray
net weight in th morning
c-wt. & eighty th motherfuckn all
limitd to th east side & fillmore music
gem spa & i cant spare a dime.
my poems & lil tomcat in your belly
teethn on raw blood too are down wif it
(totem is in th spirit house) th red-
bone hunger.[3]

Looking back on Weatherly's life and work, I don't think
it's a stretch to say that they inhabited the Blues, filled in
the Blues like a filled-in sketch now in color and depth,
helping the Blues to attain its full, great stature for which
it was destined. That it took a writer or two to make
this happen, musicians aside, is to me a curious fact.

I will have more to say about his poetry shortly, in the
above regard, but here it's important to mention the
groundbreaking anthology he coedited in 1970, *Natural
Process: An Anthology of New Black Poetry* (in which—he
insisted upon it, me a white Jew—I was published under
the pseudonym L. V. Mack, the maiden name of a young
woman who would become my first wife). To say that
Weatherly and his work were idiosyncratic —or, to use a
favorite word of his in his poems, *eclectic* —would be to
state the obvious. In any case, he was a downtown guy—a

mainstay at the Poetry Project, a participant in the Umbra Collective, who worked in Village restaurants and bars. But at that time how could he not have felt the magnetic force of uptown Manhattan? Although a participant (along with the likes of Edward Albee and others who would later be highly celebrated) in the Playwrights Horizon workshop in the West Village (whence in 1964 *Dutchman* was written in a single drunken night after a workshop session),[4] Baraka, Weatherly's senior, left Hettie and their kids along with his literary name, LeRoi Jones, to found the Black Arts Movement uptown (later returning to Newark, New Jersey, where he lived out the rest of his life with his wife Amina Baraka, formerly Sylvia Robinson, and their children). To understand Weatherly's poetry one has to consider the two poles he was pulled by once he arrived in New York from the deep South. Baldwin was of course an uptown figure, and at that time the *éminence grise*.

I thought Weatherly's writing in the late sixties was groundbreaking and had a lot to teach me as a fledgling poet. My fellow student at SUNY Cortland, Michael (M. G.) Stephens, had left school and set himself up in the East Village (as would another of us, Ron Edson, also a Cortland alum); having visited them and gotten a taste of what was happening there, the poetry especially, I myself left college at the end of 1967. Mike, Tom, and Ron were all members of the inaugural creative writing workshops at the Poetry Project, which was begun by Paul Blackburn (who would come to Cortland College to join its faculty) and whose first director was Oppenheimer; I attended Joel's workshop once, as well as readings at the Project at that time, and would see Joel and everyone else at the Lion's Head (the famed West Village watering hole for writers, poets, and journalists), where Tom was employed.

In Cortland, we three students were part of another workshop, which had been created by David Toor, a professor. David's brother worked in the same print shop as Joel. Many of the Black Mountain poets (and others who were included in Donald Allen's game-changing anthology, *The New American Poetry: 1945–1960*) thus came to Cortland to read and participate in our workshop. Eventually Weatherly was also brought to Cortland to do the poet turn.

The Black Mountain school, as it had come to be called, its poetics, was rooted in the modernist poetry of what the scholar Burton Hatlen once called "The Philadelphia Three"—Ezra Pound, H.D. (Hilda Doolittle), and William Carlos Williams, who, all still in their teens, first met in and around the University of Pennsylvania (Marianne Moore was not far off, in Bryn Mawr). In a 1986 letter, you can see Weatherly's debt to both H.D. and Pound. "I'm trying to go beyond my serious use of pun-like tropes to whole passages with that effect," he writes, possibly indicating as a purpose to make a poem in its entirety that has the unitary force of some ur-word. "The human passions are such," he says, turning to H.D and her poetry's influence in his poetry: "I hope I'm successful in what I say is a development of H.D.'s way of imaging and playing, with the jazz, blues, rnb, and country phrasing (& fugal influences[)]. We have strayed to [*sic*] far from dance music and its humanity."[5]

Years later, in a letter, he writes:

Burt, I know that you have ideas where I belong in the poet poem [these two words are written one above the other] spectrum. I claim that, broad sense, I àm a descendant of the imagists and the bluesists, and, and et cetera. I belong to the school of eclecticism; I will use any method, mode, and technology ever used so call me an eclecticist if you wish to call me something other than poet, just poet—acolyte of the syllable. Yes, the syllable; the word, the semantic content is our personality[,] it moves automatically out of our nature and nurture. We must make our poems sound.[6]

In many ways Weatherly, and another unusual poet, Ronald Johnson, are quite different. Yet their comparison is useful. They were both, let's say, "eclectic." And they both loved form and how words resided on the page; and they both shared the Pound-H.D.-Williams, and then Black Mountain, tradition.

My feeling, perhaps an exception to a widely held view, is that Weatherly didn't need to be eclectic but everything about him insisted on being exactly that, and what that was would never, could never, fit into anyone's category or description. He was a person of a number of worlds that, on their face, would have nothing to do with Alabama where he grew up, returning to

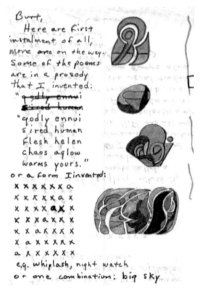

in old age, in the meanwhile living a life disparately. What pulled the threads of various worlds into a single skein was Weatherly the poet, and those who knew him, who read him, who were possibly excited and awed by him and loved him, were the larger for the grand poetic world he erected.

Some of what H.D. may have had to show him was how a word could sit on a page. He invented forms—the Glory and the Double Glory.

While the Glory and the Double Glory are entrenched in sound—as regards syllable stress, pitch, duration, rhyme, and so on (note, for example, in the diagrams here, the crisscrossing of the rhyme sound in the Double Glory), I think the *look* of a Weatherly poem was a matter he also took seriously. (Is it easier to have clean visual lines when your poem has only three syllables on a line, let's say, and only two or three lines in a stanza?)

Following is more diagramming, with some of Weatherly's explanation of these forms (note the attention he pays to consonants and their relationships to vowels).

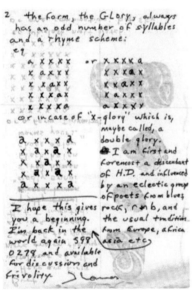

The above two images were part of a longer, now undated, letter—the envelope is missing —most likely sent to author in the mid- or late 1980s.

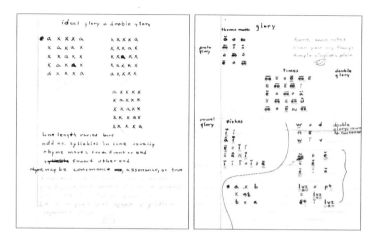

Looking at the below text, and the diagram following it, consider how many multisyllabic or Latinate words can be employed within the short line, and the short-poem form.

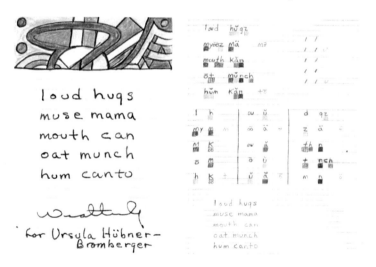

Now notice, below, how Weatherly works out the poem and explains it (n.b.: "canto" here comes from Pound's *The Cantos*).

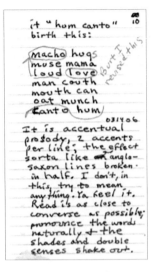

This and the four preceding images are contained within the cited letter to author, May 13, year uncertain due to blurred postmark.

Weatherly knew Pound's work inside and out—yet it was H.D. who became not so much his muse as interlocutor or confidante.

A *cotton mouf* uttered the most elegant language imaginable, was not averse to making reference to classical roots, and from them Weatherly's coming into fullness as a poet ("thomas mouths / smooth mythos / medusa / seemed amused").[7] He honored them in their bettering ("enter crete adept / erect word temple / poppy petal fumes / unset tunes never / better hd's flesh").[8] I found his poetry in the sixties and on through *Mau Mau American Cantos*, and *Thumbprint* published the following year, astonishing on a number of counts, among those his explorations well beyond the modernist purview.

What he was writing partook of a cutting-edge approach to understanding poetry that was present in the work of some other poets in those early Poetry Project workshops. Even so, his poems possessed a rigor and, let's call it, deeply intuitive grasp of, and belief in, syntax vis-à-vis particles of speech, with which he fashioned a music that was more muscular than just being sinuous. His music— which in his mature work can be experienced vividly and deeply at the same time as it's being purposely strained through an austere prosody—never departed from its sonorous values, remarkably, at the same time that in it we feel the thud of talk, of human speech.

Weatherly's poetry—erudite and adventurous—truly stands alone. At first the poetry will not disclose its erudition—not even, at first, its amazing wit and profound insights, yet, after reading some of his poems, and letting them settle in, the full magnitude and singularity of their lyric voice begins to make its presence known. Furthermore, we can find his mature lyric voice in the early poems (something I'll turn to shortly), such as this love poem from the 1971 collection:

> Nadine
> > for vlada
>
> we hold hi school hands
> fuck i mean that
> as love we workd out
> th 50s our own down ways
> dreams would be jaild.
>
> your jelly mama
> th way you walk & roll ass
> soul eyes innocent.
> black cat bone hunger
> pigmeat heifer. fuck you
> like a song chuck
> berry.[9]

103

In passing, let me note the fact that here we are seeing an American poetry (of course, "nadine" refers to the Chuck Berry song if not to something or someone else), for all its calling out of America's murderous shortcomings—which can be addressed directly, or which, as in the above poem, can simply be an immanence out of which the lyricism springs. The darkness in the lyricism is ever-present, while the élan of a Weatherly poem establishes an unexpected beauty and grace. In *Maumau* Weatherly had written:

> "South African Judge
>   Rules Family Is White,
>   Not Colored."
>
> court changen race by legal decree
>
> worn it is a gesture
> as skin, suit won in south
> mericu court i'd be proud
> declared white in new jersey
> or Georgia.   Proud   mericu
>
> experience limitd
> to these states
> i'm in for meric.
>
> whereas the meri states
> beautiful the gods the heroes
>
> if a jigaboo I spill milk
> coming he spill it going.

there are like homer's blues
themes. Black humpd under
magnolia writn
life of the great black
wasp. State
oracles divine, witch docs
sprinkle bone dust

mericus mojo

I stay here wearing thin
suitd for the climate.

New York Times
April 30, 1967, p. 86

Postmodern Blue

That the early poems' originality finally redounds to some greater art and ethos cannot remain hidden for very long. The remainder of this essay endeavors to elucidate a poetics that takes Weatherly's biographical circumstances into account. The poetics has its roots, as has been discussed, but I just want also to advance the notion that this poetics is peculiarly personal relative to his personal history. Needless to say that such an assertion may obtain to just about any poet—nevertheless, given the sweep of American political and cultural history during Weatherly's lifetime (in which he played a part), I would argue that my consideration of his life within a period that, in some respects, might be said to have been marked by extraordinarily dramatic change, enjoys a special purchase in our coming to appreciate his artistic power.

Weatherly knew the Objectivists' poetry and theorizing enough to rival them while drawing upon the lessons he'd learned especially from Pound and H.D. whom he never stopped studying. His emerging lyric voice when we were young was new news for me. His continuous meditation on language and what makes poetry would evolve, perhaps in part from his intellectual pursuits, yet I suspect that his utter mastery of the short line and condensed lyric, as evinced in the late and great volume of poetry he titled *short history of the saxophone* (in which the voice has receded while its haunting presence is felt as the essential element of the poem), is what most of all should be remembered.

Let me add to this one other thought, which has to do with what might seem like a gulf between the early work—before Weatherly seemingly let go of the need to pursue publication (or whatever it was that led him to step away from the public adulation he was earning)—and the work of *short history*. I would like to advance a thesis in this regard, having to do with at least an unconsciously developing praxis on his part, one culminating in the final section of this late book. This thesis has to do with his economy. I find in his poetry, increasingly pronounced in the late poetry, more meaning than would be possible in a larger number of words. Also, if you read through the mature book, you see the same words over and over.

These words often appear in the early books—not with such frequency, nonetheless in key poetic moments. Take, for example, the word *blues*—with its open "oo" sound, as in *boogie tune*, a key phrase of his, as well as in often-used words in his poems such as *music, loony, brute*, etc. They show off the favored "note" in the Weatherly oeuvre. What does that sound represent or evoke in our primal experience of life and death, of exquisite pleasure or pain?

The opening poem of *short history of the saxophone*, titled "musick," anticipates the multi-section fugue concluding the book, *wally*. Even so, *musick* reaches back to the early books, establishing the basis for the fugue. What might it mean to find, in Weatherly's poetry, the most highly refined as well as original *brute music*? That the following poem opens *short history* is not without special significance.

musick

bluesy subtle bluest
thence beauty blooms
sunlit bluets center
whence brutal musics
humans vent as blues[11]

Wally calls back to what I think is the greatest conception in *Maumau American Cantos*, the most powerful, raw, and graceful poem in that book, and what I regard as its signature lyric, "blues for frank wooten":[12]

blues for frank wooten
    House of the Lifting of the Head

let me open mama your 3 corner box.
yes open mama your 3 corner box.
i have a black snake baby his tongues hot.

you shake round those curves baby dont quite make the grade.
you shake round those curves baby dont make the grade.
man come home tired dont want no lemonade.

we been blowing spit bubbles baby in each others mouf.
we been blowing spit bubbles baby in each others mouf.
burst all them bubbles mama norf cold like the souf.

let me be your woodpecker mama tom do like no pecker would.
let me be your woodpecker mama tom tom do like no
    pecker would.
open your front door baby black dark come home for good.[13]

What goes relatively understated in this poem is fleshed out in its book's multisectioned eponymous poem, where *blues* repeatedly carries out its pivotal function (as shown below).

MAUMAU AMERICAN CANTOS

1

intersection

honking sirens approach at,
searchlights

honk out
FRANK

kill you dipshit fagot
motherfuckers.

& frank never know
how to outguess stupidity

the blood, the mean
woodenframe the coptic site
blues

the mans honking

dont come

at my door.

CANTO 2

the yellow brick road

for trane[14]

we trespass the blues
hanging outhouses in picture frames

a record heard
live performance
blow easily
        forgotten phrase. we bleep
        dont read music. listen
dont move dont you remember
saxophones never die.

titty toad down
remember, read scratchy
sheet music, croak
in the backyard.

CANTO 3 [excerpt]

[...] the sirens
honk at my hymns to malcolm [...][15]

CANTO 4 [excerpt]

      speak of my
      self respect

> for myself
> no success, the score is
> success, the ritual put down
> all the blues gone west
> mongers of the world unite!

CANTO 5

coon fire

the landscape was
musical cartoons.

tattoo the sound of
blood on my eardrums

taut, the tenses
i were wolfish to dance
dance the half romance
the language

& violence, music to
dance to
violate the progress:

rust at the muscle.

CANTO 6 [excerpt]

americus mojo

brown stone woman honkn outside,
my honeydew rider.
                              o deliver me   my lady, tom
reconstructed tom, dont ride no more fronts for the lily
BLACKJACK PERSHING
                         THE HIGH KITE SUCK
YOUR
                         BONES.
east fifth street sings TPF out my ears[16] the morning
     you're not here
[...]

CANTO 7

first thesis
     for m.l.k., jr.

aim   get your sights & its sound
in abstract or journal movements
to a peace settlement

old fancy western

dude shot my man

dead,
          precious lord blow off
theres no willy in th blues theres no you.

CANTO 8 [excerpt]

valley stream carol[17]

[…]
freight trains gone in last round house. home
fret no music made, no drama, shiftless
out of head gear, disorient blues takes firm
control these days keep me cool enuf collect
my thots my fingers (your river hips flow away)
swim wif th current holdn breath.
east fifth street children dont fear broken glass
come rescue me losing touch system
reality, blue singn me wif his bad mouf.
them mushrooms th stink of pool doos pussy
biography of joseph smith on my desk
life & times change again   look old
things pewter wif designs on 'em made in england
unicorn products limited go lovely
to th kick hills. my tongue is blue any form you wish
come bird   fish   worm   sing   swim
loosen th black belt.

CANTO 9

lucy belle[18]

d b a rider
ginger hips bred
you said
captain easy
go down on
river hips

new orleans
louisiana
where my mouf sings
a goat song
(th chorus line.)

CANTO 10 [excerpt]

wooten
[…]
devil lights up th day knowing
which hat to wear in his
green avenue stompers above franklin
going downtown, th robins
by Stuyvesant, nostrum,[19] utica avenue.
over wireless 'robins nest' slim harpos
blue thang. do your thang blue sea
cop the reefer   ride away
[…]

Here, in full, is the eleventh, and final, canto now in its
proper context:

CANTO 11 [excerpt]

east Corinthian

village period piece hettie
cohen got her jones, wiped th colostrum
off th mouf of his first poems
days down wif it.

east fifth street kikes have retreated to
maw of long-guyland, few ulanower cong.
a saturday holdn act from soap opera kahn.

lissen mama   right-handed-wingd
i'm head tomcat round this spray
net weight in th morning
c-wt. & eighty th motherfuckn all
limitd to th east side & fillmore music
gem spa & i cant spare a dime.
my poems & lil tomcat in your belly
teethn on raw blood too are down wif it
(totem is in th spirit house) th red-
bone hunger.[20]

I find fascinating the contrast of *Thumbprint* to the 1970 collection (such as the above). The word *blues* does not appear even once in the subsequent book, published only a year later. Yet "blue" does appear, once, in *Thumbprint*, in "speculum osiris" ("bladderwort.   Blue / frog in th harbor street"), and there are cultural cognates in "nadine" (the Chuck Berry reference, "song"), "oba skorpios" ("dirty boogies in texas"), "for billie" (alluding to Billie Holiday and ending with, on a concluding line set off from the rest of the poem, "loony tune"), and "peanut butter fly" ("let me see you boogie / woogie"). Some of the poems in *Thumbprint* may very well have been at least in development contemporaneously with those in *Maumau*.[21]

Wally, a Conclusion

Did Weatherly plan for *short history* to be his final book, a collection meant to complete a conversation he'd begun, having set that conversation going in the later sixties and then in 1970 with *Maumau*, which was the first comprehensive display of what I believe he knew full well was a new and important poetry? Aside from the discourse proper, there is in the work, as I've suggested, a remarkable compression (à la Pound's coinage, *condensare*), which is especially striking in the final book, but which was there, to be appreciated, in the earlier work.[22]

The series *wally* ends *short history* with a *grand jeté*. It is in itself beautiful, and is a most accomplished fugue that, like the blues in its structure, operates with a determinedly limited lexis. Weatherly is using his own form, the glory, as a basic prosody; yet underlying that is an interchangeability of words within a construct of beat and dense sonority. Here's the first of the poems in *wally*:

> never   muted   heart
> never   muted   heart
> eclectic blues guitar[23]

The poem develops its proposition in intervals, which holds that "in death brute's reward / an artful western music / [is] meant to true the heart" (88). This argument moves through its own set of permutations. The repetition ("never muted heart"), no doubt, is key. Contrapuntally, the opening tercet evolves on a parallel path with this:

> tulip petal larvae
> tulip petal larvae
> eclectic blues guitar (89)

The next poem, a counterpoint, begins with "never muted heart" and ties the two mini-series together in its following line, the closing phrase of the tercet's three lines (the two mini-series merge briefly in the subsequent three-liner, where the third line becomes the premise, thus pushing the conversation of the poem forward):

> eclectic blues guitar
> eclectic blues guitar
> never muted heart (90)

We have returned to the start of *wally*, while, however, our attention is fixed upon a sonic mirror, so to speak. The poem continues, from this convergence, into its culminating movement in which a repudiation, or at least a qualification, of the "western" influence, already declared, comes to the fore:

> never muted heart
> eclectic blues guitar
> hardon belly groove
> move your heady arse
> hoodoo bard from heaven (92)

The child of highly educated parents (educated in the Western tradition), Tom Weatherly was the consummate connoisseur of a literary modernism steeped in Western ideas and aesthetics. He has shown his command of the Western lyric while taking that lyric as a vehicle to elevate the blues to the great stature it deserves. In doing so he makes clear its roots in slavery, America's original sin, and American slavery's legacy. To the slave-holding white class the illiterate, the *brute*, that brutish composer and singer, creates *the* American art form, blues then jazz, finally in all its exquisite complexity, subtlety, and grandeur.

Here is how *wally* ends, arguably prompting us to reread Weatherly's early publications that, after all, represent the blossoming of an early Poetry Project aesthetics transformed into his own unique artistry:

> levee music darky
> levee music darky
> eclectic blues guitar
>
> every movie darky
> every movie darky
> eclectic blues guitar (93)

The book ends with "eclectic blues guitar." This phrase is, alas, a final statement in print of an overall conceptualization orchestrated by Weatherly himself. He was our "eclectic blues guitar."

Notes

1. Tom Weatherly, *Maumau American Cantos* (New York: Corinth Books, 1970), 29. "old envious   blues feeling" is from Amiri Baraka, "Look for You Yesterday, Here You Come Today," in *Preface to a Twenty Volume Suicide Note* (New York: Totem Press, 1961), 17.

2. Weatherly, *Maumau American Cantos*, 16.

3. Weatherly, *Maumau American Cantos*, 43. Tom and Carolyn had an apartment on East 5th Street between Avenues B and C.

4. Baraka conversation with author, Newark, NJ, early December 2013.

5. Letter to author, February 21, 1986.

6. Letter to author, May 13, year uncertain due to blurred postmark, sent from Birmingham, Alabama, with a Huntsville return address, hence probably mailed during Weatherly's years after moving back to Alabama, although he made frequent trips back to New York City.

7. Weatherly, *short history of the saxophone* (New York: Groundwater Press, 2006), 73.

8. Weatherly, *short history*, 23.

9. Weatherly, *Thumbprint* (Philadelphia/New York: Telegraph Books, 1971), 15.

10. Weatherly, *Maumau American Cantos*, 11.

11. Weatherly, *short history*, 5.

12. Frank Wooten was a chef at the Lion's Head in the West Village.

13. Weatherly, *Maumau American Cantos*, 45.

14. The great saxophonist John Coltrane.

15. Malcolm X.

16. "TPF" was the New York City Police Department's Tactical Patrol Force. Created in 1959, all its members at least six feet tall, it was meant to battle rising crime but also political foment, specializing in crowd control. Eventually it became involved in political surveillance, which was a larger NYC police initiative. The TPF was a palpable presence in the East Village, at the time this poem was written.

17. Carolyn Samuels, Weatherly's wife at the time. The reference is to Valley Stream, New York, on Long Island.

18. Lucy B. Golson Weatherly, Tom Weatherly's mother.

19. The poem is listing streets in Brooklyn; "nostrum" is Nostrand Avenue.

20. Weatherly, *Maumau American Cantos*, Cantos 1–11, 33–43. Tom and Carolyn had an apartment on East 5th Street between Avenues B and C.

21. *Thumprint*, 29, 15, 16, 20, and 23, in order.

22. As in this from Weatherly's midcareer, signaled in the word "crops":

> Art
> *for B.K.*
>
> elias built
> model poems.
>
> skies unlit
> hotly vocal.
>
> guise skill
> crops trope.

Dated December 3, 1989, in a letter to author, envelope missing.

23. Weatherly, *short history*, 87.

SUSAN HOWE, WILLIAM BRONK, HENRY DAVID THOREAU, & THE NEW NEW ENGLAND MIND

Different on their surfaces, the writings of Susan Howe and William Bronk go back to Henry David Thoreau. The veneer of his work, like a still pond, reveals the depth of the American experience, sharply the early New England way of life. The three writers concern themselves with a fundamental connection to place. The connection was visceral. This is brought to its essence in Howe's long poem *Thorow*. While *place* can be imagined as sheerly physical, there's also its spiritual dimension, especially when, though this may seem a contradiction, the spiritual is treated with an unalloyed skepticism.

It's not wrong to think of the flinty New Englander cliché. And yet this skepticism revises a concept embedded in the phrase "New England mind," which was made popular by Perry Miller in the mid twentieth century (*The New England Mind* one of his best known scholarly books). Given the time in which Miller was writing, literary and philosophical tendencies then, I wonder if he simply could not have conceived of Thoreau as someone who was untouched by his society. This was a society rooted in Puritanism. Thoreau would more readily subscribe to the idea that spiritual immanence manifests, first and foremost, through direct experience, and this gave rise to his singular understanding of the natural world—whereas Thoreau's contemporaries conceived of a "natural" world as one mediated by doctrine and language itself. Thoreau's comprehension would have less to do with what Miller termed a "religion or devotion of some kind" (*The American Transcendantalists* 373).

I locate the nineteenth-century writer's writing through Howe and Bronk—his writings were an important influence on them both. Taken together, they reveal a Thoreau who doesn't quite resemble the picture of him created by Miller or, for that matter, another canonical scholar, F. O. Matthiesen. Modern New England poets like Robert Lowell or Amy Lowell (to use either as a foil) make for an apt comparison, one in step with Miller's or Matthiesen's ideas comprising the widely accepted view. Howe and Bronk either rejected them at some point or simply could never have lived with, in the first place, either scholar's historicism.

I don't mean to claim that either Howe or Bronk has done anything like rescue Thoreau from our standard comprehension of him (as handed down by scholars, absorbed through authoritative tomes like *The American Renaissance* by Matthiesen, or *The Transcendentalists* and *The New England Mind* by Miller). It's not the case that Bronk or Howe has exactly discovered or shaped a Thoreau for our time. Yet each poet proceeds in a way that's quite Thoreauvian, though their writings might not proclaim such a thing at first. Thoreau becomes a powerful force in the shaping of Bronk's, and then Howe's, work. And seeing him like this does mean rethinking earlier New England literature and life. Through Thoreau's writing we can see Bronk and Howe creating their respective poetic identities—in response, actually, to his. And through the writing of these out-of-step poets we may, after all, with a certain nuance, come upon a Thoreau who's somewhat new to us.

The two corroborate the view of his unconventionalism, of course, both in his life and writing—whether or not we see their departure from convention as rooted in him. At a quick glance they seem dramatically different from him, as well they might in their modernism (yet different from one another, by the way). What becomes evident, however, is that they both found in him what I'll call, without irony, a *kindred spirit*. We may be able to speak of *friendship*—to put this in a very Thoreauvian way—in their respective writings coming after, having been about, and coming about through him. These texts disclose a Thoreau who fits more into their understanding of a world that includes New England history yet it's a history that accommodates their shared sensibility of friendship—friendship not to be divorced from poetry or place.

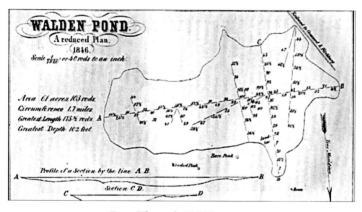

From Thoreau's 1846 Survey

Place, by coincidence, includes the Lake George region of New York (which is on the same latitude as Barre, Vermont, and not far from it). This was where Howe's *Thorow* was composed, a place understood as part of modern New

England. Bronk was raised in Hudson Falls, New York. He attended Dartmouth and put in a year of graduate school at Harvard. Both Matthiesen and Miller played roles in his early maturation; and the two scholars figured in Howe's early years as well. Bronk left Harvard early. He found its curriculum distasteful, having taken a course taught by Matthiesen. As for Howe, she knew both Matthiesen and Miller in her youth, since they were family friends, her father their Harvard colleague.

How Thoreau sees the world, himself and his art in it, is conceptualized in one way by Miller or Matthiesen, finally in another way by Howe or Bronk. Miller viewed American Transcendentalism as having come out of Calvinism. Thoreau's "approach to the particular presumed an abstract rationale," Miller writes. He does go on to say that, for Thoreau, "any given fact *could* flower into a truth" (*The Transcendetalists* 4). Matthiesen characterizes Thoreau as a writer who "often pushed to a rigorous extreme not merely the supremacy of nature over art and of content over form, but also that of the artist's life over his work" (*The American Renaissance* 154). *Place* is not absent—at least as a concept.

Perhaps, then, there's merely a difference of emphasis. *Place* suffuses Thoreau. For Bronk and Howe, also profoundly taken by place—also profoundly taken by the New England region—religion, belief, divine presence, or spirituality is nondoctrinal. This was true for Thoreau. For him *experience* is what's important. Howe and Bronk view religion or belief, or divine power or spirituality, or even presence, as potentially relevant. Nevertheless, they don't understand them in any doctrinal way. What's key for them, rather, is experience of time and place both directly and essentially. This, for Thoreau, is his *sine qua non*. The category of the *place* is the crucial element in the work of all three. How place, as such, is foregrounded in their respective work, furthermore, is critical to understanding not only each writer's peculiar *presence* in the *writing*—but also its relationship to the fact of, for Howe and Bronk, their being poets—in fundamental terms *writers*.

The difference between the old guard, and Bronk and Howe who reach back to Thoreau, to see in his work something vital to their own, with regard to *place*, becomes naming. Of the three, it's Howe, the youngest, who makes naming central. *Thorow* is a meditation on place, yet Howe has framed it with her attentions to the very act of naming. In a headnote to *Thorow*, she's found the town of Lake George—at the time a run-down, commercialized overlay of a majestic natural terrain—to be a sad "Simulacrum" (41). The simulacra of names, perhaps even of language itself, becomes the problem. She goes "down to unknown regions of indifferentiation" in her walks. "The Adirondacks *occupied* me," she reports (44). Beyond this poem, she has described "the whole Lake George area" as having "transformed my own writing." She lived "in a small cabin in an abandoned for the winter motel, beside the lake alone and out of the center of town etc. under [Thoreau's] influence in a way" (Email to author [6 March 2012]).

This self-locus is common to Bronk's poems, particularly in his 1989 collection *Death Is the Place*. Howe once said she "kept" this volume " close beside me [...]." Bronk, and clearly this collection, for her, were especially important. A further remark of hers is revealing: "[the] poems in that collection amaze me with their philosophical and poetic reach (even religious in the way I think of religion). [....] I cannot get over what he produced then, and I turn to them time and again" (Email to author [6 October 2011]).

A shared interest in Thoreau is not the totality of her connection to Bronk, and Howe may not have been especially thinking of him when she was writing *Thorow*. Still, Howe and Bronk shared a basic outlook. The look of their respective poems and their diction are different. The fact is, though, that the way in which each poet understood language, poetry, and what I'll call reality, is worth considering when thinking about Thoreau—which may lend credence to any conception of poetic lineage in which they both not only came from, but also may recast him in a light common to each.

A useful analogue for considering them together is the relationship between Bronk and Charles Olson—especially within the context of Olson's *Call Me Ishmael*. Bronk's collection of essays on Thoreau, Melville and Whitman, titled *The Brother in Elysium*, shares Olson's outlook in this early volume of his. Moreover, these two books stand in stark contrast to the studies by Matthiesen and Miller. Robert Creeley refers to *Call Me Ishmael*, in the introduction he wrote for Olson's *Collected Prose*, saying that he was "astounded" by it. "[W]e share," he proclaims, "a sense of person from a place, New England. Like the Pequod's crew, we are fact of a democracy, which does not think of itself as such but so functions. We believe in knowing, gnosis, we take over various worlds as a primary" (xi).

These are sentiments Thoreau would readily embrace. Howe's critical study, *My Emily Dickinson*, does not involve itself with Melville, and it was written long after *The Brother in Elysium*. (Bronk began his essays in 1939, his work interrupted by the war.) Her critical approach and style both place her book alongside Bronk's and Olson's, nonetheless, as New England meditations. *Call Me Ishmael*, she once recalled, "enthralled me when I first read it" ("Interview with Ed Foster" 17). As for Thoreau, I can say her approach in writing obviously has him in mind—just as it reveals a kinship with Bronk, and then as having to do with his own engagement of Thoreau.

Bronk and Olson admired one another. Bronk, however, refrained from praising Olson's poetry, claiming not to be able to get a handle on it. But this was how he spoke of most contemporaries' work. Even so, he'd spoken admiringly to me of Howe's work, in a visit I'd paid him. Olson, it would turn out, blurbed Bronk's 1964 New Directions book, *The World, the Worldless* (made possible by June Degnan, the sister of George Oppen who edited Bronk's manuscript). Olson's zeal was obvious, as was his amazing acuity. To this day I find it intriguing that Bronk, mostly because of Cid Corman (who was tipped to Bronk by Creeley), published poems in journals like *Origin*, and even showed up at Black Mountain College one day, intending to pay Olson a visit (Olson later tried to visit Bronk in Hudson falls in much the same casual way). Yet Bronk's earlier reading was in a more traditional Modernism.

The years he spent at Dartmouth, as a late adolescent, were unhappy. Even so, through his professor Sidney Cox who befriended him, Bronk met Robert Frost, read Wallace Stevens and became close with Samuel French Morse, the Stevens biographer and editor. Bronk then spent his one disastrous year at Harvard. I think the iconoclasm of Howe's utterly original poetry bears out the argument that her choice, too, would be to escape a sterile academic world, in which the approach to literature, and perhaps more broadly a mainstream Modernist poetics, was beside the point. Stylistically, her poetry aside, the critical approach in *My Emily Dickinson* couldn't be more different from that of either Miller or Matthiesen. Howe "regards herself," Peter Nicholls has commented, "as first and foremost a poet, but she is also a freelance historian in a long and distinguished line which includes writers such as Ezra Pound and Charles Olson, each of whom shared a keen sense of American history as a carefully policed regime of knowledge." ("Unsettling" 586)

I can't help but feel that a filial rebellion took place, very much what happened with Bronk at Harvard, which eventually results in the two poets' intellectual, in some sense spiritual, engagements with a number of New England and rural New York writers.[1] Thus manifested a kind of writing normally not countenanced in academe, which must have led Bronk and Howe into a vital, deeper encounter with Thoreau. Howe was granted a residency at the Glens Falls library in 1987 (near Lake George), which led to her composing *Thorow*. She visited Bronk in nearby Hudson Falls. He treated her in a way, as attested by other writers in a like predicament, which was not atypical of him. "[H]e wasn't very friendly—crusty even," she recalls. "I loved Glens Falls and the library there and that whole Lake George area. [. . .] I feel badly I didn't make more of an effort to break through the shell he presented" (Email to author [6 October 2011]).

And yet, while Bronk could be cool, even cold to people, including other writers (especially other writers?), I was surprised to learn of this meeting between them, since my own recollection of visiting him, at about this time, stands in jarring contrast. Yes, he could be diffident, in his later years increasingly less interested in any living poet's work other than his own (as he was quick to stipulate). Not long after Howe's overture, however, he spoke (as I've mentioned) kindly and even deferentially of her. And I was really struck by this, not only because he didn't do that sort of thing, but because her work seemed to me so dissimilar to his—while, possibly in his mind, her writing was closer to, let's say, Olson's *The Maximus Poems*. (When I queried Ed Foster about this period, and his memory of Bronk's feelings about her, he corroborated my own version of events, which was like his at that time [Email to author (16 June 2012)].)

What did Howe and Bronk see in the other's work, exactly? Some of this answer lies in how each of them saw Thoreau. As I continue to think about this, I grasp more securely what's become my own sense of the nineteenth-century elder as the bole of a tree—this is what takes me to, considering Howe and Bronk together, my seeing the New England experience in a new light. Was that "new" light not so new really, was it some faltering glimmer, *in nascence*, in Thoreau, in a vision, possibly a poetics, later inherited by Olson, Creeley, Corman, Ted Enslin, maybe Rosemary or Keith Waldrop? We think of them all in terms of "The New American Poetry," and they all hailed from the New England region—just as a Robert Lowell did, maybe more recently his student Gail Mazur, or a poet like Rosanna Warren (daughter of Robert Penn Warren and the scholar/

critic Eleanor Clark), also New Englanders, yet these latter poets' work is qualitatively and substantively different.

In my own search for the critical difference, I turn to Howe's concern for naming in *Thorow*, if I can hold this comparison steady in my mind. Kornelia Freitag describes the aim in *Thorow* as a striving to "[capture] the locality of Lake George," which is accomplished through reckoning its history of cultural confrontations which were at once locally specific and part of the broader process of the creation of "the New World." While the place seems disconnected from any history, Howe finds and explores the link in the language of a wide range of Western cultural texts. Indian place names (Swegachey, Millinocket) are shown to be more than relics of time gone by. They function as symptoms of the racial, economic, social, religious, or psychological repressed. (133)

For Howe, the names are of great importance: she writes that "Indian names lead [to the] understory" (*Thorow* 52). This deft coinage, "understory," refers to both a linguistic and conceptual sublayer—to a history, Freitag adds, "of the place she inspects," and still "further to the 'understory of anotherword', of great cultural texts of Western and American civilization" (Freitag 133; *Thorow* 50).

Much as is stipulated in *Thorow*'s headnote, Howe's thinking about naming, in this long poem, hints at a fundamental engagement with place, even more so at what I'd like to call *lived time*. "I was trying to paint a landscape in that poem," she says in an interview (with Tom Beckett). Her "vision" of Lake George, when she was writing the poem, had less to do with "space" and more with "time": "I was very much aware of the commercialization and near ruin at the edge of the water, in the town itself, all around—but I felt outside of time or in an earlier time and *that* was what I had to get to on paper" ('Interview [with Tom Beckett]" 20-21; in White "The Landscapes" 242). This task becomes all the more urgent: "[f]or some reason this beautiful body of water has attracted violence and greed ever since the Europeans first saw it. I thought I could feel it when it was pure, enchanted, *nameless*" (20-21).

Is there something about the New England landscape, about New England *place*, an "enchanted" place, "nameless," which gives rise to such disquiet? Naming is critical for Thoreau, famously so in "The Ponds" chapter of *Walden*: "*Flints' Pond!* Such is the poverty of our nomenclature." Thoreau's outrage is unmistakable. "What right had the unclean and stupid farmer, whose farm abutted on this sky water, whose shores he has ruthlessly laid bare, to give his name to it?" Thoreau's vitriol seems well placed, as he answers his own question:

> Some skin-flint, who [. . .] regarded even the wild ducks which settled in[the pond] as trespassers. [Let] it be named from the fishes that swim in it, the wild fowl or quadrupeds which frequent it, the wild flowers which grow by its shores, or some wild man or child the thread of whose history is interwoven with its own; not from him who could show no title to it but the deed which a like-minded neighbor or legislature gave him [. . .] whose presence perchance cursed all the shore; who exhausted the land around it, and would fain have exhausted the waters within it; who regretted only that it was not English hay or cranberry meadow,—there

was nothing to redeem it, forsooth, in his eyes,—and would have drained and sold it for the mud at its bottom. (163)

Bronk likely had this passage in mind when he composed "Flowers, the World and My Friend, Thoreau" (it appeared in his 1982 collected poems):

It no longer matters what the names of flowers are.
Some I remember; others forget: ones
I never thought I should. Yes, tell me one.
I like to hear that. I may have forgotten again
next week. There's that yellow one whose name
I used to know. It's blossoming, secure
as ever as I walk by looking at it,
not saying its name or needing to.

Henry, it's true as you said it was, that this
is a world where there are flowers. Though it isn't our truth,
it's a truth we embrace with gratitude:
how should we endure our dourness otherwise?
And we feel an eager desire to make it ours,
making the flowers ours by naming them.

But they stay their own and it doesn't become our truth.

We live with it; we live with othernesses
as strangers live together in crowds. Truths
of strangeness jostle me; I jostle them
walking past them as I do past clumps of flowers.
Flowers, I know you, not knowing your name.
(LS 217)

Howe's "otherstory" is comparable with Bronk's "it doesn't

become our truth," his "othernesses" as well as, perhaps, the "dourness" he shares with Thoreau. My picture of Howe reading "The Ponds," having it in mind when composing *Thorow*, is prompted by lines like these:

> The origin of property
> that leads here Depth
>
> Indian names lead here
>
> Bars of a social system
> Starting for Lost Pond
>
> psychology of the lost
> First precarious Eden[.]
> (52)

(Do "Indian names" seek to possess?)

Bronk writes that "The difficulties of expression led Thoreau to leave his friendships, . . . in reference to language, almost unexpressed" ("Friendship" 74). Thoreau realized poetry was the best hope for capturing the experience of place. Howe finds language in landscape:

> Eating nothing but hominy
> Scribbling the ineffable
> See only the tracks of rabbit
> A mouse-nest of grass
> (47)

She writes on paper, thinking of rabbit "tracks" as inscription.

Further on in *Thorow*, her inner voice, to herself:

Only step

As surveyor of the Wood
Only Step (48)

And shortly thereafter:

Expectation of Epiphany

Not to look off from it
but to look at it

Original of the Otherside
understory of anotherword   (50)

Howe has become the "Child of the Adirondacks" who is "taking notes like a spy." Is she acting as the good "Scout" (43) identified at the start of *Thorow*, who has put down in this place, observing a "Most mysterious river // on the confined brink" (53)? In this and other passages, she has evoked a trope Thoreau was quite familiar with, which portrays the spirit as integral to his sense of essential connection with nature and direct engagement of the tangible world. It's implicit in his accusation against Flint, the farmer who wants to drain his pond in order to sell "the mud at its bottom" (above).

The pond "was made deep and pure for a symbol" (233). Thoreau's figure here is recognizable throughout his writing. "While men believe in the infinite some ponds will be thought to be bottomless." And yet "[t]here is a solid bottom everywhere" (267). Ira Chernus has caught essential in Thoreau, which is apparent in the pond in its depth of mud, as place and figure: "beneath the finite appearances of life there is an infinite, ultimate reality that is the foundation of everything," Chernus writes. For Thoreau, in other words, "[u]ltimate reality is not something set apart from the world; it is the essence of the world and all that is in it" (Chernus n.p.).

Within the world conditioned in this way, Thoreau can pen what's now a famous passage, surely known to Howe and Bronk: "Time is but the stream I go a-fishing in," Thoreau begins, and then pushes the metaphor along to great effect: "I drink at it; but while I drink I see the sandy bottom and detect how shallow it is. Its thin current slides away, but eternity remains" (83). Chernus points out that "the 'solid bottom' of reality is actually a dynamic process of spiritual powers, which are, in Thoreau's words, 'identified with the substance of things', and from which 'they cannot be separated'" (Chernus n.p.; Thoreau 112).

Bronk could have had such a philosophical construct in mind when he wrote, in *Death Is the Place:*, as follows.

> It isn't what we say of reality
> is metaphor but reality itself
> which is. Reality as God or as
> cosmos or as, more often, both at once
>
> —whatever—reality is metaphor
> not more not less and, being that,
> is real as can be and not quite real:
> (36)

He ends the poem with a tease: "always brilliantly true and

less than whole." In *Thorow*, Howe writes of

So many true things

which are not truth itself
We are too finite   (49)

Further on, she ties in her theme of naming, of simulacra:

The expanse of unconcealment
so different from all maps

Spiritual typography of elegy

Nature in us as a Nature
the actual one the ideal Self   (55)

Names, maps—all inscriptions—fail to comprehend the natural world. Thoreau felt it was imbued with the eternal yet, in human perception, it existed in time. As Elisabeth Joyce puts it, for Howe "[t]he map becomes [...] an emblem of cultural identity that renders the incoherence and irrationality of the

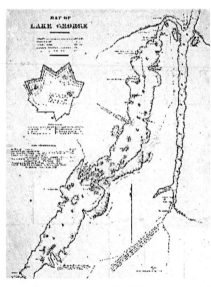

Map of Lake George circa 1850 (Inset: plan of Fort Ticonderoga)

wild into the tamed logic of civilization" (35; cf. 38).

In Bronk's essay, "The Occupation of Space—Palenque" (written prior to *Thorow*), he concurs: "The names of places are names we have given them." In considering the act of naming, he understands how the

> more precisely we try to locate ourselves, the more we are sent back to the realization that, except as we have imposed a shape on environment by occupying it, it is still as described in Genesis in the first creation, without form and void and with darkness covering the face of the deep. (*Vectors and Smoothable Curves* 22)

"The Occupation of Space" was written as part of *The Brother in Elysium*, the book beginning with a series of prose meditations on Thoreau, Melville and Whitman. In having to complete the book after the war, Bronk's writing straddled Matthiesen's *American Renaissance*, and coincided with Olson's *Call Me Ishmael*. Bronk got most of the Thoreau essays in place, for his future book of prose, before entering the service; these comprised a section of the book he titled *Silence and Henry Thoreau*. The first of these essays is titled "Friendship":

> To nourish and care for the spirit,—this was what friendship was as Thoreau saw it. [...] in its simplest, most basic form, as the force which motivated all the rest of the complex, friendship was an exalting and powerful love. It was a kind of love that went forth with no particular object in view and was wholly self-generated. It neither arose from, nor was directed toward, anything else in the world. This love without

reference is the basis of friendship in Thoreau. [....] He was almost driven to believe that a sympathy; with man and a sympathy with nature could not consist of one another, — that those qualities that bring you near to one estrange you from the other. And yet he knew that this was not so, and indeed that nature must be viewed humanly to be viewed at all [. . .].

Bronk revives a Thoreauvian apothegm: "'man is all in all, Nature nothing, but as she draws him out and reflects him'" (69-70; Thoreau, *Journals* 166).

Toward the end of *Thorow*, perhaps as Howe's way of beginning a conclusion to her poem, she writes this:

> You are of me & I of you, I cannot tell
>
> Where you leave off and I begin
>
> selving
>
> forfending
> Immeadeat Settlem
> but wandering
>
> (58)

And yet, as Bronk points out in "Friendship," Thoreau was a writer who implicitly grasped the problem and power of ineffability: "[t]he difficulties of expression led Thoreau to leave his friendships, as here in reference to language, almost unexpressed" (74). In Howe's lines, there's an open-endedness of reference that suggests ineffability.

Note, now, how Bronk continues: "Thoreau, who was

absorbed in being rather than in expression, was hesitant of names, of words, of forms of any sort. He was aware of their ambivalent power which is the power of the metaphor, suggestive of truth, suggestive of being, but such that the truth is not literally in it" (74-75). Likewise, Howe writes of "The source of Snow / the nearness of Poetry" (50). Is poetry for her, as well as for Bronk and Thoreau, an attempt to elude the dominion of naming?

Through writing, also in spite of it, Bronk considers how, "to the observer, the life lived is a kind of fiction. Actuality is a work of the imagination only" (in "The Actual and the Real in Thoreau," also in *The Brother in Elysium* 27). But what of the seer herself? Compare Bronk's comment here with Howe's "the source of snow" lines and then, from *Death Is the Place*, these two brief poems:

Vicarious

Except from our

mortality
how should
infinite
eternal know
how beautiful
the brief world
is to us?

Mundane

What we do gets so natural

feels so good to us

139

we forget what we are
and any interruption,
lessening,
even the final breaking off
seems terrible
and wrong.

Bronk may not be exclusively New England in kind. He
shares something about knowing and the spirit, though,
with Emily Dickinson. *My Emily Dickinson*, Howe's study
of her, like Bronk's prose on Thoreau, is an extended
meditation that consists of great poetry as well as criticism
and scholarship. Howe writes that Dickinson "looked right
into the nature of things / words, straight through,—to
the fearful apprehension that there was no Truth, only
mystery beyond mystery" (138). The tangible world is a
manifestation of an intangible—except, perhaps, that the
intangible might become otherwise through poetry; this
same immanence makes not only communion between
person and place possible, but communion between person
and person too.

Not unlike friendship, this way of making art is grounded in,
and dependent upon, a person's essential experience of the
natural world. Such an apprehension comes out of a duality:
on the one hand, the notion of a metaphor, on the other,
the ultimate reality of metaphor. In *Thorow*, Howe addresses
this phenomenon—so does Bronk, in a number of poems.
Thoreau, her poem's namesake, is ground for them.

The question of metaphor, the question actually of knowing,
inevitably leads to questioning the efficacy of art, indeed of
writing. The "Thursday" chapter in *A Week on the Concord and*

Merrimack Rivers is another of Howe's "favorite pieces of his writing"; she "knew it well" by the time she arrived in Lake George (Email to author [16 June 2012]). Years later, she highlights how important a particular comment by Thoreau was to her—this one having to do with artistic creation.

It's an abiding concern, to the degree that she repeats, verbatim, something she'd written decades earlier (in a letter to John Taggart from May of 1987): "'The talent of composition is very dangerous—the striking out the heart of life at a blow, as the Indian takes off a scalp. I feel as if my life had grown more outward when I can express it'" (Email to author [16 June 2012]; Thoreau, *A Week*, 329).[2] In *Thorow*, Howe makes this notation: "From the Fort but the snow / falling very deep / remained a fortnight / Two to view the Fort & get a scalp / domain of transcendental subjectivity [etc.]" (43).

Does art kill only so there can be resurrection? By way of explaining Thoreau's definition of composition, I offer this key passage from that "Thursday" chapter:

Poetry is the mysticism of mankind.

The expressions of the poet cannot be analyzed; his sentence is one word, whose syllables are words. There are indeed no words quite worthy to be set to his music. (328)

In "The Arts and Death: A Fugue for Sidney Cox," an early poem by Bronk, Henry Weinfield maintains that Bronk "[envisions] human beings" as bound to "a kind of Sisyphean attempt to get closer and closer to a truth that must always elude them." Weinfield wonders if the attempt is perhaps more true of the artist even than the philosopher: not because there is anything inherently deficient in art, and not, as Socrates supposed in *The Republic*, because art is two steps removed from reality, but, on the contrary, because it is the artist who is most driven by desire to penetrate the whole. (Weinfield 162).

Bronk's final poem, in life, had no title; it was simply this:

Art isn't made; it's in the world almost
unseen but found existent there. We paint,
we score the sound in music, we write it down.
(*Bursts of Light* 300)

In *Death Is the Place*, however, Bronk had written that "the little we know or do doesn't make the form / and nature of things" ("Worksong" 44).

What's left to say—in contemplating Howe, Bronk and Thoreau together—really has to do with the Northeastern winter, how it helped to forge a kinship, and what it might have had to do with the creative act for each of them. Bronk is *the* poet of winter. His "crustiness," as Howe has called it (above), is this very winter. Could the Thoreauvian way of seeing things have emerged apart from it—winter's stark reckoning in its demands—its severe, perhaps absolute clarity? In later years Howe remarked, about that stay in Lake George and the birth of *Thorow*:

the landscape and the frozen lake and the pines in snow wrote it. The entire lake was so frozen you could walk out to the center. I remember the terror and lure of walking out on ice.

In speaking of Bronk, and her attempt to reach him (something to be taken into account when we read *Thorow*):

> I think we have some kind of religious belief in common. If one can call it that in this secular age. A belief in the sacramental nature of poetry and of winter light (Email to author [16 June 2012]).

In this context, of what she's said, I reproduce here, simply, Howe's favorite poem from *Death Is the Place* (Email to author [16 June 2012]), entitled "Emptying Out":

> How it is like the first day now
> —the bareness between the evening and the morning
> which were the first day.
>
>   Winter now and light
>
> comes late and it is celebrant
> and just the light is enough, the idea of light,
> the waking naked to it. Then evening coming on
> and the memory of light in the eased dark
> and nakedness again, the lying down.
> (DITP 19).

The writing of either Howe or Bronk contains a desolation, often enough, but especially *Thorow*—in which the world's illusions have been stripped away. Here's a truth beyond naming after all, and the writing of it, the accession of immanent metaphor, which is a memorializing of the moment of insight. It takes a lot to survive that winter.

Howe realized she'd taken this from Thoreau. As for Bronk, and as for Lake George—she writes that this region left her with "a very particular feeling about time and the power of local history. Winter. He [Bronk] gets it so perfectly right [...]" (Email to author [16 June 2012]).

Notes

1. In passing it should be mentioned that Howe and Bronk have written eloquently about Melville, especially *Billy Budd*.

2. Cf. Montgomery "Appropriating" 739 and n. 1 on p. 752 that cites this quote used by Howe in a letter to Taggart of 29 May 1987.

Works Cited

Bronk, William. "The Actual and the Real in Thoreau," *Thoreau Quarterly: A Journal of Literary and Philosophical Studies*, 14 (Spring 1982): 26-27.

_____. *The Brother in Elysium: Ideas of Friendship and Society in the United States*. New Rochelle, New York: The Elizabeth Press, 1980.

_____. *Bursts of Light: The Collected Later Poems*. Jersey City: Talisman House, 2012.

_____. *Death Is the Place*. San Francisco: North Point Press, 1989.

_____. *Life Supports: New and Collected Poems*, New Edition. 1981. Jersey City: Talisman House Publishers, 1997.

_____. *Vectors and Smoothable Curves: Collected Essays*, New Edition. 1983. Jersey City: Talisman House Publishers, 1997.

Chernus, Ira. *American Nonviolence: The History of an Idea*. Maryknoll, NY: Orbis, Books, 2004. Online. Accessed 4 January 2015.

Creeley, Robert. "Introduction." *Charles Olson: Collected Prose*. Eds. Donald Allen and Benjamin Friedlander. Berkeley: U of California P, 1997. xi-xvi.

Freitag, Kornelia. "Susan Howe's *Thorow(s)*: The Politics of Place and Time in Postmodern Poetry." *A World of Local Voices: Poetry in English Today*. Eds. Klaus Martens, Paul Morris, and Paul Morris, Arlette Warken. Wurzburg: King & Neumann, 2003. 124-35.

Howe, Susan. "Interview with Ed Foster." *Talisman: A Journal of Contemporary Poetry and Poetics* 4 (Spring 1990): 14–38.

_____. "Interview [with Tom Beckett]." *The Difficulties* 3.2 (1989): 17-27.

_____. *My Emily Dickinson*. Berkeley: North Atlantic Books, 1985.

_____. *Thorow. Singularities*. Middletown, CT: Wesleyan UP, 1990.

Joyce, Elisabeth. *"The Small Space of a Pause": Susan Howe's Poetry and the Spaces Between*. Lewisburg, PA: Bucknell UP, 2010.

Matthiesen, F. O. *The American Renaissance: Art and Expression in the Age of Emerson and Whitman*. Oxford, UK: Oxford UP, 1941.

Miller, Perry. Ed. *The American Transcendentalists, Their Prose and Poetry*. New York: Doubleday Anchor, 1957.

_____. *The New England Mind*. 2 Vol. 1953. Eastford, CT: Martino Fine Books, 2014.

_____. Ed. and Intr. *The Transcendentalists: An Anthology*. 1950. Cambridge, MA: Harvard UP, 1978.

Montgomery, Will. *"Appropriating* Primal Indeterminacy: Language, Landscape and Postmodern Poetics in *Susan Howe's Thorow*." *Textual Practice* 20.4 (2006): 739–57

Nicholls, Peter. *"Unsettling* the Wilderness: *I* and American History." *Contemporary Literature* 37 (1996): 586–601.

Olson, Charles. *Call Me Ishmael*. 1947. New York: Grove P, 1958.

_____. *Charles Olson: Collected Prose*. Eds. Donald Allen and Benjamin Friedlander. Berkeley: U of California P, 1997

_____. *The Maximus Poems*. Berkeley: U of California P, 1983.

Thoreau, Henry David. *Journals. The Heart of Thoreau's Journals*. 1927. Ed. Odell Shepard. New York: Dover / Houghton Mifflin, 1967.

_____. *Thoreau's Walden*. Ed., Intr. Annot. Raymond McDonald Alden. No loc.: Ulan Press / JPS Norton, 2012.

_____. *A Week on the Concord and Merrimack Rivers*. Eds. Carl F. Hovde, William L. Howarth, and Elizabeth Hall Witherell. Princeton: Princeton UP, 1980.

White, Jenny L. "The Landscapes of Susan Howe's 'Thorow'." *Contemporary Literature*, 47.2 (July 2006): 236-260.

Weinfield, Henry. *The Music of Thought in the Poetry of George Oppen and William Bronk*. Iowa City: U of Iowa P, 2009.

ENID DAME'S HOUSEHOLDRY

Enid Dame's poems concern themselves with the questions occupying human thought for the last thousands of years. It's fair to say her writing is of great moment although its concerns are always focused on the moments of a life. For the most part, Dame has now fallen out of notice, since her death in 2003. But the work has stayed with me. What I still find most remarkable about her poems is their presentation. They're without the hint of pomp or pretense, and they intensely, assiduously inhabit the everyday. This is so even when they address what Dame finds to be confounding matters of Scripture.

Always there's that intimacy. Her poems have the ring of natural speech, as they ground themselves in the objects and events of the ordinary. Her work seems to me finally to be of great stature, actually, marked by a relaxed eloquence. This sense of ease conveys the impression that the poems haven't been crafted—but the reader comes to realize their intricacy and balance. They seem so tossed off and yet, if you're paying close attention, they show their elegant constructions.

In keeping with her ability to create a language of breezy contemporaneity, yet often talking of ancient biblical events, Dame establishes a tension between the modern and an eternal quotidian. It can be the source of exquisite humor, always striking in itself, meanwhile disclosing how shrewd and wise she is. Most memorable for me, in any case, is the poems' consistently tight focus on the present moment. She situates and dissects it with a graceful lyricism. She shows us the human concerns, endearingly presented within domesticity. Dame's love of householdry, to be sure, is key to comprehending her entire poetic life; the poems consistently on the human scale, never denying the grandeur of the divine, decidedly Jewish poems, they embrace a Jewish dialogue with God. So, as comforting as they are in their air of the familiar, they're disarming.

We're never quite prepared for the depth of a Dame insight, which is established within the most natural or ordinary of circumstances. Take her poem "Untenanted," which eulogizes Dame's father as it takes advantage of the cityscape in which he lived his life. The poem begins in the past, and ends in a palpable, moving present, opening with the daughter who recalls her father's life (his corpse lying in a hospital) soon after his passing. She's addressing him:

> Standing over
> your uninhabited body,
> Father,
> I kept thinking,
> "The building is still there."
>
> I could picture it: the five-floor Bronx walk-up
> where memory started, for you.

The poem moves through time, dwelling on the details of her father's childhood neighborhood; there's a shift to the recent past. The speaker is now a grown woman:

One wet spring,
you came to see me.
I showed you the ocean at the end of my block.
We stood and watched it, a caged animal,
shrunken, grey, talking to itself.
A police car crawled down the boardwalk,
rain-battered, slow as an insect.
"The city is dying," you said.

In an unavoidable, lingering sadness, the daughter contemplates the father in his old age. Then comes the succinct, gritty resolution in the poem's closing lines:

When you were dying, in another city, I was in the next room,
on the phone, arguing with a nurse.
She didn't believe what was happening.

And when I touched you
finally
you felt hard, untenanted,
yet warm,
a brick wall
still holding in the sun.

(*Anything You Don't See* 48-49)

The beloved, difficult city endures, and is a comfort. If nothing else, Dame is clear-eyed, but she's also compassionate. Yet her work never strains for either feeling or idea.

What we get from her is conversation, a rather casual conversation with someone you know, in which, we suddenly realize, a lot's at stake. The ease, the friendliness, perhaps the sense of banter with which the conversation is carried on, puts us off our guard. In the end, we may find ourselves crying out for help—needing to be saved from that we've been drawn fully into, the speaker's existential plight. Such is the nature of fate, and this theme underlies virtually all of Dame's work—fate without our being able to prepare for it, to strive to turn it, even if only obliquely, as time unfolds.

At the core of how Dame understands fate is her vexed relationship with her mother. Her poems comment upon or depict her vividly. Often the poems are very funny. At times her husband Donald Lev is a stand-in for the mother; the poems then will more subtly focus on the marital relationship. Lev was her long-time husband as well as her partner in the poetry tabloid *Home Planet News*. (Her soulmate, he died in 2018.)

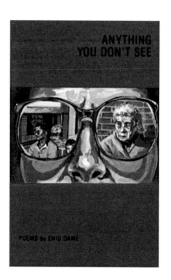

Dame possesses an ironic, wry humor. It comes to the fore most obviously in her many Midrashic pieces. In these, epic Scriptural issues are taken up—yet with the greatest nonchalance, and pointedly in the speech of modernity. They can be suddenly devastating, in their recognition of the darkness in human nature—and at times they're the light therein. Either way, they're couched in the everyday. Her writerly strategy allows us to see that what can seem distant, or cerebral, usually within the Jewish textual tradition, may become immediate and inescapable.

Particularly Dame's descriptions of men—mates or fathers—strike me as Lev substitutes; they serve as replacements and, dazzling complications, they're versions of her mother. In one or another turn-about, the daughter has come to terms with her. Frequently, the men are juxtaposed with some mother figure.

References to mothers and motherhood abound in Dame's poems (Dame had no children), often in recreated settings whose biblical aura is suffusing; some are dramatic monologues, like the "Lilith" section of "Looking for a Mother." Here is how this one begins:

> I never knew my mother.
> We never spoke.
> I knew my father's name
> but never hers.
> The grasses whisper.
> The owl moans faintly.
> The owl is never silent:

it creaks and hums and scratches.
Is one of these her voice?

(*Stone Shekhina* 14)

The state of mind of the speaker in "Day 20," one of the
sections in "Excerpts from Naamah's Journal," is as one
with "Looking for a Mother":

The rain beats on the wood
like my mother's voice pounding pounding:
Bad girl bad girl bad girl
Look at this mess! Look at your life!
You live in a sty you'll never get clean.
Dirty girl! Dirty! Dirty!

My mother treated her bread dough
like a recalcitrant prisoner
or child   something that had to be punished
her hard palm   pounding pounding it down
until it yielded sweetness.

My philosophy was different!
I tried to work with the dough
as if we were partners   colleagues
comrades in a pleasant enterprise.
Of course, we weren't equals:
the bread, eventually, got eaten.
I told myself this was what it wanted.

(*Stone Shekhina* 25)

The repetitions are incantatory, musical. They also bring the speaker's point of view to an exquisite acuity. When it comes time for her rendezvous, the ultimate showdown, with her *actual* mother, that crucial rapprochement occurs in Dame's own, contemporaneous, unfussy kitchen.

She confronts her mother there, yet seems to forgive her for her unfair treatment. At the same moment, she honors the differences between them. Dame's speaker is smart enough to know not to deny her love for her. The poem fully captures Dame's tormented reconciliation:

Yahrzeit

In Jewish tradition, it is customary to light a yahrzeit, *or memory candle, on the anniversary of a family member's death.*
The *yahrzeit* flame
is beating its wings in a cup
on the edge of my kitchen sink.
Its stealthy gold shadow
breathing along the wall
suddenly terrifies me:
like finding a bird in my bedroom
still alive   pulsating   nervous,
changing the shape of the day.

No intruder is ever harmless.
And, Mother, I've got you cornered,
fierce memory pacing your glass cage,
houseguest with nowhere to go.

I'll lock myself in alongside you.
Today, we'll remind each other
of old connections, old journeys,
from muddy, sincere Indiana
to ragged-edged Brooklyn
with all its stray cats, its ecstatic
vegetable stands.

(*Anything You Don't See* 41)

In Donald Lev's volume, *Grief*, made up of poems about Dame's dying of cancer and its aftermath, we find this uncomplicated, touching remembrance:

I helped you bathe,
grateful for the intimacy,
then we held hands,
we even joked [...]."

(*Grief* 9)

Lev's entire collection serves as the appropriate counterpart to Dame's letters to Lev and her poems that came out of this period, which she was writing nearly up to the moment of her demise. (She'd traveled to California for hyperthermia treatments, in a last-ditch effort to be cured.) Lev collected her writings of this period in a volume he titled *Where Is the Woman*. These inscriptions, attestations, document her arrival at a stage of serenity in her relationship with her mother, if not also in her struggle with her fatal disease. Time and again Dame paints a picture of domestic order, one that's consoling. And yet, in these very late writings, I wonder if she hasn't achieved the ideal human connection with another, in this case her husband, and through their relationship some peace.

Her poem "Missing" concludes as follows.

> This is a missing-Don letter. Here,
> I count the pills myself
> imagining you sitting across from me:
> your voice   your face   your hands
>   opening a bottle,
> breaking the stillness of the morning.
> We talk of poetry or friends or shopping
> over bread   cheese   almond butter
> fresh blueberries in season.
>
> Because food is a benediction
> because sharing food is a sacrament
> because shared language is a morning prayer
> because I miss the tabernacle
> in which our love increases,
>
> it is difficult to eat alone
> in this place of healing.
>
> (*Where Is the Woman* np)

In comparison, here is a passage from Lev's poem, "Scene from a Marriage":

So precarious!
Two tipsy piles of books
At the edge of the dresser,
Her reading glasses tucked
In between them.

On my side,
An even tipsier pile
Threatens from the night table.
(*Yesterday's News* 48)

Now consider this stanza from "The Idea of a House" (another of Dame's California poems):

The idea of a bedroom
under a slanting roof
pillows piled high   bright-squared afghan
tower of books on the floor,
long nights read into mornings
waiting for a familiar tread on the stairs;
waiting to be joined.

In this poem, Dame expands Lev's conceit, memorializing the domestic routine she shares with her husband:

The idea of two people
working in separate rooms;
one is fastening down words in wax,
one is cuttling garlic
tomatoes   basil   sorrel if it's spring,
spinach if it's winter,
building the soup
they will eat together, later
meeting at the table.

The poem concludes with an unvarnished hope:

The idea of a house
will persist
even when the house is sold
even when the lives lived there,
live elsewhere
and newcomers move in.
They will unpack new words vegetables
        cooking pots.
They will remodel the kitchen.
They will add another chapter
to the house's biography.

They will set up new routines
to sustain them   in the shadows
we leave behind.

(*Where Is the Woman* np)

Dame turns to the scene of domesticity regularly because this is what she came to prize most in her life. In her last poems and letters, and in some of Lev's poems of that period and shortly afterward, such as we see in *Grief*, we find the domestic—householdry—memorialized. Within this domesticity, which Dame managed to establish with her mate, she solves the pain of her relationship with her mother; likewise we see her triumph in her relationship with Lev.

Dame was known widely for her remarkable, insightful humor that holds many of her poems together. The poet Madeline Tiger aptly remarked that Dame "expanded the 'story' of our lives by moving us into history, and by bringing history forward—hilariously—into the present" (I.1). Tiger went on to point out the "ironic vein in Dame's work," which she finds "embedded in historic paradox. Laughter connects grief and survival" (II.6).

What I find most important in Dame's poems is her ultimate reconciliation, largely, with the world. Within this pact she comes to terms with her mother, a scene that's repeated, drawn with the sharpest perspective—most gracefully and with poignant symbolism in "Fruit Cellar":

> Bury your memories
> like jars in a fruit cellar.
> Let them mount high on the shelves.
> Let them wait.
> Dark jewels   in their cold nests
> they will keep.

Unbottle them later,
if you can find that town,
if you can find that house.
If anything is left from that time,
break in. Smash windows,
lower yourself to the bottom.
Reach for a memory. Crack one.
Take what you need.

Now   hold your mother
lingeringly on your tongue.
Her fruit is still alive.
It tastes as it always did:
Heavy   resonant   edgy.
It makes you think of old coats
fur-collared   camphor-scented
worn in another country.

Think of your mother preserving.
Think of your mother destroying.
Her stove: old companion,
turned against herself,
turned into an enemy,
that time she turned on the gas.
Good citizen,
the oven refused to cooperate.
Thirty years later,
she didn't need help to die.

Swallow this memory quickly.
The fruit cellar's silence
isn't empty.
It's a presence,
like a woman's disappointment
stored too long.

It can turn fruit sour,
fracture glass.
(*Anything You Don't See* 36-37)

Dame's love of daily living, that which takes place in a household, tells us of her reconciliation. It especially manifests in the caring descriptions of the husband, in a number of her poems—as in the dramatic monologue "Eve." Eve has to live with her mate's "snores"; however, they're as "comforting / as radiator steam." The poem leaves us with this plain observation: "My body is / the only home / he hasn't had to leave" (*Stone Shekhina* 13).

Dame's last poems complete the picture we have of her. Her very late poem, "Returned" ("returned" from California, the treatment having fallen short) puts her back in her home:

This is my kitchen. I am safe here.
The utensils fit themselves to my hand.
This blue-speckled pot is an old friend.
It awaits my pleasures.
The flame-red casserole with its cracked side,
its burned-black bottom;

159

the quirky veteran propane stove
are ready for new ventures.

Here I can drink green jasmine tea
at five AM and feel night drowse itself to daylight,
the leaves outside are rusty at their edges,
a sign of coming fall.
The radio moves from BBC to Mozart.
My mug is brightly colored:
a yellow large-eyed cat
contemplates orange fish,
while my real cat, fast and black, leaps on the table,
scraps of cobwebs in his whiskers.
No one can say he's in the wrong place.
Everything is right here:

the garlic with its buds snuggled like buttocks,
the ripening avocado,
the battered yard-sale colander,
the square tiles left by a former owner—
I kept them as they seemed so useful,
though I seldom use them.

(*Home Planet News* 13)

There's a rejoinder to "Returned"—another very late, post-
California poem, "Dream at the Start of a Bad Year," which
insists upon the domesticity Dame most ably memorialized:

There are two elders,
a woman and a man.
She is a poet,
he, a socialist.
They try to change the world
in the little time they live in it.
We share a language
I never learned to speak.

A table spreads between us.
A yard-sale of my treasures:
a rainbow glass   a goblet
with a bubble in its throat
a family of vessels
from the start of memory
back in the Bronx   or Wreschin
(which is now part of Poland).

I must divide these gifts
between my mentors.
(My mother's voice,
and also yours, my love,
advises me
what to bestow on whom.)

A closer look reveals
the legacy is flawed:
the edges chipped   or broken
a crack across the rainbow.

But everything's accepted—
the man impatiently,
the woman, stoic.
The table's almost empty.
A lamp remains: a golden-orange chimney
in which a candle quickens.

I reach to add this offering
to someone's pile: his? hers?
But you say, "No. Not that one.
We have to keep the lamp.
As long as we still live here,
we need the light."

(*Home Planet News* 14)

Works Cited

Dame, Enid. *Anything You Don't See*. Albuquerque, NM: West End Press, 1992.

_____. "Dream at the Start of a Bad Year." *Home Planet News* 50 [Vol. 12, No. 4] (Spring 2004): 14.

_____. "Returned." *Home Planet News* 50 [Vol. 12, No. 4] (Spring 2004): 13.

_____. *Stone Shekhina*. East Hampton, NY: Three Mile Harbor, 2002.

_____. *Where is the Woman?: Letters and Poems from California, July & August 2003*. New York: Shivastan Publishing, 2006.

Lev, Donald. *Grief: Poems by Donald Lev*. Staten Island, NY: Bardpress / Ten Penny Players, 2006.

_____. *Yesterday's News: Poems 1998-2001*. Claryville, NY: Red Hill OUTLOUDBOOKS, 2002.

Tiger, Madeline. "Bless This Garden: A Review of *Stone Shekhina*, Poems by Enid Dame." *The Newark Review* (March 2004). Online.

THE DEAD AND THE LIVING:
HUGH SEIDMAN'S LATE POEMS

In old age, many a poet ought to think twice before putting that last book together for public consumption. Easy enough to say—often the late work, when the poet had once published truly compelling, arguably great poetry, disappoints. I was in conversation with an elderly poet recently, someone who's now in the eighth decade of life (as am I). We found we were harboring the same fear —we didn't want to be repeating ourselves. We pictured rereading our late work and not seeing enough in it to warrant sharing it with the public. When we were young, reading Pound, our commitment was to "make it new."

Adrienne Rich's final book, *Tonight No Poetry Will Serve* (2011), was met with plenty of adulation. Nevertheless Julie Enszer, at the time, split the difference. The final volume, she remarked, "confirms as much as it departs" from what Rich's readers had come to expect.[1] Stephanie Burt's subsequent pronouncement, "[her] new poems show qualities that almost require the label 'late style,'"[2] comports with Enszer's judgment. While the "almost" is intriguing, Burt did characterize the collection as "explicit [...] in its return to the poet's prior work"—comparing Rich with Yeats. Why, then, the question? Do we rely on our great poets, still at work, to heed bounds we've set, our confidence in what we've celebrated, that toward which we look?

Yeats's late work has of course been the subject of so very much, justly reverential, commentary. Peter Ure points out that the challenge for Yeats was "to discover his role in a universe" he "conceived" of "as a dramatic structure."[3] Yeats confided to his diary that "one reason for putting our actual situation into our art is that the struggle for complete affirmation may be, often must be, that art's chief poignancy."[4] A substantial amount of Yeats's late work is taken to possess a power and grace equal to that in his earlier poetry. Ask someone randomly about a poet's late work; more often than not Yeats is mentioned.

I've thought a lot about William Bronk's concise, dense, late statements. They don't possess the majestic sweep of his poems at middle age (in terms of line length, overall volume, the philosophical punch in the solar plexus). Bronk's late poems, however, hold their own, and they do seem typically Bronk. For me the comparison here is with someone like Harriet Zinnes; her late poems—their ethereal, sprightly, fleetingly brilliant statements seeming to have come from beyond the veil—are exciting in their exquisite lightness yet fascination that doesn't dissipate. Zinnes's last poems are supremely graceful, intelligent, paradoxically profound in their sheer defiance of gravity. Yet I'd not be surprised to find readers of her work, over the years, keeping to mind poems of hers written when she was at, say, full strength, which they know well, feeling the late poems to be a distinct leave-taking. They strike me as drawing upon the same wellspring of insight, finally, and as possessing an eerie gracefulness— less on display in her work of middle age, obfuscated there by something grander in presentation. That earlier work, not diminished by what would come, probably remains what her readers will embrace.

There's another poet, Louis Zukofsky, needing mention in this context—as I think about Hugh Seidman, who is most noticeably Zukofsky's progeny. The difference, when it comes to Seidman, among all poets, is that in a long and distinguished career, his greatest achievement is his last volume. In this sense, then, we can view *Status of the Mourned*, Seidman's new book, and his career, apart and together, as something most rare. Published in 2018, in his seventy-eighth year and fifteen years since his last collection, this very late book, furthermore, discloses—announces—Seidman's return to a poetics from which he'd strayed, once his friendship with Rich had blossomed.

As I contemplate the significance of this work that's come very late in life, I naturally think of *Tonight No Poetry Will Serve*, Rich's final collection, and of *80 Flowers*, Zukofsky's. Like Rich, Zukofsky was a poet who broke new ground. "Poem beginning 'The'" was an inflection point along the modernist trajectory; *80 Flowers*, considered to be an early postmodernist exemplar, has yet to be fully divined. Seidman's late book includes poems about both his mentors, but it's Zukofsky's tenets that dwell within Seidman's powerfully wrought lines. All the same, each elder is more than simply acknowledged. They help to create a historical tableau. By design, the book takes us back to Seidman's youth, in order to move forward toward a present in which we witness the poet looking back, in reflection. This is an autobiography, and it is a reckoning.

The ordering of the poems historicizes Seidman's poetic development. Perhaps it's ironic that a few of them explicitly challenge the value Seidman himself finds in Objectivist poetics. First encountering Zukofsky in a class he taught at Brooklyn Polytechnic Institute, he solidified his bond with him. Seidman's rendezvous with Rich was a decade off—that second, very important friendship, which is most sensed in the poems of his midcareer. I can't help but see Rich pulling him, in some respects, away from Zukofsky. Yet Seidman's spiraling back to his origins, given the longevity of his life, makes the homecoming possible. But why, exactly, is this something I feel needs saying now?

While Seidman's last book is, I believe, his finest collection of poems, the peculiar grip it's had on me has also to do with its intent to look back in old age, and to take stock. This is his seventh book; some poets (including Zukofsky and Rich), after well over a half century of writing, have amassed a much larger oeuvre. Seidman is frugal. This quality is obvious in his poems. The writing's imbued with sheer craft and piercing intellect. Each syllable belongs

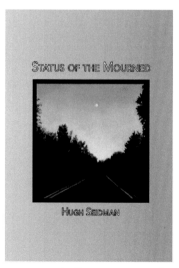

right where it is. None of the poems is very long. All of them make room for the subtle percept. They're meticulous statements, rendered in a refined prosody and shot through with obvious care.

Readers long ago came to expect such a practice from him. Three of his six prior collections have won prizes. Now, after protracted silence, comes this work of unparalleled beauty. It's ably complemented by a modestly affecting design.

The front cover features a haunting painting by Jayne Holsinger: a landscape below an evening sky, the moon appearing just above a tree-lined, heavily shaded road. The painting's mystery augurs what follows.

The other singular characteristic of Seidman's work is its ethical imperative, which is couched in the question of how to live. In this late book the presence of death is palpable; so is a commitment to being alive. The duality runs throughout the book and forms the tissue of human relationships. Seidman gives us an honest, tender, and harrowing accounting of the living and the dead, who they are, and he strives to do the same for himself. His judgments are unadorned. To read them is to exult and weep. Family and friends are glimpsed and considered.

In past and present, people live and die within the built, implacable city. Manhattan landscapes sustain the delicacy of memory—within a fading world. Remembering affords clarity. Vital sightings from the past are a necessity.

The *status of the mourned* is a conceit whose vector courses in either direction. In the title poem, "Seido Karate: 'Kino Hito No Mi Kyo No Wagami,'"[5] we look on Seidman as he is meditating with others in their *dojo*, while a *sensei* struggles against a life-threatening illness:

> butt on heels, right palm up in the lap under left
>   knuckles, thumbs touching

> I shut my eyes and shot a ray of invisible light to Beth
>   Israel hospital
> to the first female *sensei*—as the Master had instructed

tube-entwined, eyelids fluttering under the morphine—
she had not known him
and then we stood when he struck the gong

and the tears arose that I would not have accorded
myself as if then for her with whom I had no connection (6)

Seidman grieves for those gone, witnessing his own bereft state; "amid the remarkable fervor that raises the dead to the status of the living," he loves those here. His poems embrace each *status*. (The word *status*, the diction here, is curious in its abstraction, possibly suggesting the extraneous nature of circumstance, in juxtaposition to something elemental.)

In counterpoise, the poems dwell within the dead's hold upon the living. The depth of one's love for another is contingent upon keeping faith with the other's human frailty. Its constancy is dramatized in the book's first poem, entitled "Old Letter," which conjures Seidman's father. "Lava" follows it—meant to recall his mother. The two poems are a set piece. Symbolically, the parents will give birth to the remainder of the book. Here's "Old Letter" in its entirety:

Passion of the written when all whom I knew were alive
*Helping you will not in any way burden us in any way
     whatsoever*

Like the theory of the future of the visible stars
So far-flung in the blank sky that their light will not
     reach us

You being happy makes us doubly happy
You are our life and joy—no matter what the psychology
   books say

And my father in motion fated like the voided stars
One who has gone light years by now—who would
   help if he could (3)

The first line of "Old Letter" inaugurates the remembrance of Seidman's parents and establishes the entire volume's premises. The poem reveals an aching disappointment that the son still feels, yet preserving his love for his father (who didn't want him to become a poet).

Seidman understands the limits of personality, human will, and action. "Lava," the second poem, resuscitates his mother, who suffered bouts of profound depression and stints in mental institutions. The poem discloses the story of her vacancy in his youth, depicting a mother at war with her very young child:

Six-month, street-ditched tot.
Psycho mom walks off.

ECT tit swapped for Dad.
Talk about mixed metaphor!

Shocked Mom comes home.
Babe's bed at parents' bulb.

Past it, Freudian strobe.
Had that shut sonny up?

Did not talk until three.
Doc said: a spew, if ready.

Yes—fire smart, avid.
Cooled to paradox of rock.

Yet Mom spat: rotten brat.
E.g., babe nixes galoshes.

But—why not rebirth?
Not the re-screwed watts. (4)

The outrage over what is clearly the woman's neglect of the toddler hammers at us in Seidman's brief and taut, pulsing lines. Psychological cleaving between child and parent places any hope of happiness in jeopardy. Time is depicted as both physical and emotional distance, through the poem's jarring observations made palpable by its muscular rhythms (e.g., "Yet Mom spat: rotten brat"). "Lava" is suffused with the grown son's disgust and sorrow.

The opening lines of "Lava" look ahead to several other poems in which Seidman is also watching people who frequent one or another of his city's pocket parks or playgrounds: an "Old woman in black on a bench," her "Shopping cart like the metal wheeler given a neighbor" who "[fell] in the street," Seidman confides, is now "afraid to go out." The surround envelops them all—private and public in shared space—the city possessing its own living, frenetic pulse. It's as much a life force as anyone in it, a place where everyone watches everyone else. He enjoys the park's "last-of-April tulips" that are set against Manhattan's towers, their "sky-high-rent" in this "world-wide-tourist center of the universe" (42). People congregate in streets and parks hugged in by buildings. Everything's held in the moment by the city's rhythms. Beauty and callousness meet amid the noise of traffic or in relative calm under a few trees. The flaneur intersects it all.

Seidman, who sees in the present and past at once, starts in physical *place* and transports us through reverie and reflection. "Crossing Bryant Park" transcends the present moment to eulogize his deceased friend, Susan Robertson. In the poem, Seidman's on his way through the park to his job. He walks along, "1200 steps to work," going back decades to Robertson's "bridal two-step":

> Father: suicide; Mother: survivor; Sister: fatal breast.
> *Tai chi* fighter, shrink, scholarship Bryn Mawr waif.
>
> Lungs sicker than said or known.
> Phone small talk—then you were gone. (30)

Illness is irrevocable. Seidman recollects her "noduled, cut out womb" and a "[t]ransfusion, perhaps, the future tumor root." No relief from the suffering is on offer. A noble and beloved human being disappears.

Seidman's greatness as a poet ultimately lies in his capacity to identify with the other. Suffering rivets him. Compassion fails to ameliorate it. And so he's thrown back upon a bare sense of moral urgency. The problem of the random universe is that there is nothing, no moral framework, no locus, nothing to hold onto against the wind from a black hole. His poems, however, stand in defiance of that, as in "Writing and Catastrophe,'" in which "[t]o exist is to be guilty" and "[t]his is the black hole of morality." The poem's opening movement defies the reader to forget and brings us all to account:

Albania, Kosovo/Kosova, Lebanon, Nicaragua, Pakistan

No poem post "holocaust"
Irony shuts up

Body unable to speak on atrocious Earth

No poem sparks the gap—universe-narrow, atom-wide —
Between act and word

Some lover enacts no difference
Eyes bleeding, palms budding stigmata

Modern life is the "Radio alarm buzzer" that "wakes the justice by the torturers" (43–44). Another of Seidman's eulogies is for Marla Ruzicka, who founded the Campaign for Innocent Victims in Conflict (CIVIC). He depicts her as the young American woman she was, who perished at thirty in Baghdad—"her last outcry: 'I'm alive.'" The poem's extended incantation, made up of literally searing images, details how she would place herself in harm's way:

sparks rachet from the tinder
crackle from the racket of fire and light and are gone

tireless, fearless
against generals, bureaucrats, politicians

her skull touching skull
hem of her black *abaya* clenched in her fist

set on the shoulder of the unveiled woman in *hijab*
who buttresses the dark-eyed, moon-eyed child

corpuscles hiss from the splutter
flare from the pyre drafts

motes rocket, incandescence, and are lost
flecks tick from the holocausts

ingénue *face-splitting* smile
Buddha-girl California smile

petite with curly blonde tresses
pretty, peppy, fiery, vivacious

nicknamed *Bubbles* in Kabul
immolated by a *God car* on the Baghdad airport road (45)

In "Millennial," portraying a similar situation, the lack of self-regard has become a necessity. "Millennial" takes us further back in time, to the Vietnamese Buddhists who set themselves aflame in protest against America's disastrous war in Southeast Asia (the footage of their suicides ubiquitous, then, in the American media).

What was Seidman doing while people burned? "I programmed

a mainframe," he concedes. He was "[d]eferred for 'critical skills'"; at the same time, a conscientious objector performed "alternative service," though much the same kind of thing. In Seidman's genteel naiveté, what was left for him to ponder then—and now—is the moral precariousness of that life. Throughout history we find human cataclysm:

> What did I know of war?
> A brother-in-law's M-16.
>
> Words like *the fires of Dresden*.
> (Put, struck, swapped.)
>
> Car bombs leave me whole.
> What eye for what eye?
>
> Debris of the universal Kaddish.
> Blaspheming local death. (36)

He won't absolve himself. "I confess that I confess," he declares in "Unfinished Poem" (47). Yet forgiveness takes one but so far. Among several remembrances of Ed Smith, Seidman's oldest and closest friend, there is "Grand Mal," the group's linchpin, in which Seidman realizes his utter helplessness. The poem's metaphysics is nearly intolerable. His despair is his genuine form of love, as he looks on at his friend's death throes:

> salt water wracking metal
> salt water rupturing buckled metal

a melanoma a frothing at the mouth
eyes rolled up into the head

the convulsed ocean the metastatic sky
conjoined to the tumoral brain

cremation ashes beside a bed
glacier melt thinned-out beaver pelt

sand foam churned by the salt
Pied Piper child shut in the wave (17)

Seidman's grief is the grief of the world. A particular trope, which recurs throughout the book, materializes in "Grand Mal" in the phrase "buckled metal"; it emblematizes Smith's defeat.

The world's elemental, huge forces mimic Smith's primal fight, in the poem, simply to breathe. In comparing the fundamental condition of human struggle with vast exterior forces—"convulsed ocean the metastatic sky"— Seidman portrays a parallel, gruesome drama: oceans have ebbed, flowed, and surged, well before humans' presence; the single human life might end without hope or dignity. There is always the possibility of human extinction.

And there's no recourse to Smith's calamity other than Seidman's impulse to answer for it as if somehow responsible for the wretched end. His intolerable dilemma is expressed succinctly in "Frank Canned, Joe Upped"—another of the Smith poems, as a single, self-sustained line, and as a non-sequitur: "Rage: a steel bar to bite" (7). The line floats alone, on the page, between couplets. Its density, like the compression to be seen in a poem such as "Marla Ruzicka," drives home the existential atrocity residing at the core of "Grand Mal." The "steel bar" becomes the "buckled metal" of the later poem (*metal* punning with *mettle*).

This trope's subliminal associations will arise in still another poem, titled "Melancholia," which also anticipates "Grand Mal":

On Ed's way out I bragged: I found the path.
Muzzled the black pit bull at 70-plus.

Tumors in the head of my boyhood friend Ed.
Three-scalpeled, three gamma-knifed.

Metatastic melanoma—then, the grand mal.
Suddenly the ambulance woke me for a while.

Irony of Ed: Columbia imager of brains.
Claremont home hospice—a "life," as is claimed.

Ambition that enacts the acts of its plan.
To love, to work—for as long as one stands.

But underworlds smoldered and flared.
I could not forget what I could not remember.

The black pit bull again licked my hand.
Manic tongue of the clamped, adamant jaw. (13)

The "clamped, adamant jaw" is the earlier poem's "rage,"

the bitten "steel bar." Seidman's loss is irremediable. And in *Status of the Mourned* Smith's death looms so large that it becomes, in essence, the subject of the entire book. The poems about his cancer remind us of our modern affliction. The ministrations of contemporary medicine become their own insults, beyond the disease.

Suffering, which must result in death, becomes Seidman's absolute zero. "I did not understand a good death until my friend died and I had no friend," he avers in "Testament" (14), never looking away from the torment. Through loss, however, he holds himself, and everyone, within the human communion. Dying with dignity becomes paramount.

In "Envy," a sardonically playful, bravura performance, he is the object of castigation for his self-involved aspirations:

Once: Musketeer, soul chum, "brother."
Then: self-exalter, cocksure strutter.

No nameless Midas met minus a glance.
But galler, compeer, top dog, shunner.

I glared from that skewed level.
One foot in the present, one foot in the past.

Sane brain urged: let other prosper.
One wins today; one, tomorrow.

Instead: I signed the chit; I bought the myth.
200-dollar Brioni marked 29.

Silk treasure, paisley verdure.
Four-in-Hand, Pratt, Windsor, Half-Windsor.

Narcissus: unbudged, mirrored.
Knotted, noosed cravat at buttoned collar. (10)

Here, in arch irony, his vibrancy has blinded him to the importance of friendship. Seidman's sense of regret and self-accusation shaping "Envy," in some respects thematically resonant with "Melancholia" and "Frank Canned, Joe Upped," subtly, indirectly shares something else with "Grand Mal": the horror of one's undoing.

"Envy," furthermore, is meant to stand in contrast to several love poems to Holsinger, Seidman's wife. One of them, "The Longing of the New World for the Old World," completes the book. This poem's placement is also intended to serve as a counterweight to the two poems about Seidman's parents, which open the book (particularly "Lava," recalling his mother). The final poem, for another reason, rivals "Grand Mal," serving as a kind of antidote or salve. The poems to Holsinger affirm the will to live and to live well—to live meaningfully, even in the presence of calamity—or alternately, as this poem demonstrates, in the triumph of happiness.

"The Longing of the New World for the Old World" is magisterial. Complex and sweeping, this final poem gathers all of the book's concerns. The poem's setting is the shore of the Hudson River in lower Manhattan, near the island's southern tip. Across the river, Seidman can see "the far-shore monoliths" of Jersey City; slightly to his left, toward the open sea, there's the Statue of Liberty, and then the harbor.

The poem begins with a phrase that will become the speaker's refrain: "I keep my post for you at the harbor of the new world." Holsinger is embarking for Europe. He'll stand where he can see the ships entering from the ocean. "I go down at dusk," he tells his absent spouse, "and watch the sun drop." The lines suggest how this last poem is meant, figuratively, to be a paean to the world itself. In effect, they're a declaration of love. They spell out Seidman's devotion to Holsinger, yet their expansive nature comprehends a great deal more. And they sum up his life: "My father landed a hundred years ago from the old world. Take care, come home, as they say, safe and sound. // I keep my post for you at the bend of the continent" (71).

The poem's grandeur—emerging out of time and place on the one hand, on the other out of love and commitment —is enacted through long lines that contrast the book's typically shorter lines and compact statements. Seidman's words seem to expand to something much larger, in any case, within which Holsinger is central. The poem concludes much as it began, coming full circle not only to its first lines, it's implied, but also to shared and abiding concerns arcing across all the poems:

> I will think of you in the old world as I stand in the
> new world.
> This poem conjoins to the absence of Mother.
>
> This poem creates itself as the absence of Mother.
>
> No reason for the poem but the absence of Mother.
> No refuge from the absence of Mother but the poem.

180

I breathe the dark of the water that covers the last of
  the sky.

For what do the people of the old world long?
Why do they show the American film in the park
  below the
Ferris wheel in the Prater?

I keep my post for you, my river post. (71–72)

A poem like this, its capacious nature, was not possible
for Seidman when he was young. However, condensed,
staccato-like lines such as we read in "Lava" ("Six-month,
street-ditched tot. / Psycho mom walks off.") are reminiscent
of what he was doing even in his first book, *Collecting
Evidence* (the 1970 Yale Younger Poets selection). In a
way, *Status of the Mourned* returns to where Seidman began,
albeit with greater sophistication and wisdom. The closing
of the circle comports with this book as a true, faithful
summation. Seidman has come to terms with his entire
life, in retrospect.

Integral to this life has been his relationships with
other poets and their work—most of all Zukofsky and
Rich. *Status of the Mourned,* containing a sizable number
of poems written about or to each of them, also simulates
them in the persona's acts of address. The inclusion of these
poems can't help but raise the question of a poet's late work
(as Seidman must be aware). The new book, a testament,
interweaves or merges autobiography with impartial
observation. A particular irony is that when he looks back
at loved ones he sees their imperfections and failures along
with their victories.

Seidman met Rich in 1967, when he took her MFA class at Columbia. He'd met Zukofsky in 1958, when he was still quite young and therefore more amenable (than he would later be) to Zukofsky's understanding of poetry—his Objectivist precepts undergirding the appropriately titled *Collecting Evidence*. Although it molded his foundation, Seidman managed to throw off the clinamen of Zukofsky's monumental achievement and ego, to develop his own distinct poetry. It doesn't seem out of the question that Rich's tutelage was of help in this way. Still, whether or not he was a second son for Zukofsky, Seidman took that role for himself.

The poem "L.R." replicates the rhythm as well as the form of *80 Flowers*, whose first lines are "Heart us invisibly thyme time / round rose bud fire downland." Seidman reconceives the poem's proceduralist method of five-word lines as a kind of salute:

> Forked sycamore gores the moon.
> Piebald bark wrinkled like skin.
>
> Notch between here and there.
> Gash between now and then. (25)

What was then is again now.

Zukofsky had advised him, as Seidman once put it to me, to "cut cut cut." He later remembered Zukofsky's approach to poetry as "not foreign to me since I was already involved with the paring down of mathematical proofs."[7] All in all, his teaching was "an accumulated gesture." Taking Zukofsky as his "poetic father," Seidman strove "to imitate" what he was being drawn to naturally—that "spare, precise style." He later declared: "I must simply say that I loved him."[8] The musical, linguistic virtuosity, most salient in Seidman's late collection, comes from their relationship. The book can't help but make reference to that both explicitly and in the poetics on display in it.

Full-stopped lines are the norm here. They underscore concision as a daily practice. Seidman's elegance has always resided within the empirical, despite the spaciousness of the mathematical, and the book maintains a fierce commitment to specificity. The result is disclosure of delicate truth not normally sensed in the tangible world. (Perhaps, at heart, this has been the allure of Objectivist poetry.) While *Status of the Mourned* is at heart an autobiography, the vocation of poet is central in the life—and poetry may, like mathematics, invoke something else.

There's a slew of poems about Zukofsky in the book. And there's a wonderful two-poem sequence about Rich. She's admired. To a degree she's turned into a martyr and worshipped. Seidman employs italicized phrases, in his diptych to her, meant to reproduce portions of her poem "Tear Gas."[9] They reflect his own corporeal ethics evinced in his title poem, in which he describes himself as "[sitting] *seiza* before *kumite* / upon the track to no end but the speed of the hurtling body." Addressing Rich directly, in the first poem of the sequence, titled "In an Ill-Lit Formal Space," Seidman recalls her efforts just to be taken seriously:

your stare almost mocks us
your stare is the four-year-old

locked in the *closet*
*beat*ing *the wall with* her *body*

second photo: Berryman, you, Mary Jarrell
(a suicide, two suicide widows)

female prodigy fronting the phalanx:
seven dark suits—Kunitz to Penn Warren

privilege to expunge yourself
freedom to renounce the dead (69)

Seidman may recognize in Rich his own image, as that of someone whose early years were filled with trauma, for similar reasons. In any case his life as a poet is integral to a moral kinship he has with Rich. Both lives are possible, finally, only because of the vocation of *poet*. Whether or not poetry heals wounds is another matter. "I labor," he tells her in the final line of his homage, "because of you with the hope of poetry."

His homage to Zukofsky is more complex. And, as in "Zuk Tape," Seidman offers something still more intimate. The poem begins with suspense: "Bill Z's note: *Hughie here's Louis* / Craving solace of his voice (decades unheard)."[10] Similar to Seidman's "Two Poems" to Rich, each of the several Zukofsky poems acts as an element within a lengthy meditation on the elder's work, its legacy, as well as Seidman's attachment to it. The italics in "Zuk Tape" convey —as they echo the titles and lines of some of Zukofsky's works

—the sense of an ongoing inner dialogue. This is especially the case in the poem's middle portion where the poem's speaker gets lost in rumination:

> Lines in my head all my adult life
> Blown-dust texts pulled from shelves
>
> *Shorter Poems*
> ("Hear her clear mirror"
> "Come shadow come")
>
> *Bottom*
> *"A"*
> *Catullus*
> ("Miserable Catullus" to "Miss her, Catullus?"
> Paradigm of his speech/song poetics) (62)

Among the works Seidman mentions is the vivid, magically supple, and succinct lyric "So That Even a Lover."[11] Midway through "Zuk Tape" he pivots to an admission, which ends with the poem's delicious punch-line (the italics are Seidman's):

> *Objectivist?*
> *That was forced on me*
> *I had no program*
> *It was all very simple*
>
> *You live in a world*
> *I don't see how you can escape it*
> *Even if you escape it*
> *You're still living in some kind of situation*

You make things in it
You make it with the tools of your own particular craft
In this case words
I feel them as very tangible

Solid so to speak
Sometimes they liquefy
Sometimes they airefy
But those are still existent things

(And finally after 40 years
I catch "little wrists"' sexual "do") (63)

What comes across in the suite of Zukofsky poems is a picture of Seidman, a highly accomplished poet looking back upon three careers, and coming to a resolution about his poetry as well as poetry itself. This entire configuration is held by one or another form of memory. To remember, for Seidman, is also to ponder the lifelong vocation of poet.

What could it mean to "labor" in obscurity? Zukofsky had done so and was profoundly disappointed by that. Seidman ends his poem "L.Z." (echoing Zukofsky's purposeful echoes of Shakespeare) like this:

Failure has nothing to be lost.
If bile offend, shall love deform?

Happiness/unhappiness—the great tautology.
Lineage master of the song.

So-called cup of bitterness.
Three times full and running over. (61)

"So-called," indeed.

Notes

1. Julie R. Enszer, "'*Tonight No Poetry Will Serve*' by Adrienne Rich," Lambda Literary, February 7, 2011.

2. Stephanie Burt, "No Scene Could Be Worse," *London Review of Books* 34, no. 3, February 9, 2012.

3. Peter Ure, "W. B. Yeats: The Later Poetry," *The Review of English Studies* 16, no. 63 (August 1965): 328.

4. Ure, 329.

5. The Japanese phrase can translate, roughly, into English as "yesterday the other person, today myself."

6. Hugh Seidman, *Status of the Mourned* (New York: Dispatches / Spuyten Duyvil, September 2018), 16.

7. Emails to author, October 11, 2009, and December 29, 2018. In an interview, Molly Nason asks, "You went from mathematics and theoretical physics to writing poetry. What caused that shift?"—to which Seidman explains: "I started writing poems and also became a lover of mathematics at around the same time, at about the age of 14—i.e., the age of puberty. Before that I had been a kid growing up on the streets of Brooklyn. After that I entered, for good or bad, into the life of the mind. And, I did not give up one (math/physics) and start the other (poetry), but rather I had been doing both all along."

8. Hugh Seidman, "Louis Zukofsky at the Polytechnic Institute of Brooklyn (1958–1961)," *Louis Zukofsky: Man and Poet*, ed. Carroll F. Terrell (Orono, ME: National Poetry Foundation, 1979), 100.

9. The will to change begins in the body not in the mind
    My politics is in my body, accruing and expanding with every
    act of resistance and each of my failures
    Locked in that closet at 4 years old I beat the wall with my body
    that act is in me still[.]

10. "Bill Z" is the poet Bill Zavatsky.

11. Little wrists,
    Is your content

    My sight or hold,
    Or your small air
    That lights and trysts?

    Red alder berry
    Will singly break;

    But you—how slight—do:
    So that even
    A lover exists.

CODE AND SUBSTRATE: RECONCEIVING THE ACTUAL

Part 1

I recall the poet and art critic Corinne Robins talking about what she believed was the core of an artist's practice. Above all, in her view (one she shared with her husband, the sculptor Salvatore Romano), the materials are most important—which the artist manipulates, basically by hand. This fundamental, physical engagement is the essence of the artistic act.

People more readily understand this primary connection when thinking about tools or craft, rather than art. A carpenter builds a cabinet by hand, using a saw, hammer, and nail. This is *craft*. A painter, let's say an expressionist painter, applies paint to a canvas. This is *art*. In an interview, the painter James Little was once asked about "influences" he could recall, which "might have contributed to [his] early interest in the arts." The abstract colorist tells the story of what for him was a revelatory moment.

Little's father had taken him to work, when he was a boy, at a construction site. Watching what was going on there, he was entranced by what the laborers *did*. The youth was particularly fascinated by how they were pouring concrete. A highly successful artist, Little now volunteers to his interviewer a piece of advice: the pouring of concrete "should be done manually." He says he was fascinated by the "masons," how they "would spread it out."

189

Little's seminal experience led to a form of art viewers talk about as *purely aesthetic*. His childhood experience at that construction site, in some nascent, semiconscious way what he was understanding, "had a strange influence on [his] sensibility toward surface, even to this day." Little's painting would come to be characterized by what he then says: "I just like the idea of taking this medium, this material and transforming it—making it do something other than what it appeared to want to do" ("In Conversation"). He was touched, so to speak, by what could be *done* with that material.

Although the line between art and craft may be meaningless in the minds of many people nowadays, even nonexistent for all practical purposes, Martin Heidegger's mid twentieth-century distinction between the two can still be of use if we want to think clearly about art. (I might add the distinction is pertinent if we want to think about the nature of poetry.) In his essay "The Origin of the Work of Art" ("*Der Ursprung des Kunstwerkes*") the critical difference between the work of art and the work of craft has to do with *use*. What Heidegger calls *equipment* (*das zeug*)—technological artifact—is involved with skill, design, even inspiration. Equipment is an artifact meant for a task. Heidegger would want to say, in contrast, that art has no task, or at least no practical task. Art is useless.

A critique of an art installation titled *Floating Piers (2014–16)*, created by the artists Christo and Jeanne-Claude, takes issue with Christo's claim that the physical manifestation of their art was "purely aesthetic" (Watson "Shooting Down" *Hyperallergic*). Over many years, the grand-scale nature of this artist-couple's work employed natural landscape merged with technological artifact, which could yield visually stunning effects. Their efforts beckoned crowds of people who interacted with their artworks, engaging them in a physical as well as psychological way. *Floating Piers* was sited on Italy's Lake Iseo and the adjacent town of Sulzano; the "piers" were covered by 1,076,391 square feet of vivid orange-yellow cloth.

Regardless of whether or not they might be seen to have some kind of use, Christo's salient remark about them was telling—and it drew the ire of the article's author, Mike Watson, who quotes Christo as saying the artwork had been made "for ourselves"—the piers were "totally unnecessary"—adding that they "don't serve for anything except to be a work of art; like all of our works they need to be lived [...] you need to physically go through" them (Watson par. 1). Watson conveyed his annoyance over this claim for a "purely aesthetic" achievement, basing his complaint on Immanuel Kant's monumental *Critique of Judgment*, pointing out the substantial financial and social consequences of the piers installation—which, in Watson's words, "impede an artwork from being a purely aesthetic experience" (par. 1).[1] Sociological and economic repercussions are, Watson would say, unavoidable.

His dispute relies on "[Kant's assertion] that one can only have a purely aesthetic experience if it is free of any judgment regarding the goodness or usefulness of a given object or phenomenon" (Watson par. 1).[2] The social and financial collateral damage from these (useless) piers—the various forms of cost to the lake and Sulzano—cannot be overlooked; Watson questions the artistic merit of the project. By challenging the aesthetics of the installation, he also seems to want to undermine Christo's rationale.

However we might feel about Kant's conceptualization of art, aesthetics, the sublime, even judgment, it's worth noting that Heidegger finesses certain of Kant's contingencies (these Watson points up—e.g., a possible relation to ethics, as well as the status of an aesthetic judgment in relation to the sublime and perhaps to beauty). The younger philosopher does this by taking us back, with a specific purpose in mind, to the ancient Greek viewpoint, which lies at the root of the Western intellectual—artistic, possibly aesthetic—tradition. Hence he lends a powerful lucidity in thinking about art and/versus technology (to use his terms, in thinking about *equipment* versus a *work of art*). The distinction is key.

Kant's *sine qua non* of an aesthetic judgment—that it be free of contingencies, such as a determination of goodness or usefulness—highlights a crucial effect at stake in the toggle switch between *useful* and *useless*, which is set out in Heidegger's essay. (Christo echoes this western philosophical line of thinking.)[3] The ancient Greeks, Heidegger points out, designated both art and craft with the root word *technē*. In a work of *craft* or *equipment* (a technological creation) the materials making up the craftwork "disappear," Heidegger says, from our attention to it ("The Origin of the Work of Art" 24 ff.); or rather, they go unnoticed. We attend to a further end beyond the technological artifact of the tool *per se*; this end has to do with the purported *purpose* of the tool.

It's the opposite in art. In a work of art, the very materiality of the artwork comes to the fore, fills our attention.[4] Heidegger implies that this coming-forth into our awareness, which we might experience as purely sensory, as ideated or both—as *aesthetic?*—is integrated within our act of attending-to the artwork as something we have a sense of, even if we're not paying attention to the fact of its material ontology. A figurative painting, like Van Gogh's pair of shoes (Heidegger's example), contains a narrative; nonetheless the viewer gains a sense of what helps to make the narrative exist on the painting's canvas in the first place—composition overall, brushstrokes, pigment, thickness, etc., as we move closer to the elemental nature of the art object. The materiality, that which we attend to in the artwork, is absent in the piece of equipment—replaced by the consciousness of the equipment's purpose.

A "mere" shovel, for instance, which is such a piece of equipment, is viewed and understood precisely as a tool. We are likely more ready to appreciate, to understand, this shovel as a tool if it's seen, let's say, leaning against the side of a house. Our attention is not on the shovel's honed wooden shaft tipped by a tempered and shaped metal handle on one end, on the other an equally tempered piece of metal designed for the purpose of removing snow. But what happens when we encounter the shovel leaning against the wall of an art gallery, when there's a small plaque bearing a title for that "shovel," which someone, let's say an artist— let's say Marcel Duchamp—has given it?

Another way to think about this duality is to consider poetry. Writing is a technology. The aesthetics of a poem became possible with the advent of literacy. Before the invention of writing, poetry was *done* for the purpose of keeping a tribe's memory intact. Techniques we now think of as elements of verse were once simply mnemonic devices invented to serve a collective memory, for the telling of it as performed at tribal gatherings. The historian-poet constructed a matrix holding rhymes, rhythms and epithets, and formulas of phrase. These could be retrieved, could be remembered and performed; the techniques of remembrance later were active memory (cf. Walter Ong's monumental *Orality and Literacy: The Technologizing of the Word* and a wealth of scholarship since). Verse, since writing's invention, language arranged according to designs created in preliterate times, is prosody no longer serving a practical purpose.

Duchamp's shovel, if it were being used to move snow, would be taken up in one's hands and maneuvered with one's arms, as an instrument by which someone clearing a sidewalk or driveway might be injured from the strain of the snow's weight (which is Duchamp's not very clever joke). His so-called "readymade," which he titled *In Advance of the Broken Arm* (1915), was a mass-produced shovel put on display, a purported work of art that resides within our visual and cognitive engagement of it as something quite material. *In Advance of the Broken Arm* has been comprehended by artists, critics and scholars in ways that don't account for the work's absolute material presence— furthermore its presence as a mass-produced object, which could come to be seen as beautiful (here, I've gone beyond Heidegger's essay).[5]

I mean to pun when I talk about the hand holding the shovel. In his other writings, where he contemplates the use of tools (within discussions of Being or *Dasein*), Heidegger organizes the concept of *tool* according to two categories: *zuhandheit* and *vorhandheit*—*zuhanden* to mean there by nature or ordinarily existent or "hands-on," and *vorhanden* to mean fabricated or in readiness or simply at one's disposal, or "before one's hand" or "close at hand" (cf. *Being and Time* 408–9 / *Sein und Zeit* 357–8). In the latter case, writes Iain Thomson, "we come to experience ourselves as isolated subjects standing reflectively before a world of external objects, which we thereby come to experience as standing over against us in the mode of something objectively 'on hand'" (Zalta, *Stanford Encyclopedia of Philosophy*).[6]

This perception of Duchamp's shovel is so regardless of whether or not this *readymade* (*made* in a factory and *ready* for *use*) is to be considered as a work of conceptual art—*conceptual* as long as the work embodies, supposedly foregrounds, an overriding *idea*, aesthetic value ancillary in this engagement of the work). In modern and contemporary commentary, the material substrate of a work like *In Advance of the Broken Arm* is not fully recognized for what it is, while there are obvious ways in which the ancient Greek *technē* might lead to our thinking of conceptual artworks as ultimately lacking a material significance.

Part 2

The poetry of the North American avant-garde has been, uniquely, involved with art. Craig Dworkin's study, *No Medium* —a scholarly discourse as well as personal and objective meditation on art and poetry—prompts me to think about the *readymade*. Not unrelated to it, Dworkin considers the completely black or completely white painted canvas, and Robert Rauschenberg's erasure of a Willem de Kooning drawing in 1953 (as one of the defining gestures of postmodernism), as well as artifacts like Ronald Johnson's *RADI OS* (Johnson's erasure of the first four books of Milton's *Paradise Lost*) and Stéphane Mallarmé's *Un Coup de des* (1897) that's foundational within the context of these other works. *Un Coup de des* is a poem and a work of art. It foresees the potential of N. Katherine Hayles's scholarly book, *Writing Machines*; written more than a century later, to be both an autobiography and *objet d'art* (the book was designed by Anne Burdick). Hayles meant for her book to be a bridge, on the one shore writing and print, on the other computing. Her central concern in the book, actually, is for digital expressivity. When I think about "digital expressivity," I recall Little's remarks about painting, which for him is "taking" a "medium," that is to say "material," and "transforming it." The question Hayles might have wanted to ask is if coding, which has its practical purposes, can also be artful (at least in Heidegger's terms).

Writing Machines shows a potential even Hayles may not have seen—insofar as she realizes what inscription is and how we've been shaped by it over time. Her 2002 book is a prelude to later studies by her; yet it has not been superseded by anyone's critical study.[7] Chiefly, what she has had to say about the efforts, logistics, involved in producing the very artefact *Writing Machines* as an object in itself, a highly designed physical book, is remarkable. It might seem odd, on its face, for me to note that her book can be easily read, but I'm making a certain point here she'd agree with.

Why should a book be an object whose text is meant to be read? A subsequent book, *Credit*, by Matthew Timmons, published seven years after *Writing Machines*, is really not meant to be read (I suspect Marcel Broadthaers, specifically his art books, were an influence on Timmons, and before them Mallarmé's late work). *Credit*'s physical presence is powerful, and it can be said to be materially beautiful. The fact that its purchase price is quite steep is another element in this work's *conceptualization*. Not only might you not need to read the book; you also need not purchase it (a point taking me back to Watson's complaint about Christo and Jeanne-Claude, and to Kant). A collection of credit card offerings and dunnings, *Credit* is a book we might think of as literary art. (I first encountered it at an AWP convention.) It's usually taken as conceptual poetry. Like *Writing Machines*, however, it's an *objet d'art*. For me, the material presence of the book is obvious.

Flarf, too, like conceptual poetry, possesses an obduracy. Insofar as it depends, furthermore, on internet discourse for its grist (for the linguistic material with which to construct a poem), it celebrates text as digital event, even as a Flarf poem is normally composed for the page. Timmons' book *Credit* can just as easily be taken as Flarf. A primary element of Flarf is making use of language gleaned from the internet (it's possible some of the credit card offerings the book reproduces were sent online). The offerings have been recontextualized, however.

Stein and the Objectivists, principally—in some respects especially Williams, who enjoyed personal relationships with some of the Objectivists—worked from the material, written statement on the page, yet worked to undo statement in response to it. These Modernist poets' artistic acts were a reaction to the very idea of the written, printed text. In contrast, conceptual and Flarf poets, more demonstrably digital poets, do not concede the Modernist monumentality of that text. Dworkin doesn't arrive at the notion of sheer materiality, its artistic or poetic value. He spends little ink (I note my anachronistic phrase) in explaining what is art's powerful assertion of the material. His profound insights about illegible or disappeared art (again, Broadthaers a forerunner), or conceptual poetry or art, are of crucial importance in and of themselves, and they can be appropriated to further ends involving digital poetry/art.

John Cayley, in an essay titled "Time Code Language," takes the materialist position, stipulating that "One of the defining characteristics of poetic writing is its attention to the materiality of language" (307).[9] While some might find this stance can be overly broad, sweeping—it leaves aside what he may mean by *poetic*—it does call attention to the nature of language at least in more recent experimental writing, specifically to this writing's *textures*. One of our foremost digital poets and scholars writing about digital poetry, Cayley's pronouncements wield a lot of heft.

Texture is not an irrelevant notion when it comes to digitally programmed poetry. This poetry can be thought of as language in visual flux—on the screen, not on the page. I don't see how this idea of texture, however, differs from the material presence to be found in poems by, for instance, Gertrude Stein or Louis Zukofsky (in stark contrast to the writings of contemporaries like Amy Lowell or Edna St. Vincent Millay). But Cayley has singled out something crucial about the present avant garde, which was set in motion by Modernist literary innovation. Often seemingly radical Modernist experiments were operating under a shifted intellectual and aesthetic paradigm, engendering a poetics apart from predecessors'.

In large, the paradigm shift emerges from Enlightenment thought, including Kant's *Critique of Judgment*; it's preceded by Isaac Newton's theorizing of a three-dimensional universe. Rethinking of the atom in the nineteenth century leads to Einstein's theories of Relativity early in the twentieth, and later Bohr's model of atomic structure, and Heisenberg's Quantum Mechanics and Uncertainty Principle. These scientific developments, technological innovations in tandem, affected people's understanding throughout the disciplines; the arts could not have remained immune to them. Circa 1900, a profound transformation in the arts was already well underway.

Dworkin doesn't delve into this macro-shift but he's finely attuned to its nuances. He writes about Jean Baudrillard's work (which comes much later). In discussing Baudrillard's book *L'Autre par lui même*, Dworkin examines notions of "transience and dematerialization," the "transparency and disappearance" of texts—taking him to his focus on the practice of erasure in art and poetry (à la Broadthaers). It's inevitable, then, that the question of aesthetics has to be addressed.

Dworkin's meditation on erasure, perhaps unintentionally, takes me back to Cayley's claim about the nature of the *poetic*. Erasure is neither disappearance nor dissolution, according to Dworkin. It's not an end of something, since we can "look as well," he explains,

> at the opaque material remainder, and the inescapable residuum of recalcitrant physical matter left behind when certain inscriptions do not occur as expected. In the absence of inscription, the substrate can be seen not as a transparent signifier but as an object in its own right, replete with its own material properties, histories and signifying potential. (9)

This argument doesn't merely obtain to erased text. Setting aside his comprehension of art as a phenomenon of presence-absence, which has to do with an approach to avant-garde poetry and art in which a material "substrate" is there to be *read*—almost as after the fact—I want to underscore my point about Modernist poetry and art in which this later work is rooted. Since the start of the twentieth-century, the materiality of the work is what increasingly has occupied the foreground of aesthetic, as well as intellectual, engagement of that work.

Part 3

Do poets ever talk about poetry in the way Robins and Little talk about art? I think of the Objectivist poet George Oppen's notion that language is not to be trusted. In his Daybook he wrote that "words are a constant enemy: the thing seems to exist because the word does" (53). In his poem "A Language of New York" he cautions: "Possible / To use / Words provided one treat them / As enemies."[10] Are Oppen's sentiments in harmony with those expressed by an artist like Little? Or with Robins' reduction of art to the visceral working of materials with an artist's hands? Little remembers the pouring of concrete and shaping it, the sensuality of it, the awareness of its material existence. What's the difference between concrete and words? Oppen talks of *building* a poem as what happens at a construction site. Here's the first half of his poem "The Building of a Skyscraper":

> The steel worker on the girder
> Learned not to look down, and does his work
> And there are words we have learned
> Not to look at,
> Not to look for substance
> Below them. But we are on the verge
> Of vertigo.

In making great art, great poetry, is there a moment of "vertigo"? Might it happen when we avoid looking "below" words for "substance"? We mix ingredients to make and pour concrete, maybe smooth it out, like constructing strings of words, syntax. Concrete and language, words.

What's the difference between philosophy (or, let's say, political diatribe, or basically theorizing of one sort or another), on the one hand, and poetry on the other? To echo Cayley: What's the difference between prose and poetry? What does language do, or what do words do (as Ludwig Wittgenstein in *Philosophical Investigations* asks, or J. L. Austin in *How to Do Things with Words*)? What possibly can poems *do*? Is it better to ask of what are poems *made*? Once words could be written, the inscription read, poets conceived of their praxis differently from how shaping words were viewed in preliterate times. Instead of memory-keeping, for the first time there was an aesthetics of verse. The difference is stark.

The troubadours had many possibilities for agreements of sound, by the late eleventh century, as provided them by Old Provençal. Nearly all western verse forms used today come from them (the sonnet indirectly but only because troubadours fled the Albigenisan Crusade to Sicily, where that specific form would first emerge).[11] At the height of the era of the book, with the Industrial Revolution— when photography, cinema, and a number of writing technologies like the typewriter were affecting people in powerful ways—experimental poets became all the more aware of their linguistic *materials*; at that time, these were written or printed texts. Words were not only more visual; they became more material too.

The materiality of writing, the written text residing over

against the poet, becomes ever more apparent. Oppen thinks of writing when he thinks of language; and, as a deeply philosophical poet, he's also realizing language's problem. So is someone like Stein. She wished, rather in keeping with her friend Pablo Picasso's artistic intentions, to put pedestrian syntax under such strain that words themselves, in their material existence apart from their capacity to invoke abstract thinking, could be savored for themselves—*seen* as such, felt. What did it mean to type a word on a piece of paper, afterwards to look at it—not a handwritten word containing a personality, instead a word disconnected in some new and striking way from the creator of that word, who was contemplating it, within its composition on a typewriter, just as it was coming into visual form?

In her groundbreaking study of Modernist experimental typography, *The Visible Word*, Johanna Drucker points out that innovative uses of typography, typography's very presence, in effect constituted an "insistence upon the autonomous status of the work of art (visual or literary) which veritably defines the founding premise of modernism"; that insistence itself rested "upon the capacity of words to claim the status of *being* rather than *representing*." To be sure, for various Modernist movements—Cubism, Futurism, Dada, Vorticism and others—in order to make such a claim, "the materiality of their form had to be asserted as a primary in-itself condition not subordinate to the rules of imitation, representation or reference" (10-11).

A transformation within the writer had taken place, which would continue along the same trajectory—hence the claim about coding Cayley makes, one that Dworkin must have intuited, in his involvement with conceptual poetry. To describe the transformation is to comprehend a shifted cultural milieu. This was typified by people's experience of early cinema, who entered a movie theatre for the first time, emerging from it utterly transformed, now in possession of a novel concept of self. They saw themselves in motion, in action, objectified. Over "there" images of human beings were witnessed, on a screen, conceptualized in some new way, through self-identification. The images were moving through time, as it were; narratives were created, so there could be an identification with the story on the screen, with the person on the screen—the person "over there" existing within a new dimension.

For Ezra Pound, H.D., and William Carlos Williams, the world stood apart as a nascent image. The trio gave birth to Modernist poetry (Burton Hatlen referred to them as "The Philadelphia Three," their having met at the University of Pennsylvania when they were still in their teens).[12] They create Imagism. All a reader has to do to get a sense of the upheaval they were caught up in is to look at their spacings on the page. Oppen, a later Modernist, read these three poets assiduously. He was befriended by Pound and Williams. If, for Oppen, who was one of the principal Objectivist poets, words were the enemy, then his viewing of them as such could have come from his sense, possibly not just subliminal, of alienation—simply, just being situated apart from them. The words *physically* existed when he looked at "his" words on a typewritten page; they were *over there*. How did the Objectivist poet avoid the trap of language when constructing a poem—a set of signs, linguistic designs, *inscriptions*? Inscription possessed a resistance or friction. Might it be, then, that the "recursive" nature of reading material language did not so much depend upon a semiosis? To read an Oppen poem is to engage it in the way one views or engages a work of art, not just a sculpture but a painting as well, its tactile existence, especially a Modernist painting.

Dworkin eventually posits *media* as the embodiment of social investment—accordingly defined semiotically, beginning with his mention of a "substrate" (cf. above), within the context of Baudrillard's thinking and as contingent upon, Dworkin writes, "not so much the play of presence and absence that has animated studies of inscription, but rather the recursive realization that every signifier is also itself a sign" (9). My alternative approach might take as its metaphor the *dark matter* in space, which supports matter we observe; the dark matter is unreadable. Our present moment is partly defined by an identifiable unknown. There's an opacity, an unreadable element within our calculus of discourse, our epistemology. Art or poetry, without mystery or the inexplicable, possibly without the enigmatic, is finally not really art or poetry.

Part 4

In his postmodernist paintings, Little's striations of color are striking, his overall composition exhilarating. With his mature work most of all, the color's material *being* is *there* on the canvas. It's extant there because he's put together pigment, oil, honey, and other ingredients of his paint in unique ways—over hours, days in which he's mixed the elements. In his mind the materials eventually make one color and density, or another. The merging of the two allows Little to create a sheer visuality, which includes resonance, in some other medium including the canvas.

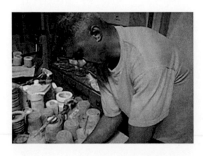

Little stirs, heats, stirs, cools—stirring, heating, stirring—over and over until some experience of the paint *per se*, which he's *made*, comes to fullness—so that the *meaning* of his abstract paintings, if we may talk like this about a truly abstract painting, involves its physicality, and even its sculptural values. There's a useful distinction to be made between Little's abstractions and those of a painter like Mark Rothko. (Abstract paintings by someone like Barnett Newman or Morris Louis, with whom Little has been compared—their vertical striations—don't make for as apt a comparison.) I'll say in hindsight that Rothko's work—which was also the product of many cycles of mixing, heating and cooling, stirring—is undoubtedly a forerunner.

The difference between Little and Rothko, these two abstract colorists, taking into account their complex processes of creating color and texture—to be more 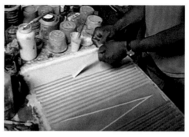 precise how they each create the *affect* of color, color in and for itself—has precisely to do with this affect. For Little, it's something that allows him to avoid what he'd call *illusionism*.

While I don't think illusionism is an apt synonym for *spirituality,* there's something like this in Rothko's paintings—which has often been articulated as the sense of the spiritual (hence the Rothko Chapel in Houston). Rothko achieved this in great measure through his own arduous and protracted process of preparing his materials, of processing them. Possibly it was not for him to choose to be quite as abstract as Little. Even so, the older artist's protracted involvement in his materials for their own sake was necessary to achieve the end he did. Little's notion of illusionism, however, takes him to *flatness,* which in turn takes us more deeply into abstraction itself.

Little characterizes himself to Celia McGee, who's paid a visit to his studio a few years ago, as "a strong believer in [. . .] something physical and perceptually tangible." Well, so is Rothko. More to the point, though, Little also says, by way of explanation: "I'm not interested in illusionism, the way a lot of abstract artists are. I'm interested in flatness, the flat plane, and materials that keep illusions at bay"

(McGee and Little, "Driven to Abstraction"). The spiritual as illusion?

Was there a story-telling, a narrative quality Rothko could not, or would not, avoid after all? What *is* abstraction? I think of "The Increasing Abstraction of Language," a poem by William Bronk (whose intense relationship with Oppen had a salutary effect on both poets' writing). Bronk paid attention to the textures of words and syntax as if, in the verse line, there was an existence all its own there, apart from any rhetoric integral in it. In this poem Bronk tells us he's

> [. . .] amazed at the way the language survives
> other structures: we go on talking as if
> we had never lost all we come at last
> to lose, the time and place the language described
> [etc.].
> (170)

In an untitled poem, Bronk realizes that his "are invented words and they refer / to inventions of their own [. . .]." In an abstract painting, the problem of language never enters into the picture (pun intended)—but is there an author of the painting?

Part 5

Jacques Derrida writes, beginning *Of Grammatology*, that "the problem of language has never been simply one problem among others" (6). We might appreciate how the philosophical attention to language paid by someone like Derrida (*Of Grammatology* may have inflected the intellectual and artistic climate of its time) lends an important perspective on the midcentury emergence of word art. Well after the initial thrust of Modernist aesthetics and thought, the coming to the fore of the material, and well after the experimental typography movement Drucker has analyzed, the new form of word art begins to be created by the conceptual artist Joseph Kosuth—in a still newer mode, it's furthered by the artist Jenny Holzer.

When Holzer first exhibited her language-as-art productions they were understood, including by her, in none of the ways that had to do with the sheer materiality manifesting in the various media of her word art as it was to evolve. Following upon Kosuth's innovations in the 1960s, which included the making of paintings that were written statements, in 1978 Holzer felt herself no longer to be restricted to the traditional artist's canvas. She first called her writings *Truisms*. Trained in the Whitney Museum program, steeped in both Western and Eastern philosophy and literature, she began to see how her writings "could be simplified to phrases everyone could understand." Her sententious truisms were printed and displayed "anonymously in black italic script on white paper." She'd affix the written-upon paper to building facades, signs, and telephone booths in lower Manhattan. Arranged in alphabetical order and comprised of short sentences, her "Truisms" inspired pedestrians to scribble messages on these posters, making verbal comments. Three years later, she created *Living Series*. This time her "word art" manifested as short and simple statements on plaques made of aluminum or bronze (Art History Archive).

Her mediums were becoming more durable, substantial. I highlight the evolution of Holzer's artistic vision and practice to point out that her work evolves at the midpoint in a progression of art development. Her art serves as a synechdoche[13] not merely for the twentieth-century's merging of North American art and poetry. What she did with her art-as-writing goes beyond the achievements of someone like Kosuth. Hers is qualitatively and ideologically different. Her linguistic statements (visual statements) are physically embodied over time in ever more solid substances—aluminum, brass, stone—eventually neon lighting. The ontology of the artwork, at this point, is the glass and chemicals of the light installation. The artwork is its glow.

The arc of a word-artist's evolution (can we conceive of Holzer as a language-artist?) prompts me to ask a series of questions: *What does it mean to make marks? What is writing? What is formal language?* Also: *What is physicality?* And: *Can there be an aesthetics of conceptual art? If the artist rather than the poet is doing the writing, must the writing itself be taken to be significant, or must the writing be comprehended as part of some larger gestalt?* The fact of Holzer's neon light works (Dan Flavin and others continue the practice) asks us to attend a transforming concept of physicality. A broader framework for thinking about all of the twentieth and twenty-first century's avant-garde artists and poets might rest upon realizing materiality-cum-presence in their work as both over-determined and undermined with respect to the physical.

Possibly the material is being interrogated for its nature. This would invite us to situate these artists within an intellectual construct marked by a conceptual shift away from Newton's classical physics, away from certainty or determinacy. In 1935, Ludwik Fleck publishes Genesis and Development of a Scientific Fact in which, Peter Quartermain reports, "the assumption [. . .] that scientific facts are flat, impartial, neutral, objective," is no longer tenable (Quartermain 271).

In time the sense of solidity located in Newtonian physics and Enlightenment reasoning (along the lines of Kantian judgment) is vitiated. Straddling the turn of the twentieth century, science and technology have already become radically transformed. Milestones in science include Einstein's theories of Relativity, shortly thereafter Bohr's remodeling of the structure of the atom, Heisenberg's Quantum Mechanics and Uncertainty Principle, and then the Einstein-Poldosky Rosen Paradox (also in 1935). In their respective moments, all these helped to reconceive our understanding of world, substance, and time. Einstein's four dimensions with time included, is superseded by models of many more dimensions, postulations of alternate universes and the like.

Breakthroughs in physics lead to digital technologies. Alongside strides made in computing, there is genomics that has helped to establish coding as the conceptual and intellectual paradigm of our present era. The modern photograph led to Impressionism. Film anticipated our analogous, transformational moment of space-time dramatized in the experience of digital technology, a rethinking of real and virtual. In *Chaos Media: A Sonic Economy of Digital Space*, Stephen Kennedy refers to digital space not merely as "an alternative realm or [. . .] a real/virtual dichotomy but as a lived experience of space that is facilitated and/or augmented by technology" (3). Just as the notion of *self* evolved in a certain direction, with human psychology affected by the technology and art of cinema, more than a century ago, so too, today, digital technologies have their effect on us. As elements of human expression they impinge upon our art making, at the same time altering us psychologically, and aesthetically.

Prior to 1900, Mallarmé is composing *Un Coup de des* (1897). He overrides the technological limitations of the book's structure (e.g., syntax crosses the book's gutter); this, along with his spacings of words, announces a new poetry whose linearity is tested in the extreme—for the ultimate purpose of bringing forward language as material fact. American poets, artists and others attended the 1913 Armory Show in New York City. It was a revelation for Williams. Along with Cubist art, they encountered Duchamp's *Nude Descending a Staircase* (1912).

While this painting can be read in a number of ways, the mechanistic look of the "nude" figure is especially compelling. The visual field of early cinema was, relative to later film, inadvertently revealing of its construction; the jumpy sequences of still images resemble the descent of Duchamp's nude. Sequences of still photos by Edweard Muybridge were an influence on Duchamp, the conception of his *Nude* (Malamud 68). In this way, an artist might gravitate to a machine aesthetic—ever more pronounced in Duchamp's *readymades.* The nude descends the staircase, depicted in visual phases. Its collective imparting of the sense of motion, a moving-through of an intuited space-time, was also evoked in a 1913 sculpture by Umberto Boccioni (the principle painter of the Futurist movement—though not represented in the Armory Show).

Titled *Forme uniche della continuità nello spatio* (*Unique form of continuity in space*), Boccioni's figure appears to be walking forward. The sculpting suggests motion most of all. As one turns away from the viewing of this work, the temptation remains to read phases of motion into it. The figure's contours—featuring curved planes making up a quasi-abstracted anatomy, its head and musculature resembling hydrofoil design, not organic tissue—uncannily suggest simultaneously flow and resistance. Another of the Futurists, Mario Sironi, paints a Cubist-like, mechanistic looking female dancer, *Ballerina*, in 1919. To view it a century later, it's impossible not to be reminded of Duchamp's 1912 *Nude.*

Did Duchamp wish his supposedly human figure, shown walking down stairs, to be conveyed through an anatomy resembling, let's say, an erector-set construction? Metal pieces of a child's erector-set, units for assembly, looked like steel girders used in constructing tall buildings. The Home Insurance Building in Chicago, considered the first skyscraper although only ten stories high, had been built by 1885, followed by the Metropolitan Life Insurance tower in New York City in 1909 and then, in 1913 (the year of the Armory show), the Woolworth Building. Wildly popular throughout most of the twentieth century, the Erector Set was first manufactured that same year, 1913.

In 1913, Duchamp creates his *Bicycle Wheel*. Four years later, he exhibits *Fountain*, a mass-produced ceramic urinal he turned upside down and signed "R Mutt" (scandalous, it's now the best known of his readymades). *In Advance of the Broken Arm* (*En prévision du bras cases*), the snow shovel, was created in 1915. A decade later, Fritz Lang and his wife Thea von Harbou, visit New York for the first time; she then writes a screenplay and novel, giving rise to the futuristic *Metropolis*, whose filming was begun that year, the film released in 1927. Lang later said: "I looked into the streets—the glaring lights and the tall buildings—and there I conceived *Metropolis*" (Minden and Bachmann, 4). The film's aesthetics, despite its storyline, reveal an enchantment with the technology of the period (nonetheless, the plot is markedly anti-technological and anti-capitalist).

It's possible to see this same tension in Duchamp's *Fountain* and his earlier *Nude*. The visual power of *Metropolis* betrays any anti technological pose. The *readymades* perhaps came out of some unanticipated break-through insight, one coalescing in *Nude*. These were also anticipated in Fernand Léger's narratives (paintings of his were included at the Armory show). Leger's machine aesthetic recovers something of the world preceding the Industrial Revolution. In their lathed forms, the limbs of his people are at once inorganic and organic.

Part 6

Conceptualism and Flarf are the more recent versions in poetry of the Modernist explosion. I'll include digital writing with them, although it's impossible to account for an identifying aesthetics or artistic practice that can be claimed within the Modernist lineage, when considering digital artistry, simply because its medium is instrumentally determinative in and of itself, and it is so to a degree unimagined by earlier poets or artists (the closest predecessor might be the neon glow of a Holzer or Flavin, and yet the neon is a function of analogue technology). Yet if the question of *medium* is common throughout the avant gardes of modernism, postmodernism and whatever label we might choose for our present time, then digital writing can in fact be grouped with conceptual poetry and Flarf. Looking back from the present does show us how we were shaping our arts and ourselves leading up to this moment, as has been true in earlier moments along our timeline. There is also, in fact, a greater progression no one in its midst can either see objectively or on which a reliable prediction can be made.

Intellectual paradigm shifts are the predicates for what, among most readers of poetry at least, may seem disconcerting innovations in the now. I choose to call conceptual poetry, Flarf and digital writing *imaginative* practices, yet I'm mindful of how they're respectively theorized—such as in Marjorie Perloff's study *Unoriginal Genius: Poetry by Other Means in the New Century* (2010) or Dworkin's and Kenneth Goldsmith's *Against Expression* (2011). More recent work is typified by, as its title suggests, the rather droll *Riddled with Imagination: A Conceptual Poem* by Kelsie Anne Sandage (2015).

As a consequence of digital technologies in particular, all these practices, which now can be seen as akin to early developments in cybernetics and, more recently, artificial intelligence and robotics, have brought forward questions surrounding embodiment and prosthetics. They're compelling issues within the digital writing/digital art community. Preceded by criticism in a variety of intellectual communities, most vividly in the related fields of robotics and artificial intelligence, the questions being asked are as significant as the conceptual, Flarf poetry, and digital writing movements, which ineluctably raise them.

The issues migrate into the realm of art as concerns the question of sheer materiality, especially pressing when it comes to poets whose poems are driven by creative choices grounded in an awareness of language as material, or to a painter like Little who pursues the abstract flat, two-dimensional color and surface. Inevitably these issues will be recontextualized.

What awaits is the paradox of disembodied, or dematerialized, art as typified in the exploitation of the neon light's glow. The glow is being reimagined within a physics that comprehends our biology. In the field of digital expressivity people think about a poetics of computation. In the biological sciences, quantification plays an increasing role. The end result of these newer intellectual developments will not be the body's abjection, however; quite to the contrary, already there's a deeper realization of its beauty. I think of Stephanie

Strickland's work, its indebtedness to scientific disciplines it mines for images and themes, demonstrating with them the splendor of the manifest natural landscape. Her poetry has always been on the page, for several decades on the screen as well. She writes from within her awareness of the present, as we all now live in more complex ways with robots that become our rivals.

The solidity, and tactile nature of one of Little's paintings is material art; so are Holzer's or Flavin's neon installations. And so is Strickland's digital "poems"—such as *True North* (1997), *Vniverse* (2002), *slippingglimpse* (2007) and *Hours of the Night* (2016), a number of them outgrowths from a print-only version—whose transmogrifying visual effects are both mesmerizing and embracing. "Reading" a digital poem is to be incorporated within it. *Embodiment* represents a key to deeper understanding of ourselves and our artistic productions. And *embodiment* as metaphor is an aid in trying to comprehend digital poetry and art.

High Modernism—including the experimental typography Drucker has examined, which got underway in 1909—indirectly pushed forward the materialist impulse; avant-garde poetry is rooted in Williams and Stein, also the Objectivists, who revered Pound and the other Imagists and yet possessed their own intuitions about language and writing, which the Imagist and Vorticist aesthetic programs failed to realize; a focus on the material is not necessarily a focus on *image* or in some way even on *object*.

218

If we leap forward to post-World War Two North America, what becomes clear, finally, is that High Modernism distantly anticipated the work of an artist like Holzer who stands, chronologically, at a key point along the trajectory of North American avant-garde poetry. These are the forbears of later American avant-garde poetry and poetics. The three formations of present experimental work I've cited can, after all, be traced directly back to them.

A Possible Conclusion

The monumentality of the Modernist avant-garde poem, whose source is the poem's material language, is today facing its greatest challenge by the very presence of digital technology. Thus Hayles analytically describes "[t]he materiality of an embodied text" as "the interaction of its physical characteristics with its signifying strategies" (in Cayley 307). It's not that the text on the page, composed before digital text could have been imagined, did not possess "its signifying strategies," but rather that the digital work dramatizes them by virtue of how its coding manifests on the screen. The difference here may be how the idea of *embodiment* is approached.

Part of the test is to comprehend what *prosthesis* might mean in a highly technologized, digitized environment. Digital technology might suggest the conceptual dissolution of the body proper, insofar as we can understand how the organic and technological can merge (this starts at least as early as Donna Haraway's *Cyborg Manifesto* in 1985). When physicality and mechanics become increasingly vitiated as concepts, a process made vivid in digital coding, prosthesis as an element in artistic production comes to the fore. Even the notion of *hybridity* fails to comprehend the paradigmatic shift in art and intellectual discourse in our time. Hybridity is a basic tease in Flarf in its search for internet language. The very act of Flarf creation is informed by a general sense of mutation or transformation, which are a consequence of our daily involvement with digital technologies.

In Samantha Gorman's digital work *Pry*, the *prying* apart of lines of words on a touch-screen, with one's fingers, allows for new text to appear between them. We're drawn to (re)read the poem/ artwork there on the screen, with its new information, within a new context and flow. In using *Pry* the natural body has become a part of the 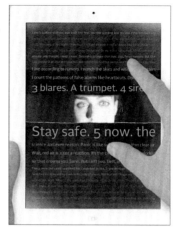 artwork as it unfolds through time—to be sure, as the user/reader becomes integrally involved in *Pry*, the human actions an integral element of the work of art/poetry. *Pry*'s text, a dynamic text, a prosthetized text and prosthetic extension of the human user of that text, is some of what another digital writer, Ian Hatcher, intends in his hard copy book of poems titled *Prostheses*, a work purporting to be poetic and yet it's critically theoretical in purposively, albeit understated, ways.

In discussing what he means by "codework," Cayley takes us closer to the heart of our present circumstance, by explaining that codework "brings inner workings [of digital text] to an exterior, especially when such work is manifested as a generative cross-infection of text and code-as-text, of language and code-as-language" (308). When might the reader/user of the digital text become a part of that text? The digital poet is working from *within* writing. Would it be better to say *prior* to writing *as writing* (as in Gorman's title *Pry*)?

Cayley is making a case for the aesthetics of code, and yet code is that which resides "behind" the poem on the screen. He's suggesting that the reader needs to include, in the appreciation of the digital poem, what's happening artistically at the level of code. (Has the the Heideggerian distinction between "equipment" and "the work of art" dissolved?) Does the reader, at least psychologically, become part of that code?

Considering how Dworkin reimagines Baudrillard's theorizing of the equivocal nature of text, we should include Cayley's key observation that the digital poem is made up of *codework*. Cayley argues that experiencing a digital poem is engaging its "complex surface." The digital poem "bring[s] the traces of an interior archive of code into the open." Cayley might want to say the code of the digital poem "reconceals itself by generating a complex surface 'over' itself" (308). It's fair to claim that the aesthetics of the digital poem resides in, or at least includes, what I'm forced to describe as its underlying coding.

"Computation invites us to consider nothing less than a new material existence—a new *digital* reality," Andrew Klobucar argues (in "Programming's Turn: Computation and Poetics" 3). Hayles has pointed out that, in this reality, "the object itself is not a pre-given entity but rather a dynamic process that changes as the focus of attention shifts" (Hayles, *How We Think* 14). Klobucar finds himself aligned with Dworkin, which is to say that materiality is being put into question by him. He observes that the ones and zeros of digital computation work fundamentally differently than what we typically understand as modes of symbolic representation in that the patterns they produce via alternating signals of "off" and "on," something or nothing, cannot be considered to signify or somehow render prior entities. (4)

Nevertheless, the coding is linguistic, insofar as it's inscription—although it's more in keeping with a quantum *real* than an Enlightenment *real*. And yet the below-the-surface aspect of the digital poem is also a part of what makes conceptual and Flarf poems.

Conceptual poetry and Flarf each differ from digital writing insofar as what lies "below" their conceptualizations, such as is made manifest to their readers, does not directly drive their respective linguistic surfaces; their "below" serves as a deeply *contextual* immanence. The reader of the digital poem may elect to make specific forays of a textually-analytical nature, which would lead to speculations about the underlying digital programming giving rise to a "surface" text. Even so, implicit in both conceptual and Flarf poetry is an intuition about this textual dynamism. This intuition most often takes the form of an unconscious assumption, which makes Flarf and conceptual poetry operate. It has been said that there's no such thing as *conceptual poetry*, that there's only conceptual art.[14]

That assertion is incorrect—once we comprehend conceptual poetry within the greater context that includes digital writing. Of course, the material practices of the avant garde rest upon literacy. Better to say they rest upon

Derridean *écriture* (a term or concept, as Eric Gans puts it, which "[retrieves the] literal meaning of *writing* as opposed to speech"). Yet what digital technology fully exposes is the non-solidity of the Enlightenment *material.* What must we think of *mechanics* now, not only after Heisenbergian *Quantum Mechanics* but also after the elimination of the physically stable *text* with which Klobucar, Cayley and Hayles concern themselves? Their somewhat shared approach informs the contemporary practices of Flarf and conceptual poetry, as well digital writing. The kind of thinking being engaged in, its nascent form, has engendered these contemporary practices. The latest manifestations of the avant-garde reflect our societal shift to *code* as the reigning intellectual, scientific paradigm—surely in the sciences, also in the arts.

Notes

1. It's hard to know to which section(s) of Kant's *Critique of Judgement*, discussing aesthetics and/or art, Watson refers, but given that he is objecting to large amounts of money put in play with an art installation, like the one in Sulzano, he is perhaps thinking of Section 2.8 (Kant 1892), the section on aesthetics and morality

2. Cf. the second part of *Critique of Judgement* (1892).

3. See, for example, Section 2.5 of *Critique of Judgement* (1892).

4. Here is where, arguably, Heidegger is going beyond Kant; and in my argument the crucial point would have to do with Heidegger's elaboration of the quality of technology and as can be related to materiality.

5. Heidegger does not discuss Duchamp's works.

6. Zalta, *Stanford Encyclopedia of Philosophy*. Consider in this context Heidegger's grouping of *equipment* and the *work of art* as having "an affinity [...] insofar as it [i.e., the artwork] is something produced by the human hand"; all the same, the artwork possesses a "self-sufficient presence" ("The Origin of the Work of Art" 29).

7. Sandy Baldwin's recent book, *The Internet Unconscious: On the Subject of Electronic Literature*, might, from a certain perspective, be seen as superseding Hayles's work, yet as I am construing *inscription* it does not. Nevertheless, Baldwin's opus is invaluable and pertinent to my discussion, precisely so because it argues, contrary to what I propose, a distinction between the *literary* and *code*—whereas I, for my purposes, need to see both as one semiotic system ultimately, as will be made clear below. Also, Baldwin wishes to view *embodiment* and *text* as, in the final analysis, one experience on the part of the singular user, so that text is obviated. My contention would be, however, that in the digital poem the text holds its own—indeed, if it did not then how could we really any longer consider the digital poem to be a poem? Even concrete poems by their nature preserve the textual, inscripted, dimension.

    The differential force, Baldwin might be saying, would be *performativity*. Baldwin writes that "the most complex multimedia, mixed reality, what have you, [may be] the edge of plaintext in performance. Performance means this separation, the synechdoche of plaintext and performance" (144). In his concluding chapter, while discussing the program *Second Life* as a kind of "mapping," he quotes René Thom to assert that "all semantics necessarily depends on a study of space—geometric or topological" Thom 275; Baldwin 71, 163). Finally Baldwin dwells on the issue of intimacy, and I point this out here to observe that the literary-artistic history of the North American avant garde (with which I am principally concerning myself) might usefully be characterized according to the sense of distance, a dynamic of text and writer/reader that arises due to an alienation from the text as material on the page. For Baldwin, finally, that "dance is lost, the dancer elsewhere," and for him "[t]he point is about intimacy" (164).

To be sure, digital poetry and art are a threshold onto the realm of robotics, artificial intelligence. While I find it necessary to include Baldwin's farsighted analysis in my own examination—helping me to bracket it—I need also to observe that Baldwin is presenting us with a human lifeworld now grounded in digital technology.

8. Dworkin says that Rauschenberg's erasure inaugurates the "dematerialization" of visual art. I take his point within a timeline of events in the art world I can't discuss in this essay due to space issues. What I will say here is that the idea of dematerialization becomes possible because of the growing attention and focus upon materiality; and Duchamp's readymades—while I'll argue in this essay that their material state is pivotal—have mostly drawn commentary, not that it's wrong, on the quite immaterial ideations these readymades portray.

9. Cf. Roman Jacobson's essay "What Is Poetry": "Poetry is present when a word is felt as a word and not a mere representation of the object being named..." (in Drucker *The Visible Word* 29).

10. Oppen, *New Collected Poems*, 116; cf. Cope, *George Oppen: Selected Prose, Daybooks and Papers*, n. 2, p. 250. Oppen, *Selected Prose, Daybooks and Papers*, 53). For a particularly informed and perceptive discussion of Oppen's, let's call it, linguistic skepticism, see: *Oppen: A Narrative* by Eric Hoffman (148-50).

11. The best scholarship on this I know of is Paul Oppenheimer's *The Birth of the Modern Mind: Self, Consciousness, and the Invention of the Sonnet.*

12. Conversation with author in 2004.

13. I am grateful to the poet, critic and painter Thomas Fink for my borrowing of this term here, from a conversation we had about this matter in 2016.

14. I myself have said this in *The Argotist Online* (2006).

Works Cited

Avnisan, Abraham. "Electronic Literature Presentation at the Kitchen." New York: The Kitchen, 2016.]

Baldwin, Sandy. *The Internet Unconscious: On the Subject of Electronic Literature*. New York: Bloomsbury, 2015.

Baudrillard, Jean. *L'Autre par lui même: Habilitation*. Paris: Editions Galilée, 1987.

Berry, David M., and Michael Dieter, eds. *Postdigital Aesthetics: Art, Computation and Design*. New York: Springer, 2015.

Bolter, Jay David, and Richard Grusin. *Remediation: Understanding New Media*, rev. ed. Cambridge: MIT Press, 2000.

Bronk, William. "The Increasing Abstraction of Language." *Life Supports: New and Collected Poems*, rev. ed. Jersey City: Talisman House, 1997.

Bullock, Allan. *The Double Image Modernism*. Edited by Malcolm Bradbury and James McFarlane. Harmondsworth: Penguin, 1991.

Cayley, John. "Time Code Language: New Media Poetic and Programmed Signification." *New Media Poetics: Contexts, Technotexts, and Theories*. Edited by Adelaide Morris and Thomas Swiss. Cambridge: MIT Press, 2009.Pp. 307–34.

Cope, Stephen. *George Oppen: Selected Prose, Daybooks and Papers.* Edited by George Oppen. Introduction by Stephen Cope. Berkeley: University of California Press, 2007.

Derrida, Jacques. *Of Grammatology.* Translated by G. C. Spivak. Preface by G. C. Spivak. Baltimore: Johns Hopkins University Press, 1976.

Drucker, Johanna. *The Visible Word: Experimental Typography and Modern Art, 1909–1923.* Chicago: University of Chicago Press, 1994.

Dworkin, Craig. *Reading the Illegible.* Evanston: Northwestern University Press, 2003.

Dworkin, Craig, and Kenneth Goldsmith, eds. *Against Expression: An Anthology of Conceptual Writing.* Evanston: Northwestern, 2011.

Dworkin, Craig. *No Medium.* Cambridge: MIT Press, 2015.

Emerson, Lori. *Reading Writing Interfaces: From the Digital to the Bookbound.* Minneapolis: University of Minnesota Press, 2014.

Fleck, Ludwik. *Genesis and Development of a Scientific Fact.* Chicago: University of Chicago Press, 1979.

Gans, Eric. "Chronicles of Love and Resentment." *Ecriture* from Barthes to GA. No. 388 (January 30, 2010). Available online.

Gorman, Samantha. *Apple App Pry.* Los Angeles: Tender Claws, 2015. Available online.

Hatcher, Ian. *Prosthesis.* Seattle: Poor Claudia, 2016.

Hatlen, Burton. Conversation with Burt Kimmelman, 2004.

Hayles, N. Katherine. *How We Think: Digital Media and Contemporary Technogenesis*. Chicago: University of Chicago Press, 2012.

_____. *Writing Machines*. Cambridge: MIT Press, 2002.

Heidegger, Martin. *Being and Time*. Translated by John Macquarrie, and Edward Robinson. Oxford: Blackwell, Tübingen: M. Niemeyer, 1993.

_____. "The Origin of the Work of Art." *Off the Beaten Track* by Martin Heidegger. Translated and Edited by Julian Young, and Kenneth Hayes. Cambridge: Cambridge University Press, 2002. Pp. 1–56.

Hoffman, Eric. *Oppen: A Narrative*. New York: Bristol, UK: Shearsman 2013; New York: Spuyten Duvil, 2018.

Kant, Immanuel. *The Critique of Judgement*, 1892. Available online.

Kennedy, Stephen. *Chaos Media: A Sonic Economy of Digital Space*. New York: Bloomsbury, 2015.

Kimmelman, Burt. "A Critique of Conceptual Poetry (Interview on Conceptual Poetry, an Interview with Burt Kimmelman, Part of a Forum on Conceptual Poetry Arranged by Jeffrey Side)." *The Argotist Online* (March 2016) Available online:

Klobucar, Andrew. Programming's Turn: Computation and Poetics. *Humanities* 6:27 (2017). Available online.

Little, James, and Benjamin LaRocco. In Conversation. *Brooklyn Rail* (May 2009). Available online.

McGee, Celia, and James Little. "Driven to Abstraction [Interview with James Little]." *Art News*. January 1, 2011. Available online:

Malamud, Randy. *An Introduction to Animals and Visual Culture*. Hampshire: Palgrave Macmillan, 2012.

McDonald, Travis. *Sight and Sigh*. Chicago: Beard of Bees Press, 2011. Available online:

Minden, Michael, and Holger Bachmann. *Fritz Lang's Metropolis: Cinematic Visions of Technology and Fear*. Lake Placid: Camden House, 2002.

Ong, Walter J. *Orality and Literacy: The Technologizing of the Word*. London and New York: Routledge, 1982.

Oppen, George. *New Collected Poems*. Edited by Michael Davidson. Preface by Eliot Weinberger. New York: New Directions, 2002.

_____. *Selected Prose, Daybooks and Papers*. Edited and introduction by Stephen Cope. Berkeley: University of California Press, 2007.

Oppenheimer, Paul. *The Birth of the Modern Mind: Self, Consciousness, and the Invention of the Sonnet*. Oxford: Oxford University Press, 1989.

Perloff, Marjorie. *Unoriginal Genius: Poetry by Other Means in the New Century*. Chicago: University of Chicago Press, 2010.

Quartermain, Peter. *Stubborn Poetries: Poetic Facticity and the Avant-Garde*. Tuscaloosa: University of Alabama Press, 2013.

Robins, Corinne. 2009. (Talk on Ekphrastic Poetry), Roundtable on The Art of Poetry and the Poetry of Art: Ekphrasis in the Contemporary Poem. *Paper presented at the New Century Poetics: A Poetry Colloquium, Centenary College,* Hackettstown, NJ, USA, Fall.

Sandage, Kelsie Anne. *Riddled with Imagination: A Conceptual Poem.* San Francisco: Stevens Books, 2015.

Strickland, Stephanie, with M. D. Coverly. *Hours of the Night* First exhibited at the meeting of the Electronic Literature Organization, 2016.

____, with Cynthia Lawson Jaramillo and Paul Ryan. *slippingglimpse.* 2007. Available online.

____. *True North.* Eastgate Systems. 1997.

____, with Cynthia Lawson Jaramillo. *Vniverse.* The Iowa Review Online. 2002.

Thom, René. *Mathematical Models of Morphogenesis.* Translated by W. M. Brookes. Hemstead: Ellis Horwood, Ltd., 1983.

Timmons, Matthew. *Credit.* Los Angeles: Blanc Press 2009.

Watson, Mike. 2016. Shooting down the Purely Aesthetic Aspirations of Christo and Jeanne-Claude's Piers. *Hyperallergic: Art and Its Discontents.* Available online.

Wittgenstein, Ludwig. *Philosophical Investigations.* Oxford: Blackwell, 2009.

Zalta, Edward N., ed. 2016. Martin Heidegger. In *Stanford Encyclopedia of Philosophy.* Stanford: Stanford University Center for the Study of Language and Information, Available online.

OPPEN→SCHWERNER→HELLER→ FINKELSTEIN (TRACKING THE WORD)

"To practice the skill
while sojourning among strangers

Dreaming inscriptions
inscribing dreams

Waiting
for the next word."

- from *Powers (Track Volume III)* by Norman Finkelstein

Toward the end of his three-volume serial poem, *Track*, Norman Finkelstein reflects on his act of making poems— on what may be his duty as a poet, a Jewish poet who "[dreams] inscriptions"—presumably to be written down. The story of writing and the story of the Jew course together, sometimes merging. Finkelstein—a secular Jew, intellectual and poet, whose interest in the ideas of Judaism begins in his youth—explores what it means, in essence, to be a Jew. He does so in a peculiarly writerly way, seeing in Judaism his personal concerns about writing and thought, writing and knowledge, writing and spiritual grounding.

To get a secure grasp on Finkelstein's poetic project, especially *Track*, requires some acquaintance with the poems of George Oppen, Armand Schwerner, and Michael Heller—all Jews by birth and of successive generations leading to Finkelstein. The four poets form a lineage that's both personal and aesthetic, each elder mentoring the younger. (Heller, the immediate elder, who has written extensively about Jewish theology, ideas, literature and culture in his poems, analytical essays and prose memoir, has been in conversation with Finkelstein about them for years.) This consecutive enlarging coheres in *Track*, taking the form of love for the written *text*, this love transmuted into a writerliness in their poems; each poet attends to the act and effect of inscription.

The lineage "tracks" the development of postmodern poetics in which writerliness is a hallmark. In my taking Oppen as a starting point—he was one of the original Objectivist poets (as defined by Heller in his critical book *Conviction's Net of Branches*, and by others)—my following-through of the four poets becomes a narrative of postmodernism's development. I come forward in time by way of influence/mentorship/friendship, like Matryoshka dolls, one doll enclosed inside the other. Each of the poets has read deeply in the work of the others. Oppen (1908-1984), Schwerner (1927-1999), Heller (b. 1937) and Finkelstein (b. 1954) represent four successive generations of American poetry.

Finkelstein's Jewish identity is crucial element in all this. Starting with his early poetry (and critical prose), he's been wrapped up in his acts of reading and writing as a way of thinking about the world and himself. This is especially so in *Track*, and in this work it's been especially the writing. *Track* expresses this complex of activity, intent on acknowledging religious, cultural and poetic lineage. *Track* sets out not only to position Finkelstein's life and

233

work within a continuum of Jewish writing and thought; it also does so within a broader continuum of poets, many of them Jewish. The three-volume sequence is a work of monumental self-exploration, but especially as a poet and Jew. And as a meditation on the civilized act of inscription, it establishes an identity for Finkelstein. This, for him, is a way of understanding Judaism in secular yet spiritual terms.

The tension between thought and writing in these generational poets is integral within the Judaic tradition—yet the four, as adults, have lived secular Jewish lives, the secularism throwing into relief, paradoxically, their Jewish orientation. Another, related tension in their work has to do, largely, with the Jewish Diaspora—which involves the poets' sense of displacement and decenteredness. The sense of exile, in their respective understanding of the written word, comes through image and theme. Indeed, the written word not only estranges the poet—most of all the postmodern poet—who is the language user; as well it establishes, and intensifies, the Judaic sense of exile (an exile, ultimately, from the word, even from the Word, of God). Jewish estrangement has been epitomized in the historical fact of the Diaspora. And it's not farfetched to claim that the Jewish sense of exile results from acts of reading and writing, these acts the very heart of Judaism even in its early stages of development. Finkelstein, and his poetic forbears, exhibit a tension between orality and literacy; they're profoundly aware of the simultaneous alienation from the word, and the magisterial construction of an identity as a literate person, indeed as a writer, and as a Jew, which that writing manifests—all of these only possible through writing.

The alienation that writing has produced in the world, as Walter Ong and others have shown (cf. especially his landmark book, *Orality and Literacy: The Technologizing of the Word*), allows for a level of abstract thinking that's given rise to modern science and to *literature* in the modern sense of this term. This is a literature in which the *self*, the inner world of the human being, can be both plumbed and displayed; in short, it's a literature of the self. Oppen, Schwerner, Heller and Finkelstein, in this order, have provided a poetry that's written down, that's aware of its writtenness, and that concerns itself with its own manifestation *as* material language—with all the implications of it, such as fixedness of discourse, which it invokes. The fixedness, that resultant monumentality, has shaped Judaism, starting with the inscription of the Ten Commandments.

Arguably the Jewish Holocaust—its definition lying outside of history whose continuum might be marked with the Ten Commandments on one end, or perhaps the destruction of the Second Temple, and on the other end the present (a present, however, conditioned by the recent Holocaust past)—destroys the Jewish lineage. Edmond Jabès, for whom the Holocaust image of the "burnt book" looms large, questions how anyone might recover from such a calamity. An impossible event, the Holocaust is the quintessential consequence of physical exile. There can be a progress, nevertheless, Stéphane Mosès insists, a moving forward: "lines drawn in the ash already organize themselves in the more complex forms of traced letters." He points out that "they signify nothing" in and of themselves; and yet, when they're "placed end to end," they form a text. In this way, beyond the impossibility of speech, words would reappear, first as forms, as graphic configurations, as hieroglyphs that would designate only themselves, then once again as words, forever stripped of all claim to embodying a meaning given in advance. These are words that no longer re-present. They are "words of exile," haunted by an absence more original than any origin, by the loss of that which we perhaps never possessed but which, irreparably, we mourn. (82)

While none of the four American Jewish poets has considered himself to be, in any doctrinaire way, observant, each absorbed the fundamentals of a Jewish outlook on life, and specifically the central position that *text* occupies in a Jew's life—even Oppen, who had little or no formal Jewish training or influence in his early life, and who thought of his Jewishness mostly as an otherness (whereas Schwerner, Heller and Finkelstein were more steeped in Jewish texts, through family and upbringing). This absorption helps to explain the fundamental writerly motivations and effects in their poems, which is to say the poetry's awareness of itself as written text and as poem. In all four of them, the poetry responds to the condition of "an absence more original than any origin" (above). Their work, attuned to the Jewish condition that is, at some basic level, constituted by the two poles of the oral and the written, and the celebration of the self that emerges out of that co-equal contestation, figures a self decidedly literate in temperament.

Ancient Judaic, orally-instigated Mishnah is to be contrasted to literary Midrash. But even the Mishnah is mediated by its recording, and thereby its inevitable altering of its sayings, which may in fact have been instigated to a degree through writing.[1] Inevitably, as Beth Sharon Ash remarks, "the destruction of the second temple, the severe oppression of the Jews by the Romans, and the rise of Christianity," are followed by "the compilation of oral law"; in other words there was a "[yielding] to the imperatives of canonization." As a consequence the Jews, "as a people," in surviving this devastation, would forever depend on the cohesiveness of [their] texts" (66; cf. Jaffee "Spoken" 84 ff., Schiffman 154, and Neusner 184). That Oppen, the most secular of the four American poets, least explicitly addresses the issues of exile and writing, as they intertwine, as well as the epistemology and ontology of the written word, is not surprising. His poems do, though, disclose a sensitivity to these issues, and this sensibility, as evinced in the poems, has had a profound effect on his successors.

In "Party on Shipboard," for instance, from Oppen's 1934 collection *Discrete Series*, we find the observation that "One moves between reading and re-reading, / The shape is a moment" (NCP 25). Reading and noticing the manifest world that lies beyond the text constitute moments whose shapes can be realized in poetic statements. Writing, too, is a focus of attention. From the start Oppen "addresses the act of poetry," Gavin V. Dowd argues (125). The poet "write[s] *of* writing." He speaks of a piece of "Paper" presumably he is writing upon, which, when "turned, contains / [his] entire volume" (Dowd 124; NCP 33).[2] Oppen can be skeptical about the possibility of knowing and conveying anything other than a partial intention or meaning; writing, in its finitude of signification, exemplifies this. The skepticism is typically Jewish. His understanding of inscription, as well as its effects in the formation of the self, are evident in many of his poems. Oppen may be contemplating the sense of simultaneous union and estrangement—which a writer, particularly a Jewish writer, experiences—in creating her or his text, for example in an alternate version of his late poem "*If It All Went Up in Smoke*." In his autobiographical reminiscence of Oppen, John Taggart describes him as caught up in the "difficulty / of writing the poem," which is driven by "the fact" that "confronts the Jew again and / again" ("[Notes]" 309; Taggart "Walk Out" 79). Oppen's poetry—a key to poetic Objectivism, which is arguably the first stirrings of American postmodern poetics, insofar as it attaches an importance to the *facticity* of the made poem, in other words its *material* nature—strives to enact that simultaneity. The poem doesn't so much describe the world as bring it into being. Reality exists through writing. Oppen's notion of a *discrete* series, which partakes of this term's mathematical meaning, involves an accretion of percepts, and this, observed in toto, forms a larger significance. Oppen's last published poem ("Till Other Voices Wake Us") describes his arriving at the title of the collection:

[…] writing

thru the night (a young man,
Brooklyn, 1929) I named the book

series empirical
series all force
in events the myriad

238

lights have entered
us it is a music more powerful

than music [...].
(NCP 286; cf. NCP 357-58)

Oppen's poetry is instrumental. Another way to say this, perhaps, is that for Oppen the task of "Objectivist poetics," to borrow from G. Matthew Jenkins, "was no longer to shape the world but rather to encounter the world" (410). As Charles Bernstein quips, "Oppen's is an engendering witness" (240).

The name *Discrete Series* serendipitously describes the textual status of the Torah, its gaps of signification, its interstices, which constitute an outlook on the possibility of knowledge, one that could have come down to Oppen within the milieu of secular Jewish intellectual life in which he was raised; even secular Jews have had instilled in them, arguably enough, certain attitudes about the world, knowledge, writing, and self—these a composite Oppen takes up throughout his career, all embodied most fully in his favored term *clarity*:

> Clarity, clarity, surely clarity is the most beautiful
>   thing in the world,
> A limited, limiting clarity
>
> I have not and never did have any motive of
> poetry But to achieve clarity
> ("Route" NCP 193)

The language resists a full knowing or telling, and this partial silence—a core element of Oppen's poetics ("Clarity // In the sense of *transparence*, / I don't mean that much can be explained. // Clarity in the sense of silence" [NCP 175])—is epitomized in the written word that must be read either silently in one's mind, or aloud with an echo of the oral, but which cannot be challenged, as Ong points out, in order to gain an explanation of its ambiguities. Oppen's struggle is with the substantiality of the written. Yet, oddly, the written word stands mute, inert.

In earlier periods, when literacy was competing with orality, Ong observes, "[w]itnesses were *prima facie* more credible than texts because they could be challenged and made to defend their statements, whereas texts could not (this, it will be recalled, was exactly one of Plato's objections to writing [in the *Cratylus*])" (96). Oppen's poetry contains gaps, fissures; there's always a tendency toward creating white space and silence, evident even in his 1934 collection, *Discrete Series*. The tendency becomes less pronounced in his middle collections but returns in full force in 1972's *Seascape: Needle's Eye* and *Myth of the Blaze* 1972-1975 (NCP 211 ff.). And these interstices should be bracketed by acknowledging Jewish commentary over thousands of years.[3] Daniel Boyarin observes that "the narrative of the Torah is characterized by an extraordinarily high degree of gapping, indeterminacy, repetition, and self-contradiction" (39)—all of which are the result of the Torah's "own intertextuality"; for it's "a severely gapped text, and the gaps are there to be filled by strong readers, which in this case does not mean readers fighting for originality, but readers fighting to find what they must in the holy text" (16).

The word, that is, only comes into its own with acknowledgement of silence or blank space from which it emerges and is held in place, much like death "holds" life. The presence of Yahweh, a faceless god, is the most fundamental absence. However, it's a verbal, written sign. Erich Auerbach famously noticed, when comparing the literature of the ancient Jews with that of the ancient Greeks, that action and meaning of the Greek literature were "foregrounded," while the essential mystery of the Hebrew deity remained within the realm of the unmanifest, as background. Hence the Jew, in acts of reading, and of writing too, ushers God, ushers presence itself, into the light of day. Likewise, Oppen's poetry invokes the world rather than describing it. The word is worshipped by Oppen, the Jewish poet, through his fetishization of it. It's the scene into which the god finally appears. This engrossment in language, especially in writing, involves presenting language within the context of death, silence, the blank visual field on the page of a book. As early as 1934, Oppen has set out the agenda that Schwerner, Heller and Finkelstein will adhere to, while they exfoliate his ideas and methods.

The ellipsis in an Oppen poem, Taggart has explained, "connects the moves of" the thought process, "and reminds us that something has been left out" (Taggart "Deep Jewels" 164-65).[4] Yet something has also been put in—"a keeping still" ("Walk-Out" 42)—indeed, a "more silent silence" ("To Go Down" 277). His gaps "remind us of the silent ground out of and within which words exist [...]" (281, 282). This "silent ground" resides within Oppen's work and in the world at large that Oppen encounters daily. His peculiar "gap" is, Taggart adds (quoting from Oppen's Daybook), "'a flaw', [...] 'the space of the mind', [...] somehow the essential thing about man, the essential human thing. It is 'a besieged and doomed sanctuary' 'on which being presses', and it is our 'home'." This flaw, which exists within us, is likewise the flaw within "the larger poem as perhaps we ourselves are in the larger scheme of things" ("To Go Down" 278).

"Myth of the Blaze" (1975) dramatically demonstrates the importance of ellipsis and silence for Oppen, a late and poignant poem concluding his work and life, in which he enacts epistemological and ontological meditation through a most distilled and graphic language, a final engagement with something that's occupied him throughout a long career:

> night—sky bird's world
> to know to know in my life to know
>
>
> what I have said to myself
> (NCP 247)

In this stylistic return, late in life, to brief and discrete utterance, which was typical of his first book, Oppen's exhibiting a comprehension of the limits of textuality, replicating the circumstances of scripture. It's only possible, finally, to have knowledge through the written word, yet the promise of that word—in its residual nature, which is that knowledge will be complete—is not kept. Thus exile, and the written word, together pose a separation from the world,

from God, even from the self. Oppen comments, "I believe //
in the world // because it is / impossible [...]" ("Myth of
the Blaze" NCP 247-48). What has he said, what will last,
what will be clear, as clear as the silence against which
utterance makes itself felt? "Words, cannot be wholly
transparent," he points out (in 1968, in his long poem
"Route" [NCP 194]), "And that is the 'heartlessness'
of words" (194). Given the limitations of language, as
represented in written language, Oppen realizes that his
poetry has to be singular, has to use language to gesture
toward some truth beyond it, and so his poem
"Historic Pun" (also in 1968) ends with the declaration,
"Semite: to find a way for myself" (NCP 189).

His thematizing and stylizing of writing's disjunctive nature
sets the stage for Schwerner's tour de force epic poem *The
Tablets*, which is supposed to be a translation of the
world's earliest Sumerian inscriptions, and which imagines
the world view and psychology of orally-based human
beings as they're being first transported into the world of
literacy. Within apparently primitive enunciations, now
being written down, Schwerner discloses the cognitive and
spiritual crises writing engenders, both on the part of the
ancient "speaker" whose words are being translated, and
that of a character Schwerner creates, who is referred to as
the Scholar/Translator, and who will be described by
Finkelstein as "an erudite schlemiehl" ("Wallace Stevens"
151). Both people—the primitive turned semi-literate and
the Scholar/Translator—must come to terms with the
imitations of signification as well as the alienation occuring
when the written word stands between world and reader,
calling attention to itself. In the case of the ancient proto-
Sumerian speaker (or speakers), there's a marked naiveté,
what the Scholar/ Translator refers to as "the unsullied

literary imagination evident in the texts which are the object of my studies, a power generously evident in the work of the so-called scribes, who were of course redactors, a vector we usually ignore" (Tablet XXVI, p. 71). Schwerner's distinction between redactor and scribe is a useful one. For the devout Jew is surely the latter, someone who contests and enlarges the Hebrew scripture penned by human beings—but of course the heritage of inscription, in Judaism, reaches as far back as the covenant with Moses. Willard Gingerich said of Schwerner's work, especially its sensitivity to issues of translation:

> [it recalls] the paradox of our essential condition: that the inescapable and necessary ground of our being is the voice of the Divine; but the Divine steadfastly refuses to speak. Therefore, we find ourselves, age after age, forced to translate an immense silence, a translation whose purpose is to obscure the forgery of its source: the inarticulate Divine. (18)

Schwerner's poem opens with an appropriately enigmatic statement: "All that's left is pattern* (shoes?). / *doubtful reconstruction" (p. 13). The statement brings into being the question of coherence and simultaneous doubt, which are germane to the conditions of Judaism; the bimodality of the Torah, its perceived limitations and implicit invitation to exegesis, lies at the heart of religious devotion in a way that is unique to Judaism. Samuel Tobias Lachs observes that

> [s]tarting with the concept of Israel there is no *ab initio* commitment to supernatural authority that fosters theocentrism. Rather, it sets up a man-centered

and man-directed philosophy in which man, himself, creates his society, promulgates his laws, and ideates God on the basis of his needs and his conception of the world. He then sets up paradigms of an ideal society and creates the means whereby these ideals are concretized and effected. He projects these ideals and values from the societal level to the divine, which in turn serves as a model of perfection to be venerated and imitated for the perfection of self and society. For the Jew, this meant the creation of the instrumentality of the Torah, which to the revelationist, is the will of God; to the humanist, it is the expression of the creative genius of the Jewish people, itself a form of divinity. (31-32)

Schwerner's Sumerian speaker emerges in the text as a human being first standing apart from the divine. The Scholar/Translator finds himself, oddly enough, drawn to this figure. The key to Tablet I indicates the proposed translation, "shoes," as being supplied by a character called the Scholar/Translator, and the asterisked phrase is also indicated as a "doubtful reconstruction." The composite term, "Pattern (shoes)," comes up repeatedly, in various contexts, in a number of the Tablets; finally, late in the poem, in Tablet XXVI, the Scholar/Translator reflects upon this, remarking, "I often feel all that's left for us is pattern, the millennial juices having been subject to so much repetition" (p. 70), probably not realizing he's internalized the text he's been working on. Oral poetry thrives on repetition that's a mainstay of oral tellings, but what's interesting in the Scholar/Translator' comment is that, through continual encounters with a written text, repetitions have actually transformed thought. Indeed, the visuality of the tablets being translated and annotated is underscored by the next statement:

As I age and my eyes weaken I do not read fewer books, but I finish a smaller proportion of the ones I take on. [....] The history of my mind besieged by 5,000 years of written documents is the history by turns of a weary and oppressed animal and that of a repeated and sometimes galling insistence on confronting and mastering the unabsorbable. (70)

Schwerner's well aware of the power of inscription, its push on humanity toward civilization, as exemplified in the Scholar/Translator—a symbol of civilization—insofar as writing is, arguably, the single most significant technological change in the history of humanity. Commenting on the passage in Tablet I, the Scholar/Translator pronounces it "interesting," adding: "We find ourselves at or near the very point in time where the word, concrete in origin, shades off into abstraction" (15). At times quite humorously, he's being pulled in two directions at once, primitive and civilized. The divine does not appear in either realm. Yet the text marks its absence.

What's important to see in *The Tablets*, not only in its actual words but also in a coding the Scholar/Translator uses to indicate missing passages, confusing passages, and so on, is that writing itself is being celebrated, specifically its element of pure visuality. Brian McHale first describes *The Tablets* as "concrete poetry"—but then corrects himself to mean "'material' poetry" (256). Its visuality, in any case, is being emphasized. Even more than Oppen, Schwerner has created

a poetry rich in spatial event: gaps and dislocations, marginalia, shifting typefaces, strings and grids of

nonalphabetic signs, pages of musical notation
(Tablet XII) and even a mandala (between
Tablets XII and XIII), and [...] "ancient"
pictographs, tiny biomorphic icons newly minted
using font-generating software. (255-56)

It's no coincidence that the first review of *The Tablets*
appeared in *Art News* rather than a literary journal.
Schwerner celebrates writing's ontology, interested in the
gaps in meaning writing both provides and showcases.
This understanding of text is decidedly Jewish. In one of
this poem's supremely comic moments, the Scholar/
Translator becomes completely caught up in the self-
reflections on his task: "Some days I do not doubt that the
ambiguity is inherent in the language of the Tablets
themselves; at other times I worry myself sick over the
possibility that I am the variable giving rise to
ambiguities" (31-32). As Finkelstein comments in Track,
making reference to Schwerner's work,

In the tractate
on the mastery of meaning

Recently delivered
and newly translated

The lovers of fate
came into the Presence

Standing
in an empty space.

\#

But in the tractate
on the mastery of mastery

Came upon a scribe
in an empty space

Before an empty book
indistinguishable from the others

Lining the shelves
but still empty.

(*Powers: Track Volume III*, pp. 216-17)

Schwerner extends a tendency in Oppen's Objectivist poetics toward understanding and celebrating visual language as a phenomenon worth contemplating in its own right. This appreciation of the written is related to Oppen's affection for the usually least significant linguistic elements. Oppen starts a press in the 1930's called TO Press, and his 1965 book is titled *This in Which*. He says in an interview, speaking about the smallest particles of our language, "[t]hat's where the mysteries are, in the little words. 'The' and 'and' are the greatest mysteries of all" ("Poetry and Politics" 38; cf. Berry "Williams-Oppen" 111).

Oppen shares a poetics with Louis Zukofsky who titles his long poem, simply, *"A"*, his collected essays *Prepositions*, and one of his major shorter poems "Poem Beginning 'The'." The small particles of language are interesting, in fact principal for the Objectivists, who understand language, to use William Carlos Williams' description of a poem (echoing Stéphane Mallarmé) as a "machine of words." The particles of language are the cogs of the machine and thus its essential feature. They're its emblem of linguistic materiality. The machine, it turns out, is made tangible in writing; it's in the visual field that these small linguistic elements can be made to stand out. Written language is overtly material (as implied in the title of Oppen's 1962 collection, *The Materials*). Schwerner comments in Tablets Journals / Divagations, an appended section of *The Tablets*, which reflects on the work he's been making, that

> Words whirl, hesitate, change, are still, move in transit phrases, whirl still. ...a field generating the Scholar/ Translator along with the presented materiality, transformable materiality, of the word, the part-word, the utterance. (143)

Writing, while existing over against the language user, the poet, is alive. As it describes the world, it also calls attention to itself, to its own beauty and power, possibly to its status as an enigma, and it can even define the poet. This understanding of language can be seen to hearken back to the Hebrew notion of Torah in its pristine standing as law but also, at once, an unfulfilled text that must be complemented by the devout's very human commentary.

All of this orientation toward language-and-world underscores a truly hilarious moment in *The Tablets*, when the Scholar/Translator has arrived at his ultimate inability to cope with the text before him. The moment is paradoxically rich, linguistically and also, in a very straightforward way, aesthetically—visually—while pointing to the simultaneous semantic power and distancing effect of written language. As noted, *The Tablets* employs a number of graphic marks to indicate translation variables and to contextualize the translation's written English (although one tablet is written in what the Scholar/Translator calls "proto Icelandic"); the marks also show the translation, in a kind of middle stage, as fully realized, coherent expression that emerges, as it were, from the white space of the page.

The marks used are: "..." that is meant to indicate "untranslatable," "+++" meant to indicate "missing," "(?)" meant to indicate "variant reading," "[ ]" meant to indicate "supplied by the scholar translator," and a circle with a plus sign in it, which is meant to indicate "confusing." Here is the totality of Tablet X's coherent language; of course, the language is anything but coherent, but it does nod toward Objectivist poetics and commemorates written language as an aesthetic and semantic machine (only the central portion of this Tablet is being reproduced here):

++++++++++++++++++++........++++++++++++

+++++++ [the the] +++++++

++++++++++++++++++

........++++++......++++++

The other side of verbal expression, silence or the blank

page, is the fact Oppen knew so well. As if to enlarge upon what Oppen was driving at, Schwerner comments in Tablets Journals / Divagations that

> The immense difficulty of defining a self, of assuming an identity, goes along with this [i.e., with "setting up categories of the real and unreal as tenable hypothesis"]. In poetry then silences and lacunae should *be*—and being, act—and the often arbitrary distinctions between concrete and abstract, real and unreal, sane and mad, objective and subjective seem increasingly irrelevant. To demonstrate the arbitrariness by the processual flux of the poem … Destroy the point of view: who's speaking? to whom? and the rest of it. (135-36)

In Tablet X we can find a similarity of motivation between this purported transcription or translation and the Judaic emphasis on calligraphy, on the sheer physical beauty of the written word. But the visual aspect is not a concern of the Scholar/Translator who's fallen into ineffability. As for Schwerner, in Tablets Journals / Divagations, as he is reflecting on the work he's making, he extemporizes on issues the work raises; the notes here are disparate and yet illuminating: "since metaphysics is not art, the artifact must exist in time, and be partial, and be—to however small a degree—'constructed'. Is this sad?" (130). And then, a short space later, on the same page:

the poet is a namer.

there is no nuclear self.

there is no nuclear self.

The made thing, poem, artifact, product, will appear to the maker as Other and yet give the pleasure of recognition, to breed other discoveries. The voices in the made thing, poem, object, need no ascription by the maker. He does not know the necessary identity of a voice or many voices. They speak him in a way he later discovers. The locus appears later. (130-31)

What happens to the name, and to the act of naming, with inscription? One key line of Tablet XIII reads: "this tablet-clay hating me separated from its name" (66). Finkelstein observes that this statement, and its surrounding lines, "record a psychic, even a spiritual crisis, brought on by the loss of immanence and the recognition of a space, a 'great emptiness' [Tablet XIII], between the perceiving subject and the perceived object" ("Wallace Stevens" 158). In his poem, Schwerner proposes a speaker/writer/reader in the throes of an existential dilemma. The person who is speaking through this inscription—in this case it may be the scribe, in any case he's to be taken as a writer— "experiences [. . .] objects," such as the clay inscription,

> as hating him; they are named, but the act of naming has lost its magical, unifying power, for the objects are now 'separated' from their names. Language, or at least written language, may be the source of this problem, which is why the tablet-clay, the writing medium itself, is the first object mentioned as hating the speaker. (Finkelstein "Wallace Stevens" 158)

The power of naming is an important feature for Schwerner's successors, Heller and Finkelstein, related by them to the act of writing. Unlike Oppen, Schwerner, and Finkelstein—who, each in his own way, displays a penchant for dramatic graphics—Heller writes about uncertainty, self, and world in a straightforward, mostly uneventful, way as far as graphical innovation or complexity is concerned; however, residing subtly behind his poems' epistemological and ontological queries is an acute sensitivity to textuality and language in and of itself, and this sensitivity is part and parcel of his protracted meditation on Judaism as well as personal Jewish identity. Questions of time and exile figure centrally in Heller's work, particularly in his understanding of language be it oral or written, and he can play on the tension between the oral and inscribed. "The history of the Jews as given in the Pentateuch, half 'fact' and half 'fiction' or 'legend'," he comments in his memoir *Living Root*,

> establishes primarily, via this very indeterminacy, the possibility of endlessly being rethought. Time, even narrative time, is a series of musical phrases, repeated motifs, rises that later fall, and falls that climb to new heights. I wanted to be a writer, a memorialist, I once jotted in my notebook; I would look back, not even aware that such looking placed everything that ever happened in one context and one context only: infinitude. So then, what was anything: a rule, a life, a book? (33)

Against infinitude can be placed the utterance, indeed the inscription that (unlike evanescent speech, going out of existence as it's spoken) suggests simultaneously the fragility and duration of time. It can also suggest exile—in the wandering of meaning like the Diaspora, a life lived although the sense of certainty, of home, of a transcendent signifier that is a name, and so in communion. The question of naming, central to all four poets, lies at the heart of Judaic tradition. To be nameless can suggest being lost. Therefore, in the work of these poets, nouns are especially significant in their signifying the tangibility of things. I think of Oppen's remark in his now famous 1968 interview: "nouns do refer to something; that it's there, that it's true, the whole implication of these nouns" (161; cf. Berry "Language" 311). And, in a 1993 interview of Heller, his essential attraction to Oppen is put this way: "What I'm really interested in, in someone like Oppen, is the idea of knowing where you are and finding, as he puts it in a line—where the known and unknown touch" (51; cf. Oppen NCP 182). Perhaps, then, in some sense all names resonate the name *Jerusalem*, as imperfect mirrors of this signifier.

Finkelstein expresses this imperfection succinctly, in the second volume of *Track* where he writes the word "Jerusalem" on a line by itself, followed by a line in which "Jerusalem" is written backwards and upside down, as is, and on a subsequent line the phrase "an exile" (p. 64). What has been accomplished in these lines is the actualizing of exile, in essence a namelessness. One attraction of the written name is its material actualization. In the written word's ability to stand apart from the language user, someone stands apart from her or his own very language; hence an alienation, an exile, is put into effect. The Jew's sense of exile comes as much from a history of psychic displacement, which is derived from acts of reading, and, in response to that reading of writing, from physical displacement. "Following the destruction of the Temple," David Stern explains, the text of the Torah became for the Rabbis the primary sign of the continued existence of the covenantal relationship between God and Israel, and the activity of Torah study—midrash—thus became the foremost medium for preserving and pursuing that relationship. Understood this way, the object of midrash was not so much to find the meaning of Scripture as it was literally to engage its text. Midrash became a kind of conversation the Rabbis invented in order to enable God to speak to them from between the lines of Scripture, in the textual fissures and discontinuities that exegesis discovers. (31)

In fact, exegesis also exploits those textual gaps, and by so doing it deepens the sense of exile—even, paradoxically, as it brings the exegete closer to the divine, in an act of cleaving or what Heller likes to call "adhesion." Finkelstein maintains that "Jewish writers are faced with a continual frustration. Unable to effect what might be called an existential closure in their work, they are compelled to accept *the exile of the text*, living, as Derrida says, 'the necessity of interpretation as an exile'" (*Ritual* 7). Elsewhere Finkelstein has said that, "[l]ike Oppen, Heller is always ready to acknowledge our fundamental estrangement from everyday life, even as we are in the midst of it, even as it is the only thing we believe we know. 'What do we believe / To live with?' asks Oppen [. . .]. No poet writing today takes the question more seriously than Heller" ("On the Edge" 68; NCP 52).

The facticity of a photograph, another form of inscription, gives rise for Heller to an extended meditation on the Jewish life of his ancestors in "Bialystok Stanzas"; at one point he interrogates the possibility of communion:

Light—
The scene filled with photographer's light

This sparsely furnished room
In the corner of which
A china-closet Ark

The old men
Under green shaded bulbs
Reading Torah

The prayers are simple.
To what they think larger
Than themselves [...].
(EF 28)

His concept of adhesion is a part of this. The photograph, and now the poem, memorialize exile as well as the Holocaust, in this poem; and as inscription, he points out in *Living Root* while quoting Walter Benjamin, Heller beholds and adds his own "posthumous moment" he likens to "the Kabbalistic ideal of *Devekuth* or 'adhesion' which is itself surrounded by notions of light and seeing, and the need to articulate [...] that which can not be put into words, the Holocaust" (33). Within the seemingly endless continuum of textual commentary that in itself, for any commentator, invites further commentary— words, especially written words that cannot be prompted for elucidation as one might question a living speaker, never can say fully, completely what they purport to say—there is also the writing that arises out of persecution. Leo Strauss comments that "the truth about all crucial things is presented exclusively between the lines." The literature of persecution "is addressed, not to all readers, but to trustworthy and intelligent readers only" (25). Scripture is at once separate from the truth of the divine, standing apart from its author and reader, alive in its own materiality, and is potentially an expression of the divine as well as hope for communion with it. *Devekuth*, a "cleaving to God" (Low par. 3), expresses that apartness and simultaneous oneness. This is the irony of the written word, with which the Jew must always contend, who has to read and in effect to write, to comment, on the written law in order to pray. To be sure, "Jewish theophany is verbal," Ash writes; it's "a continuous unfolding of divine creativity through interpretation, rather than a revealed Divinity as spiritual presence (*ousia*), as in Christianity" (67).

Heller's work has always contained an extraordinarily distilled quality, consistently taking up the same concerns over many years. In his more recent poems, however, his motifs, such as the ontology of text, have come to the fore. Writing becomes the cerebral expression of the human condition, which is formed by the human being's capacity for logic and yet which is disappointed by its inability to address fully the circumstances of a life. Thus Heller, in his poem "Cyclical," considers "[t]he calculus on the page, the numbers and symbols, the operands and constants, transparencies and theories. Only these thwart an interminable bruising against reason" (EF 155).

The conditions of a life lay siege to the best reasoned articulation of existence. Writing can go beyond this impasse, though, while it gives rise to abstraction in the history of humanity, and bespeaks the ability to reason: "And what was writing? *A snail's slime down the walkway! Nothing more natural to the creature*, he wrote bitterly" (EF 156).

Basically, Heller is continually testing that elasticity between oral utterance and written declamation. In a poem he dedicated to Schwerner, "'We can only wish *valeat quantum valere potest*'," he alludes to *The Tablets*, speaking "of words hidden behind logograms, // indicative of first things, / the need and desire to speak, // to bring back the body" (EF 158). Another poem by Heller, "Winter Notes, East End," written in memory of Schwerner, notes that "The blank page" is "no mystery. Composition is, composition is. . . ." Here he echoes Oppen's now often-quoted lines, "The self is no mystery, the mystery is / That there something for us to stand on" ("World, World—" [1968] NCP 159). Once again, Heller's referring to the irony of inscription that memorializes and yet fails to grasp reality. Perhaps we "stand on" our written words. Heller's final section of "Winter Notes" ends movingly, and again evokes *The Tablets*. Schwerner's grand opus demonstrates how primitive intelligence eludes capture by writing, yet, paradoxically, is remembered only because of it:

Scouring words for the relieving aura,

breathing deeply old vocabularies of sea,

of pine, ever-present tinge of salt. Panoply of
stars, planets. But often

one can't find what is being searched for,
the galaxy seemingly drained of that covenant.

Thus it is written out for syntax's rules,
for the untranslatable memory of black holes,

for voice, for love and against concept.
(EF 166)

Heller's work resonates the well worn phrase "the people
of the book," and he often identifies himself as being able
to trace his existence back to scripture while he realizes his
own writing as a kind of Midrash, or otherwise secular
commentary, on scripture and Jewish legacy stemming from
early written beginnings. Ash notes that "[w]hile Augustine
ultimately counsels the devout to throw the Book away,
the [ancient] rabbis believed that even God was beholden
to the task of interpreting Torah" (67). But an ideology of
interpretation ineluctably leads to an endless production of
texts, with the self locating itself within and among them.
In this context, Jabés has commented that

> Jewish writing clears a passage between two
> imprecise and indefinable points. It is the passage,
> sometimes carried along by words—which are only
> the infinite mobility of thought—sometimes
> anxious to bear witness, to engage others in the
> total experience in which it has become involved.
>
> The split is, for Jewish writing, a burst of life,
> evidence of a renewed bond with the unknown.

From the silence of writing, to the written silence, the Jewish book, in the meticulous copying of God's book, will forever remain incomplete. (30; in Mosès 88)

Heller's poem, "Autobiographia," a work framing Heller and all Jewry within the twentieth-century's cataclysmic events, begins with the core question for any Jew:

Weren't you given a text? To honor the congregation, the organ dulcet,

the cantor's hum, hymnal of Europe's East, steps of sound made fugal

but laden with a weariness (joy for another day), history transmogrified

into plaint upon plaint, to be ushered into manhood, to be brought other's pain.

Early on, the Shekinah gone into exile. Most of that century you saw

not love but power, cruelty, the face which laughs against the sun.

(EF16)

This poem is a part of the Jewish heritage in its persona's attempt to understand himself as a poet vis-à-vis a textual tradition, as well as within the context of his rabbinic forbears, about whom he writes explicitly in other poems and in his memoir. "The supreme value of Rabbinic Judaism, the continuity of Israel," Ash remarks, derives from the paradoxical situation of the exegete's submission to the oldest revelation at Sinai and yet freedom for new interpretation of the Divine Word through the strange midrashic conversation. This intertextual dialogue, conducted for thousands of years by multiple voices who understand one another as contemporaries, must also continually reformulate meanings relevant to the adjudication of current problems in Jewish life. Since the text is central to this historical process, the boundaries between the Word and its interpretation are more fluid, more open to narrative retelling than we usually imagine for scripture. (68)

In Finkelstein's second volume of *Track*, Jews are "[c]arrying torahs / as they have / been given" (157). It is important to realize, as Jaffee explains, that the written Torah was not only a source of wisdom and law; it "was also a cultic object. Ceremonially conveyed in a procession during the liturgical rite of the synagogue, the scroll communicated metalinguistically, marking the tangible presence of God, and serving as a relic of the reality of convenantal revelation" (88). Still, the scroll is a text, one that invites a textual response as a complement, although completion may only be the ideal. In a world conditioned by a divine mystery, what can the manifest truth be? "In some versions" of it, Finkelstein may be saying in the first volume of *Track*, "there are many versions / and in some versions only one // around which the commentators / weave endless versions / as if to explain" (21). Perhaps wistfully, as if to complete this thought, the third volume of *Track* imagines the end of such commentary, that which the commentators are ostensibly seeking:

As one who would gather
all things into presence

Gather all things
before they disappear

Would give them this charge:
gather unto yourself

All that is you
All that is here.
(212)

Who is the "you" Finkelstein addresses? It is likely to be a posited Jewish self, one whose identity is that of a literate, who engages the word of God as, in a sense, an equal. The word only comes into its own with an acknowledgement of the silence or blank space out of which it emerges and which holds it in place-again, like death "holds" life or like the unseen Yahweh gives rise to a purpose in the manifest world.

The acknowledgement of silence, of an ellipsis, is necessary in order that, ultimately, there can be a merging with that word, a *devekuth* (as Heller would say), through the act of writing, finally through the act of poetry, a poetry that responds to a written text. Finkelstein finds himself drawn to the Judaic tradition as a "[p]oet, critic, [and] Jew" ("'The Master'" 415). In an autobiographical essay he explains that "there came a time when I began to read, to think, to feel, and to write through Judaism—through my Jewishness—in a way that I had not done previously" (416). Benjamin comes to have great influence over him, also a guiding spirit for Heller. "Benjamin recognized that the Jew's subservience to the text," Finkelstein notes, "which had always been richly problematic, took on, under modern conditions, a heretofore unknown historical resonance" (418).

The Jewish poet makes history, his own and the world's. The word is worshipped by the Jewish poet, perhaps especially by the postmodern Jewish poet, through his valorizing of it as the scene into which the god finally might appear. This monumentalization involves presenting language within the context of death, or God, or silence, or alternately the blank visual field. The Jewish poet is a witness, simultaneously, of the unseen and the material world he brings into being. The text is the Jew's reality, and it is a source of his exile as well.

Notes

1. Martin S. Jaffee, in "Ontologies of Textuality in Classical Rabbinic Judaism" reports that "the Mishnah shows many signs that writing was used in its composition" (87); this statement is presumably a reflection of his article, which he cites, "Writing and Rabbinic Oral Tradition: On Mishnaic Narrative, Lists, and Mnemonics" (123-46).

2. The title of the poem these lines come from is "Drawing," and so it may be surmised that Oppen is not talking about writing per se, but in fact my argument is that the visuality of writing and drawing, the marks one might make on a page, for instance, underscore the literate human being's imposed distancing from her or his own creation, own language.

3. I have argued, in "George Oppen's Silence and the Role of Uncertainty in Post-War American Avant-Garde Poetry," that these gaps and more largely Oppen's silences are a reflection of his understanding of physics' Relativity and Quantum Mechanics, and I still believe that this is true, but his Jewish orientation, and particularly his relationship to text, written text, in and of itself, cannot be discounted.

4. See Kimmelman, "George Oppen's Silence and the Role of Uncertainty in Post-War American Avant-Garde Poetry," 148, 150, and ff.

Works Cited

Ash, Beth Sharon. "Jewish Hermeneutics and Contemporary Theories of Textuality: Hartman, Bloom, and Derrida." *Modern Philology* 85 (August 1987): 65-80.

Bernstein, Charles. "Hinge, Picture." *Ironwood* (Fall 1985): 240-44.

Berry, Eleanor. "Language Made Fluid: The Grammetrics of George Oppen's Recent Poetry." *Contemporary Literature* 25.3 (Fall 1984): 305-22.

_____. "The Williams-Oppen Connection." *Sagetrieb* 3.2 (Fall 1984): 99-116.

Boyarin, Daniel. *Intertextuality and the Reading of Midrash.* Bloomington and Indianapolis: Indiana UP, 1990.

Dowd, Garin V. "'Connect-i-cut': George Oppen's Discrete Series and a Parenthesis by Jacques Derrida." *Angelaki: Journal of Theoretical Humanities* 5.1 (April 2000): 123-28.

Finkelstein, Norman. "'The Master of Turning': Walter Benjamin, Gershom Scholem, Harold Bloom, and the Writing of a Jewish Life." *People of the Book: Thirty Scholars Reflect on Their Jewish Identity.* Eds. Jeffrey Rubin-Dorsky, and Shelley Fisher Fishkin. Madison, WI: U of Wisconsin P, 1996. 415-26.

_____. "On the Edge of Being." *Denver Quarterly* (Winter 1998): 66-76.

_____. *The Ritual of New Creation: Jewish Tradition and Contemporary Literature.* Albany, NY: State U of New York P, 1992.

_____. *Track* [containing all three volumes, *Forest, Columns,* and *Powers*]. Bristol, UK: Shearsman Books, 2012.

_____. "Wallace Stevens, Armand Schwerner, and 'The Thè.'" *The Wallace Stevens Journal* 24.2 (Fall 2000): 151-60.

Gingerich, Willard. "Sacred Forgeries and Translation of Nothing in the *Tablets* of Armand Schwerner." *Talisman: A Journal of Contemporary Poetry and Poetics* 21/22 (Winter/Spring 2001): 18-26.

Heller, Michael. *Conviction's Net of Branches: Essays on the Objectivist Poets and Poetry.* Carbondale and Edwardsville: Southern Illinois UP, 1985.

_____. *Exigent Futures: New and Selected Poems* Cambridge, UK: Salt Publishing, 2003. Cited as EF.

_____. "An Interview with Michael Heller [with Edward Foster]." *Talisman: A Journal of Contemporary Poetry and Poetics* 11 (Fall 1993): 48-64.

_____. *Living Root: A Memoir.* Albany, NY: State U of New York P, 2000.

Jabès, Edmond. *Le Parcours.* Paris: Gallimard, 1985.

Jaffee, Martin S. "Spoken, Written, Incarnate: Ontologies of Textuality in Classical Rabbinic Judaism." *Voice, Text, Hypertext: Emerging Practices in Textual Studies.* Eds. Raimonda Modiano, Leroy F. Searle, and Peter Schillingsburg. Seattle and London: U of Washington P, 2004. 83-100.

Jenkins, G. Matthew. "Saying Obligation: George Oppen's Poetry and Levinasian Ethics." *Journal of American Studies* 37.3 (December 2003): 407-33.

Kimmelman, Burt. "George Oppen's Silence and the Role of Uncertainty in Post War American Avant-Garde Poetry" *Mosaic: A Journal for the Interdisciplinary Study of Literature* 36.2 (June 2003): 145-62.

Lachs, Samuel Tobias. *Humanism in Talmud and Midrash.* Rutherford/Madison/Teaneck, NJ: Fairleigh Dickinson UP / London and Toronto: Associated University P, 1993.

Low, Colin. *Notes on Kabbalah.* 1992. 23 October 2005. Online.

McHale, Brian. "Archeologies of Knowledge: Hill's Middens, Heaney's Bogs, Schwerner's Tablets." *New Literary History* 30.1 (Winter 1999): 239-62.

Mosès. Stéphane. "Edmond Jabès: From One Passage to Another."
    Studies in 20ᵗʰ Century Literature 12.1 (Fall 1987): 81-92.

Neusner, Jacob. "Scripture and Tradition in Judaism, with Special
    Reference to the Mishnah." *Approaches to Ancient Judaism.*
    Vol. 2. Ed. William Scott Green. Chico, CA: Scholars P,
    1980. 173-93.

Ong, Walter. *Orality and Literacy: The Technologizing of the Word.*
    London and New York: Routledge, 1982.

Oppen, George. "An Adequate Vision: A George Oppen *Daybook*." Ed.
    Michael Davidson, *Ironwood* 26 (1985): 5-42

_____. *New Collected Poems.* Ed. Michael Davidson. Pref. Eliot
    Weinberger. New York: New Directions, 2002. Cited as
    NCP.

_____. "[Notes for the *Primitive* Poems]." *Ironwood* 31/32 (1988).
    Cited in Taggart "Walk Out" 75.

_____. "Oppen on His Poems: A Discussion [Interview with L. S.
    Dembo]." *George Oppen: Man and Poet.* Ed. and Intr.
    Burton Hatlen. Orono: National Poetry Foundation, 1981.
    197-213.

_____. "Poetry and Politics: A Conversation with George and Mary
    Oppen [with Burton Hatlen and Tom Mandel]." *George
    Oppen: Man and Poet.* Ed. and Intr. Burton Hatlen. Orono:
    National Poetry Foundation, 1981. 23-50.

Schiffman, Lawrence H. "The Temple Scroll in Literary and Philological
    Perspective." *Approaches to Ancient Judaism.* Vol. 2. Ed.
    William Scott Green. Chico, CA: Scholars P, 1980. 143-58.

Schwerner, Armand. *The Tablets.* Orono: National Poetry Foundation, 1999.

Stern, David. *Midrash and Theory: Ancient Jewish Exegesis and Contemporary Literary Studies.* Evanston, IL: Northwestern UP, 1996.

Strauss, Leo. *Persecution and the Art of Writing.* 1952. Chicago and London: U of Chicago P, 1980.

Taggart, John. "Deep Jewels: George Oppen's *Seascape: Needle's Eye.*" *Ironwood* 26 (1985): 159-68.

_____. "To Go Down to Go Into." *Ironwood* 16.1-2 (Spring/Fall 1988): 270-85.

_____. "Walk-Out: Rereading George Oppen." Chicago Review 44.2 (1998): 29-93.

STEPHANIE STRICKLAND'S UNIVERSE

"Seen scientifically, the universe is a strange and vastly unknown entity with many different interlocking dimensions. It does not refer to a 'whole' or a totality, but to something smaller than its parts, each one potentially exceeding it in detail and complexity."
- from *Ringing the Changes*

Like the *universe*, true *poetry* will never be what you think it is. The more we discover, the more we realize we don't know what we thought we did. Poetry isn't what you think it is. Stephanie Strickland reveals as much.

The natural world, the stars, ask us to think about the world in all its heartbreaking abundance. We might feel at home in it, even when our ever more fine ways of articulating *world* also show us why, no matter how hard we try, we never arrive somewhere. Perhaps poetry is, or is meant to be, about never arriving.

We learn by osmosis. The beauty of science may transport us to what Heidegger called "nearness." Yet even the near is not poetry. And even Stephanie Strickland, one of our great minds and one of our great poets, cannot tell us what poetry *is*. Yet her poems, in their linguistic reach, in their perhaps magical ability to be both simple and complex at once, disclose her communion in the world. In this I find the essential value of her work. In reading her, I come closer to poetry.

Recipient of accolades and prizes, Strickland is one of our foremost digital poets. She began her writing life on the page, soon thereafter to become an early practitioner of poetry in code. Often, now, she combines media in her work. Yet, all this time, she's remained committed to print, to books.

The digital poem may hint at how the complexity of the universe can also be beautiful in its clarity. A recent book of hers, *Ringing the Changes* (2020), is a long procedural poem comprised of complexly arranged, appropriated texts. Their order is generated by computer code to match sequences based on the ancient art of tower-bell ringing as it was practiced in seventeenth-century England. Patterns are both abstract and organic configurations, both historical and of the now, both complex in realization and beautiful in elaborated embodiment. These ringing patterns are now understood as group theory symmetry operations (something Strickland explains in the book's appendix).

There's a reading of five of the "changes" from *Ringing the Changes* on Vimeo, recited by seven participants (one for each bell). They're performing texts sampled from writers who probe the changes in our entangled virtual and real worlds. Here's one of these texts:

> Evolution and computation should not be treated as incommensurable processes but as divergent models of a single type of development. If computers are stupid, then so is evolution, and consequently they share more with each other than either does with us. (2 ff.)

What's arresting in both the video and the book itself is

the comparison in our minds of the bells with the texts' words. "Just as metal bells have overtones you can hear," Strickland writes in the appendix, "book bells have 23 texts (or overtones, as it were) that you can read" (163). What's really interesting to me, which may be a key to understanding our present era, is "the differences ordering and context make," and how "a generated order refuses the fixed hierarchy of attention print normally enforces" (164). The order itself is not merely a fascination. One of the 161 circulated and recirculated texts in the book stipulates that "[t]he good is outside history, not less present then than now, not more present at the end" (17 ff.).

Ringing the Changes, this entire book—which is as much poetry as any of her exquisitely lyrical, even when complex, poems to be accessed in either pixels or print—stands as a repudiation of inscription in and of itself. At the same time, this inscribed book anchors the recorded recitations from it, which are a work of art in place and time. I need not, here, make a foray either into questions of authorship or conceptual poetry/art. Yet I must say that, in listening to the readings from the book, I do begin to sense *time*. Poetry takes forms I'd not have expected. Some of these obtain in *Ringing the Changes*, the harmonies of algorithms engaging communities of persons.

While this book stands qualitatively apart from Strickland's other works, I understand it as belonging within her oeuvre. I see and hear, I read the book along with her other creations, which span the firmly tactile world of print and the ethereally tactile world of digital text. Her artistic imprint is unmistakable. It's worth mentioning that even her early work was a fully mature poetry, newly arrived. There's no difficulty now in seeing the endeavor in the one medium informing, at times explicitly belonging to, the other. Her graceful turns and leaps of thought, in either realm, are prized for their radiance.

I hold her recent new and selected poems, *How the Universe Is Made*, in my hands and I contemplate how space and words, arcs of thought, allow poetry to come into being. I reflect on how the pathways within the haunting, fleeting presence of digital expression—which dazzled me from early on—are deeper, more resonant when writing takes the imagination for a ride. It's worth emphasizing that Strickland's informed, scientific intuition is a principal source of her aesthetic power. She possesses a knowing, singularly fluid way of seeing, which is made material in her poems' prosody. Her orchestrated lines absorb the reader within a plenitude.

She's not the first science-oriented thinker to have succumbed to an infatuation with the manifest world, its symmetries and quirks alike. The observed and natural include equally the made and given in her writing. She's a visionary—although, unlike William Blake, she has no use for the fantastical. The realized world is fantasy enough. Like Blake's, her incisive language, its music and discernment, provide us with elements we've been missing.

The abiding, protean image or state of being, in her work, is water. Here are the opening lines of "Constant Quiet" (from *Zone : Zero*, 2008):

constant quiet
    intercostal
        intercoastal green *&* silver
        muscled gillflesh slipping into
    opens out of
constant quiet

constant quiet
    Mississippi
        overflowing built a levee
        longer higher than the Great
    Wall of China
constant quiet

The vista of the poem expands, the poem's formal structure a constant—until the sixth, final stanza:

constant quiet
    who can open
        who can
        hold it
    constant
quiet

In 1993, Strickland's extended verse meditation, *The Red Virgin: A Poem of Simone Weil*, drew more than the usual public attention. The collection's profound sympathy with and comprehension of Weil, as heroic figure, installs this intellectual woman within her historical tableau. Strickland's portrait of her as champion and redeemer of suffering is in keeping with the twentieth century's great cataclysms: workers' struggles, the horrors of colonialism, holocaust, war. Particularly in "Soul Learns Everything from Body," we start to understand Weil's magnificent selflessness:

The bird forgets
        but the trap does not. Cassandran,
her harsh voice worrying, probing: *If any*
human being show need of any other, a little
or a lot, why does the latter run away?
I have much experience, on one side or the other.

Everything from the body:
        a boy
running down the field can *read* so well, his hands
are unimpeded, have already caught the pass;
reached out before
        he saw. Finally
not to *read* at all: hands alone
fly up, whole body shaping the air, weaned, immediate.

The soul learns turning,
inclination,
fatigue:
to be worn down.

The body,

unastonished by reduction; it feels

what can be shown:

> that there exist remarkable

leafless trees of blossom,

> > tiny

back and forth of almond, long, touched, wands of

> pink

that shudder down their whole length and are blown

> to the pavement

almost at once—

Strickland published *V: WaveSon.nets / Losing L'una* in 2002, as a companion volume to her digital poem *V : Vniverse* (also in 2002), and precursor to *V: WaveTercets / Losing L'una* (2014) along with its digital companion, the *Vniverse* app (2016). She has refigured the concept of *virgin* as her own, with all its weighty implications since ancient times—a past when concepts were inscribed on bone as symbolic motif.

"If you understand virginity," "WaveSon.net 1" begins,

> you understand abstraction, you understand V—
> V which is flight, and you understand VVV,
> i.e., ric-rac, the earliest recorded

> symbolic motif, Cassiopeian breasts pouring forth
> a Milky Way, a.k.a. zigzag,

world-over water, meander, serpentine
cupmark U adjoining its inverse, upsidedown

U (please imagine), yourself
optimizing, as you do not lift but leave
your point (become pointed) pressed hard
to bone to pull that bone

writhing on your point, twist it one way,
then the other—a rhythm method making
your water mark.

Strickland is one of our most expansive intellects. Her lissome, relational thinking lies at the core of her artistry. She'll never abandon her verse for something else, as she aggregates experience to it. I would call this creative process "the formality of occurring"—borrowing this phrase from a much later poem of hers, "Unsolved Problems" (in *Dragon Logic*, 2013).

Some of Strickland's recent poems remind me of the great tenor saxophonist John Coltrane, who ultimately put down his horn to thump his chest while singing/chanting—reaching for some primal genius within him, which itself was his connection to the world per se, the love supreme. Here's "Black \ White":

meter- . . . . . made . . . . . screaming . . . . . *wah wah*
. . . . . brass
mutes . . . . . gag
swallow . . . . . gel-cling flame

vet cemetery in the Wasatch . . . chestnuts . . . flags
brick
unutterable softness . . . low
down . . . wall
    climb in . . . climb over . . . quiet

split \ \ \ spilt / / / silt
domino / /
\ \ \ \\ drama // / / /

disappeared . . . . . trousers afloat . . . . . float
in the moonlight . . . . . button black a shadow
drowned and soaking
white in the moonlight . . . . . haunt
    haint . . . . . zomboid . . . . . flow of clothes

in the twofold . . . torn . . . fold . . . tangled . . . river-
entangled
pole . . . pier

Water is the image, the ghost, which runs through this book. It's a way of knowing that, in its resilience, in its eventual uncontainability, is a metaphor for the universe. In the first poem of *How the Universe Is Made*, "Seeing a Medusa" (from *Give the Body Back*, 1991), Strickland attends to a

drifting bell-shaped medusoid form, a jellyfish, a creature
that "resets" when it's damaged, somehow persisting within
our own human fluidity (all phyla as one):

Only that tinge of crimson-pink
like cyclamen flashing
drew me down, made me see you

in the heave of the wake, all
pale-jelly innard
on your side, resisting nothing

in the wash of green glass, clear gray, the waves
calm today, steady, as you slap
up and down in their hands— a nest

of tentacles rolling with the foam,
then hanging, white with poison. You collapse
an inbreath of water, shudder. Glide.

Gone, before I grew faint
leaning over the boat: gone,
before I even knew

it was you—alive! Not knowing. Reliving
the blow, remembering: you, torn out, despised
and flung dripping to the waves.

"Seeing a Medusa" evokes birth, motherhood, persisting renewal. In *"Hello Dear I Need Your Urgently Reply,"* Strickland's current manuscript, a poem about her dying father (which is dedicated to him), titled "Keeping Company with You: Coma," reprises the imagery and conceits found in "Seeing a Medusa" composed decades before. Here, too, in this later poem, water is integral to the setting, as is the breath of life:

—the gills still swimming

with you, breathing for you, tumbling backward
toward some

future. Shallow breath.

A passing shiver. Your dream of light,
knowing no other

time, moves inside

rocking shadow of water, as if some
one still

stood on the broken

patio, haggling for hours
the price of a pool

lamp, its broken cord.

Water as image defies the empirical, yet water makes science possible. Strickland's fluid knowing draws many dimensions together to become the single utterance. In the moment making itself known to her, there is possibility—which is typified in her late poem "Apparency Not" (from The Body Obsolete, the new poems section of *How the Universe Is Made*, 2019). She never looks away from *appearance,* and allows for juxtaposition, association, confident of poetry's residence therein:

> Apparency not eye-wash, as in hog-
> wash, a costume or mask of zero weight;
> apparency not eye candy, either, however
>
> much it *is*, at times—who would count all
> bower bird display, every stray blue petal
> a reproductive cog? Apparency
>
> could be eye-wash, cleansing or smoothing
> glitchy codestreams, eye-and-eyemind finding
> an attractor, focus (filter) acting truly
>
> —usefully. At first. Indeed, *appear* as you are
> (as if it could happen) gurus advise tricksters,
> fakirs, posers; and Puritans say so, too,

but mean the reverse, mean re-fashion
(apparently finding soul a frozen, yet
attainable (code) object, written just once).

I think of Dickinson "apparently finding soul" when I read this poem. Strickland rises to such an occasion. Is "apparency" another form of "allure"? Here are the first two stanzas of "There You Are," from her current manuscript, with a similar regard, in contemplation of semblances:

Allure, as it happens, doesn't lure me—is no lure.
Direct full-on beauty, now and here,
drops me to the ground, overwhelmed, magnetized.
Allure lives over there, beyond the glass,
down an untaken path, over the hill.
There *you* are,
    there they go:
    so goes it.

Selkies seek human status. Peter Pan hangs on
to magic. The world is a hard pearl
in a hollow shell, retreating from earth-rim-spin
erosion, constant, instant abrasion. A river
sorts the pebbles. Harder—hollower.
There you *are,*
    there they go,
    so goes it.

This is the sensate world that for Strickland includes, vital to the senses, love for another. For her it's the world of human knowing—not first of the universe but instead of self and other—also the very world this poem, in its direct address to another, brings into being. The last two stanzas seem a natural direction for Strickland's persona to head into:

> Hello, my name is De-celeration,
> Flo, from the gated compound down the road,
> Biomass-Genes-Memes-*&*-Norms;
> I chain-bind, thicken and slow, for a while, organic
> body-flock-plume-group mind.
> There you are.
> > There *they* go.
> > So goes it.

> Only systems of loss have attractors.
> For ecstasy, choose A, another way to grow
> by drift. Have you met the other Flo?
> Whom we don't know as well— Fountaining
> spinning, turbulent sift, Vast-Plasma-All-Over.
> There you are,
> > there they go,
> > so *goes* it.

I don't think these closing stanzas represent some other side of Strickland, for example in their modulations of diction (such as "turbulent sift, Vast-Plasma-All-Over," juxtaposed with the repetition of a seemingly casual refrain, "so goes it," which is subtly altered each time). The very social setting of the poem (the pun on "Flo"—"Flo" who's "from the gated compound down the road") is conditioned as much by her awareness of interpersonal dynamics as by forces that make an outer cosmos manifest, beyond the compass of New York City. The flow and swirl of genes, as well as stars, is not out of mind.

Strickland's vast body of digital poetry is more than this essay can accommodate. I hope it's enough to say that the transformative effects of her digital poetry are, simply, mesmerizing. Of her many digital works, I'll cite here just five (nearly spanning her career as a poet, some of them outgrowths from print-only versions): *True North* (appearing earlier in print, then released as hypertext in 1998), *The Ballad of Sand and Harry Soot* (also 1998), *Vniverse* (2002, 2014), *slippingglimpse* (2007), and *Hours of the Night* (2016). Experiencing them is to be incorporated within them. (Such is the nature of digital expression in the hands of the capable poet.)

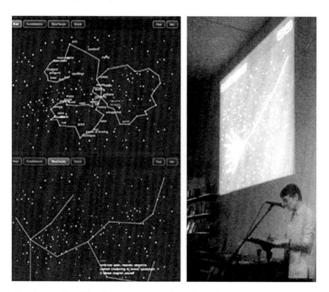

Stephanie Strickland presenting and reading from the *Vniverse* app.

The range of artistic possibility that digital poetry displays comes through, even so, in the print poem "There You Are." The poem's premise involves the semblance of a very personal voice. In this regard it's worth setting "There You Are" side-by-side with, for instance, "Presto! How the Universe Is Made":

On your Mark, one first O/riginal Form; *Get set*, a second
angular Segment; *Go*—the next step, a Rule replacing
each straight side in the first by the second; if I take

a box and for each side of that box substitute a cone
or peak, to make a kind of star—then do *again*
what I did before: take the star-box

and where I find a straight-line replace it
with a peak, to make a *starrier* star, nesting the shape
even deeper in the figure, re-placing

peaks to make a Star-in-the-Box! Or, a Diamond-heart-
Star at *every* level (a shape self-similar); a shape
of extreme complication, in only a few—in five—

iterations, it already reads as texture and is rapidly
sinking as it plummets, repeating, into bonded
lock, where photons mediate, shunting between

heavy center, vibrant orbit. Or *deeper*, look. No,
look, a quantum leap: the burst box—the born star—is re-
emerging on the line, on the line *or/and* . . . . Repeat:

The voice of both these print poems is, to my ear, the
same. Either poem, in its own atypical way, takes me back
in history to verse *summa*s such as, in the Middle Ages,
Cosmographia by Bernardus Silvestris (also known as *De
Mundi Universitate*—hence Strickland's *How the Universe
Is Made*). Even further back, of course, is *De Rerum Natura*,
the classical exemplar by Lucretius who, for all intents and
purposes, launched this scientific-encyclopedic genre of
writing.

What Strickland has accomplished that's new, which is
abundantly evident throughout her oeuvre, is a grasp of
the complexities of our presently known world. These hint
at how much we really still don't know. Nonetheless, there
are patterns. Strickland is a poet of, and thinker about,
patterns. Yet even these can dissipate. *That's* where we
locate her combined intellectual and artistic contribution.
Strickland's work, like poetry we can never know, resides in
the tenuousness of our knowing—which is where her work
takes us—and where we'd be wise to dwell.

VANESSA PLACE, KENNETH GOLDSMITH AND THE DISENCHANTMENT OF ART

Prologue

Over lunch with Michael Golston in the spring of 2015, I got more than a fleeting online mention of what had occurred at the "Interrupt 3" conference, which was held in early March at Brown University. I was dumbfounded—puzzled and fascinated by it—as I tried to comprehend the utter scandal of the conference's keynote event. It struck me as, in its incomprehensibility, in its unreal nature, an episode of madness lifted out of a darkly comic, dystopian, white supremacist novel. Surely this could not have been satire.

Shortly after my sidewalk lunch with Michael on a glorious spring day, New York City being what it's always been for me—the thrill of more people than can be imagined out after the long winter, alive to the moment at cafés, in parks, art galleries and museums, perhaps an early-season open-air concert—I was lunching outdoors with another Michael, Michael Heller . We'd put down not far from the southern-most stairs leading up to the High Line, which is adjacent to the plaza of the Whitney Museum. We almost forgot about seeing some art, caught up as we were in our conversation, in trying to fathom what had happened.

It was not merely the sheer obliviousness of that keynote, at "Interrupt 3." It struck us as being without compassion, without sense, perhaps beguiled by a fascination with masquerading as cleverness—the scandal of it, now by mid spring, having taken on a life of its own, well beyond the precincts of avant-garde poetry and art. I think we were held by our sense of shame—much as in lines from Roethke's great poem, "My Papa's Waltz": "My mother's countenance / Could not unfrown itself." What struck us that afternoon, as I reflect back on it now (writing from home where I'm sequestered in the midst of another American tragedy, an out-of-control pandemic), was the vacuous nature of the *poet's* implicit claim for the Conceptual act. That such hurt and wrong could come from this, that it may have been unforeseen, is itself a shock. It was, after all, a debased prank—by someone who (and this is what shocks me most) could have been unaware of its consequences. It was as if, somehow, in the self-serving nature of it, in its commission, the grimmest aspect of amorality had been put on display.

Finally, Michael and I, having paid our check, headed over to the Whitney, to allow ourselves an immersion in the magical world of *art*. There, I came upon a particular work: John Baldessari's *An Artist Is Not Merely the Slavish Announcer*. That composite photo gave rise to the essay that follows here. (Once I'd finished the essay, I sent it to Michael Boughn and Kent Johnson, the editors of the now-defunct *Dispatches from the Poetry Wars*, who were glad to publish it—quite fitting for the occasion.)

Part 1

In March 2015, the best known of North America's conceptual poets was the keynote reader at "Interrupt 3"; the conference was held at Brown University. The title of the reading was "The Body of Michael Brown."

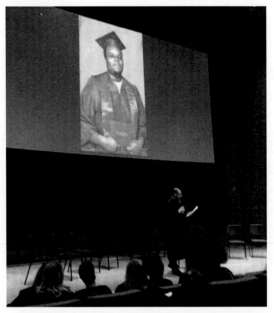

Kenneth Goldman reading a new work
The Body of Michael Brown, the autopsy report

Brown had been recently murdered by police in Ferguson, Missouri. With Brown's high school graduation photo projected on a large screen behind him, Kenneth Goldsmith gave a recitation of the deceased's autopsy report from the past August.

Metropolitan Forecast

D8 I the new york times tuesday, september 11, 2001
Metropolitan Forecast
today Less humid, sunshine
High 79. Noticeably less humid air will filter into the metropolitan region on. Brisk winds
from the northwest. High pressure building east from the Great Lakes will promote mainly
sunny skies. Daytime readings will peak in the lower 80's.
tonight Clear, lighter winds
Low 62. Skies will be clear overnight as high pressure crests near the Middle Atlantic
Coast.
Humidity will remain low, and temperatures will fall to around 60 degrees in many spots.
tomorrow Mainly sunny
High 76. Sunshine and just a few clouds will fill the sky. Breezes will turn and blow from
the
south ahead of a cold front approaching from Canada.

- Kenneth Goldsmith, from *The Day*

Goldsmith's poetry involves appropriation. His long poem, *The Day*, for example, is a "retyping, without [...] semantic alteration, [of] an entire day of the *New York Times* (Stephens 5-6).[1]

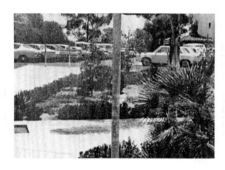

AN ARTIST IS NOT MERELY THE SLAVISH
ANNOUNCER OF A SERIES OF FACTS,
WHICH IN THIS CASE THE CAMERA HAS
HAD TO ACCEPT AND MECHANICALLY
RECORD.

An Artist is Not Merely the Slavish Announcer...,1966-68
Photographic emulsion and acrylic on canvas
59 1/8 x 45 1/8 inches
Courtesy The Estate of John Baldessari

289

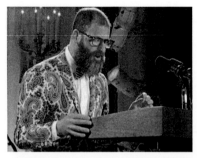

Yet his recitation that day at the poetry conference changed the report, resituating the description of Brown's genitals—so that Goldsmith's final utterance was the report's characterization as "unremarkable" ("Racial Controversy" Brown U newspaper). Immediately the *Guardian*, *Huffington Post*, *Art in America*, *Art News*, *Hyperallergic*, the *New Republic*, the *Rumpus*, the *Quietus*, the Poetry Foundation's *Harriet* Blog, *Jacket2*, and other media reacted. Eventually the *New York Times* weighed in; and there would be a long feature in *The New Yorker*.

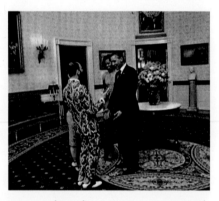

Already a media darling, in 2011 Goldsmith had given a poetry reading at the White House.

A factoid about his Brown reading has gone unreported. The painter Larry Rivers' "eulogy" at Frank O'Hara's funeral, in 1966, consisted of a reading of his autopsy report, just as it was written.[2] Goldsmith began his career as a RISD-trained sculptor. He's someone who absorbs everything around him; and he's tuned into our condition of information overload. He might well have known of Rivers' graveside recitation.

The conversation within the wider liberal world in the fall of 2015 was dominated by the blockbuster memoir, *Between the World and Me*, by Ta-Nahesi Coates, which won the National Book Award. He'd received other prizes. He, too, was a media darling.

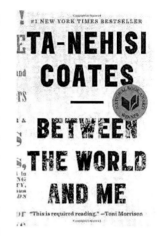

His article "The Case for Reparations" was *The Atlantic*'s cover story a month after Goldsmith's White House appearance. When the book was rolled out, commentators like Charlie Rose and Brian Lehrer, however, sought to unpack its key term, *the black body*—a novel concept in the mainstream although, two decades before, Dorothy Roberts' study, *Killing the Black Body: Race, Reproduction, and the Meaning of Liberty*, had appeared.

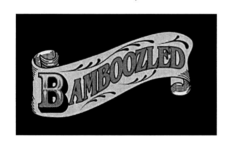

And in 2000 Spike Lee's *Bamboozled*—a piercing essay on the hegemony of American racist culture, which posed as a comedy-drama— arrived in theatres. Coates's book begins as a letter to his adolescent son:

> Son,
> Last Sunday the host of a popular news show asked me what it meant to lose my body. [….]That was the

week you learned that the killers of Michael Brown would go free. The men who had left his body in the street would never be punished.

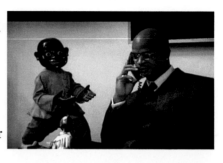

[Y]ou know now, if you did not before, that the police departments of your country have been endowed with the authority to destroy your body. (5)

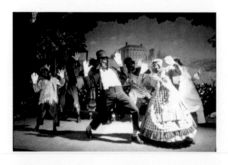

Lee's film examined the fabric of America's racist culture—its language, artifacts, sense of humor. As if picking up where the film left off, Coates observes that "all our phrasing—*race relations, racial chasm, racial justice, racial profiling, white privilege,* even *white supremacy*—serves to obscure that racism is a visceral experience[...]" (12). Lee's cultural take had focused on minstrelsy.

In 2013, a Key and Peale comedy skit shows scandalized attendees at a Black middleclass funeral.

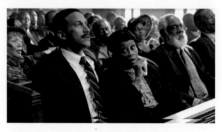

They're having to watch a recovered film montage showing the deceased during his young years in Hollywood.

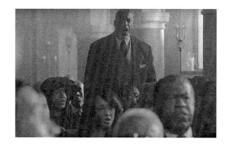

He played unimaginably demeaning roles then.

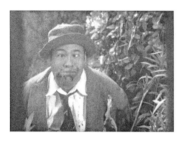 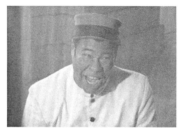

In our history, the *black body* has been under visible threat. Derision leads to violence. *Strange Fruit*, the great Billie Holiday song (written by a Jewish communist high school teacher from the Bronx) fails to mention a conspicuous fact of many Jim Crow lynchings: the mutilation of their male victims' genitalia, often after death, which James Baldwin dwells upon.

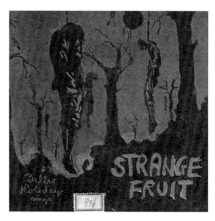

Coates's terminology evokes the European commodification of human beings. Commercial disputes in the transatlantic slave trade were inscribed in American law. M. NourbeSe Philip's 2011 poem titled *Zong!* responds to the ill-fated voyage of the slave ship Zong whose human cargo was thrown overboard due to a deficient supply of water. The ship's captain was sued in 1781 for negligence. Legal judgment went against the ship's owners. The judgment's language, codifying slave commercialization, also opened a protracted discussion on human rights.

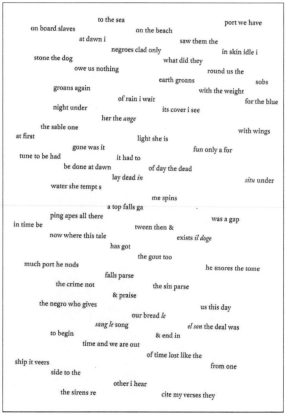

(from *Zong!* by M. NourbeSe Philip)

Part 2

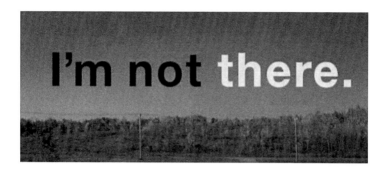

Four years before Goldsmith's White House visit, Coates's *Atlantic* article and Philip's poem, all in 2011, seven years after Lee's film, another film, which Wikipedia calls a "biographical musical drama," was released. About Bob Dylan (although he doesn't appear in it), *I'm Not There* anticipates the Brown reading and its blowback in cyberspace, then in RL—*real life*—taking the form of death threats against Goldsmith, cancelled appearances, etc.

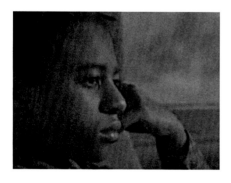

One character in *I'm Not There* features a young Marcus Carl Franklin at about the age of Trayvon Martin. A year before the Brown reading, Claudia Rankine's award-winning book of poetry and art titled *Citizen: An American Lyric* had been published.

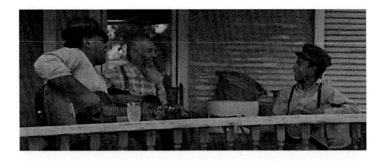

On its cover was the image of a hoodie created by the conceptual artist David Hammons. I doubt Goldsmith was unaware of either Rankine or Hammons.

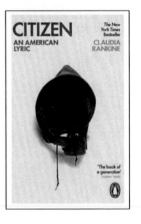

In *I'm Not There*, Franklin's character "[calls] himself Woody Guthrie; freight hopping through the Midwestern United States, he carries a guitar case bearing the slogan 'this machine kills fascists', plays [the] blues [...] and sings about outdated topics such as trade unionism [—an] African American woman advises him to sing about the issues of his own time" (Wikipedia 7 Mar 17).

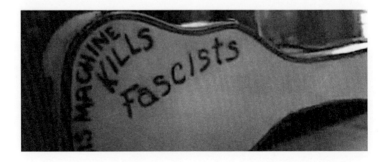

When I think of priviledged white citizens objectivizing the black body, I wonder if Franklin's character escapes the legacy of Jim Crow minstrelsy, despite the issues of social and racial justice Dylan himself has always championed, and for all the wit in this film.

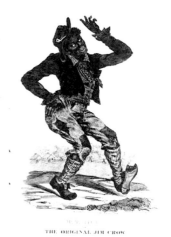

THE ORIGINAL JIM CROW

In *Uncle Tom's Cabin* Harry, the young servant, is commanded to entertain his Kentucky owner and a visiting slave trader:

> "Hulloa, Jim Crow!" said Mr. Shelby, whistling, and snapping a bunch of raisins towards him, "pick that up, now!"
>
> The child scampered, with all his little strength, after the prize, while his master laughed.
>
> "Come here, Jim Crow," said he. The child came up, and the master patted the curly head, and chucked him under the chin.
>
> "Now, Jim, show this gentleman how you can dance and sing." The boy commenced one of those wild, grotesque songs common among the negroes, in a rich, clear voice, accompanying his singing with many comic evolutions of the hands, feet, and whole body [...].

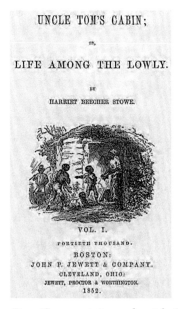

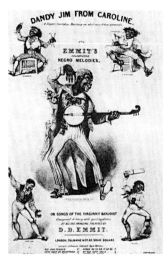

Harriet Beecher Stowe may have known that the term *Jim Crow* originated with Thomas Dartmouth "Daddy" Rice who, a white man in the 1830s, performed blackface minstrel routines as the fictional "Jim Crow," a "caricature of a clumsy [...] black slave," after Rice heard a slave singing "a tune called 'Jump Jim Crow' in Louisville [...]" (Wikipedia 7 March 2017).

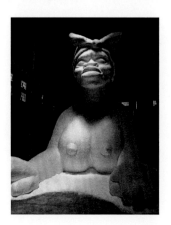

Back to the present. The year Rankine's *Citizen* is published, documenting racial micro aggressions in academe, the exploitation of the female *black body* is made the subject of Kara Walker's conceptual art installation titled *A Subtlety, or the Marvelous Sugar Baby*.

It debuted in an abandoned sugar factory in Brooklyn.

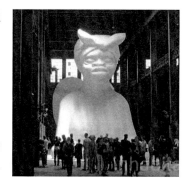

Walker's "site-specific sculpture," Roberta Smith wrote in the *New York Times*, runs the gamut in its effects. Dominated by an enormous sugarcoated woman-sphinx with undeniably black features and wearing only an Aunt Jemima kerchief and earrings,

it is beautiful, brazen and disturbing, and above all a densely layered statement that both indicts and pays tribute. [Walker combines] reality and metaphor with a great gift for

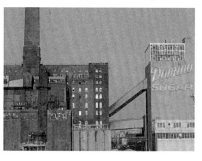

caricature, [demonstrating] unequivocally that America's "peculiar institution" was degrading for all concerned. (11 May 2014)

In *The New Yorker,* Hilton Als discussed that "peculiar institution," praising what he called *the sugar sphinx,"* who "crouches in a position that's regal and yet totemic of subjugation"—she is

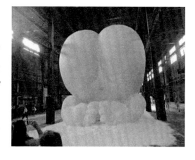

"beat down" but "standing." When "raw," sugar is "brown." By tradition, "royal chefs made sugar sculptures 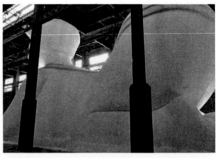 called subtleties." Walker was aware of this and the slave trade's history in which sugar cane was a staple of the triangulated shipping routes—from Europe to Africa to America to Europe: "Who cut the sugar cane? Who ground it down to syrup? Who bleached it? Who sacked it?" (8 May 2014)

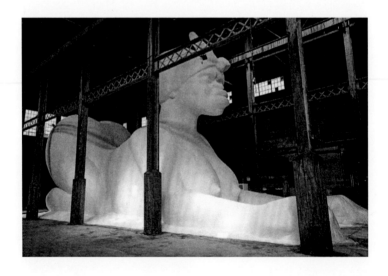

Part 3

It's possible that Walker is not aware of the second best known conceptual poet, Vanessa Place.

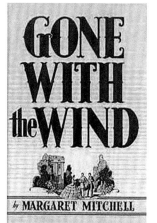

Their names are often linked in avant-garde art or poetry worlds. Their respective works push back against racism from two very different locations. Yet they've both been drawn to Margaret Mitchell's novel, *Gone with the*

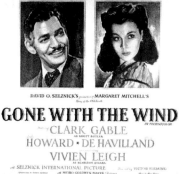

Wind, for similar reasons. I'll guess, even so, that when Walker created the sugar sphinx, she didn't know of Place's activities.

The Rolling Stones's song "Brown Sugar" was a hit in 1971, when Place was three and Walker two. It still is. The Black Lives Matter movement began in 2013 after George Zimmerman murdered Martin.

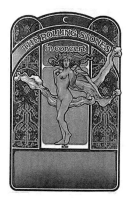

Poster for 1969 America Tour

In 2009, Place first conceived a Twitter project. It involved extensive quotations of *Gone with the Wind.* This was six years before the Goldsmith scandal in which, for him, conceptualism and white privilege would intersect—and six years before Place began to be attacked for her Twitter activity.

Two years before Martin's death, three years before Walker's "sugar sphinx," Place starts tweeting selected passages from Mitchell's novel. Along with the novel's verbatim text, she includes what's been called "Aunt Jemima iconography." She also references Hattie McDaniel, the actor who

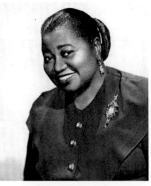

Hattie McDaniel
(courtesy Wikimedia)

played the role of Mammy in the book's film version. Place includes one of McDaniel's publicity photos. Eventually, she'll switch it in for her Twitter profile picture.

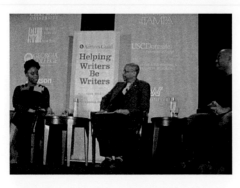

AWP 2017 Panel (left to right: Chimamanda Ngozie Adichie, E. Ethelbert Miller, and Ta-Nehisi Coates)

Some of the initial outrage aimed at Goldsmith preceded grievances voiced by Black authors who were not getting their due of publishing opportunity, critical attention, as well as academic largesse.

At the AWP conference, held in February, 2017 in DC, demonstrations spilled into the city's streets, which advocated for writers of color to have greater opportunity.

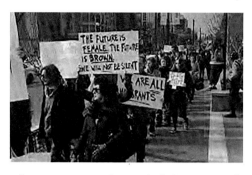

I attended a panel of young, non-white writers of various gender identities. The panel was moderated by an equally young white woman, who ended the session by volunteering that this was a time for white writers to stop writing so they could listen. (She was echoing infighting that had taken place prior to the Women's March that year.)

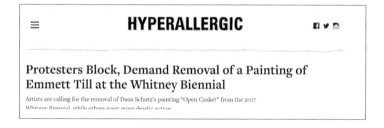

Part 4: Art as Law, Law as Art

I want to situate Place's work within a matrix of cultural formations and reformations. First, I need to say a bit more about Goldsmith.

Criticism of him, prior to the Brown debacle, had to do with his brand of conceptualism. Goldsmith fell victim to his ego. Contemplating this fall, in order to compare his conceptual practices with those of Place, I want to take us back to Marcel Duchamp's Modernist *readymades*.

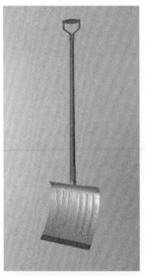

Duchamp's *readymade*, titled "Prelude to a Broken Arm," 1915

Conceptual practice is a dangerous seduction for the mediocre artist or poet; the prospect of it can seem deliciously obvious, maybe easy in some way. Recent, and great, conceptual artworks prompt me to think of how game-changing Duchamp's *readymades* actually were.

Poetic works, some by Goldsmith, hold their own. I think he blundered, however, as a result of what's been described as his self-creation; it's been integral to his artistic/literary activities. I also think his fall from grace has had to do with his immersion in digital information and media.

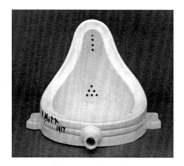

Fountain by Marcel Duchamp, 1917

Another moment, in 2011, was the publication of Robert Archambeau's often cited article, "Kenneth Goldsmith, or the Art of Being Talked About."[3]

"I like thinking about the idea of Goldsmith's books," Archambeau says. "I don't like reading them, but as he himself has said in 'Being Boring', reading them isn't really the point. They're a bit more like Duchamp's 'Fountain', which exists less to be looked at than to spark thought and to be discussed."

Goldsmith's claimed lineage starts with Duchamp, and runs through the self-promoting Andy Warhol, then on to himself, omitting mention of the great appropriation artist Sherrie Levine. Her bronze urinal was first shown in 1991.

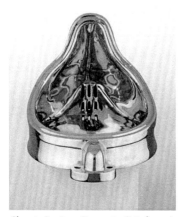

Sherrie Levine, *Fountain (Madonna)*, 1991 (courtesy wikiart.org)

"I don't share what I take to be [Goldsmith's] Oedipal desire for prominence," Archambeau continues,

> but I don't think that desire makes him less interesting or valuable. As for the embracing of the career as a medium for art: I like it. But I'm a bit skittish about the

305

particular form his embrace of the medium seems to take. He's not boring as a presence. He's got the art of being talked about down[.]"

Archambeau points to Goldsmith's interest in Warhol as "self-fashioner, working the art scene around him as an artistic medium and creating 'Andy Warhol, Art Star' as his main work. [I]f anyone is ubiquitous in the little world of poetry lately," Archambeau notes, "it's [Goldsmith]. He's not writing sonnets, [...] he's being a poetry presence."

On the other hand, Archambeau concludes as follows.

[I]n Goldsmith [there's no] indication that he's at all interested in using the career-as-artistic-medium with any kind of critical edge regarding things like status, fame, or cultural capital. Even when he says that some people might consider career-obsession "a silly game" he doesn't suggest that this might be the case because the pursuit of reputation is for chumps, a mere expression of the vanity of human wishes, or a kind of complicity with the logic of the marketplace.

In 2016, Geoffrey Side convened a forum on Conceptual Poetry, in *The Argotist* online. Participants, myself included, were asked if they agreed with Archambeau's statement that Goldsmith "often seems to believe in a linear, progressive version of artistic and literary history [...]." I answered in part with this:

[I]t's fruitless to find fault with Goldsmith's striving

for fame, popularity, "success," which has been linear
pretty much. [The Brown reading] knocked him off
his self-professed, artistic, self-evolutionizing arc. His
derailment [was] due to an apparent lack of [...]
"emotional intelligence." What is significant [. . .] is the
betrayal of his own praxis, as evinced in his tweaking of
the Michael Brown autopsy report, [which] arose from
his own ego-drive. [Goldsmith] was not fully conscious
during the modern Civil Rights struggle, and was being
far too cute for his own good. I'll accept his excuse
that he meant well. Yet he has revealed a remarkable
shallowness of character.[4]

I added that Goldsmith came "into his own with the age of
digital communication." I wonder if Michael Brown ever
existed for him as anything more than an image or data
point.

Amy King recalled the now ignored Andrew Dice Clay, to
use an apt comparison with Goldsmith, describing Clay as
"calculated in his selections, [yet] his material required very
little effort or creativity; one might even say his jokes were
'uncreative', as they seemed to be lifted or 'appropriated'
straight from the backlash culture around him."[5]

Must we view Vanessa Place like Goldsmith or Clay?
Place's tweets, quoting Mitchell's novel, of course repeated
the author's repugnant language. In an article by Aminah
Shakhur, "Why a White Poet Should Not Be Attempting
to Reclaim the 'N-Word'," she argues that,

[a]s a white artist, Place cannot reclaim [the racist]

words or [...] images as she says [in a Facebook post and elsewhere] she is trying to do. Her attempt to hold up a mirror to her fellow white contemporaries has failed. In identifying herself as a "collaborator" in racism she should be able to see how instead the project simply comes off as a reification of the racism in [*Gone with the Wind*].[6]

After my *Argotist* Q&A, Place replied to Side's same prompts. Here's her response to the question "To what extent do you think conceptualism sees itself as a serious poetic art form?":

> Someone once asked me why I was so mean to poetry, as poetry had been fairly good to me. I said that poetry wasn't someone at a party sporting a quivering lip and air of self-harm for whom I had to adopt a position of feeling concern, at least publicly. Conceptualism is a poetic practice, and hardly capable of seeing itself.

At the 2010 AWP conference, Place's quip, that "conceptualism wants to put poetry out of its misery," drew a roar of laughter from a very large crowd. When the *Argotist* inquired about Goldsmith's, and her own, "expressed [...] disinterest in poetry as having any sort of political dimension," she replied: "Being, for the moment, Vanessa Place, I believe I have said, and certainly have written, that all aesthetics has an ethics, and all ethics, an aesthetics. This would imply a certain amount of politics, given the way people tend towards aggregation."[7]

Another approach to Place's Twitter project might be to juxtapose with it what Paul Stephens maintains in his study *The Poetics of Information Overload*: "Avant-garde poetry may have a small role to play in our understanding of global information flows." And yet, he argues, "the avant garde has always aspired to be predictive […]. From Dada to photomontage to hypertext poetry, avant-garde methodology has been deeply concerned with remediation and transcoding—the movement from one technological medium or format to another" (xv).

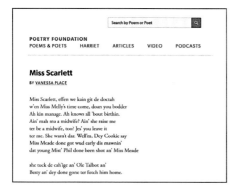

From the *Poetry Foundation* (July/August 2009), here are these notes on Vanessa Place's "Miss Scarlett by Vanessa Place":

Taken from Prissy's famous scene in the movie version of *Gone with the Wind*, Place phonetically transcribes the "unreliable" slave's words, which are then set in Miltonic couplets. Through the simple act of transcription, Place inverts our relationship to Margaret Mitchell's best-selling and beloved American epic by prioritizing the formal aspects of language over Mitchell's famous narrative. With this deconstructive move, Place illuminates the many subtexts embedded in the text concerning plays of power, gender, race, and authorship. By ventriloquizing the slave's voice as well as Mitchell's, Place also sets into motion a nexus of questions regarding authorship, leading one to wonder: who is pulling whose strings?[8]

Place's Twitter project emerged in 2009, as a result of an invitation by *Poetry* Magazine. She came to it from a background different from that of Goldsmith. In a published Artist's Statement, she explains:

> There are [now] two book versions of *Gone With the Wind* by Vanessa Place. One [...] gleans the racist language and imagery of the original. The other simply reproduces the entire book[,?] such that there are two complete volumes of *Gone With the Wind* in WorldCat.

The one is by Mitchell, the other by Place. The Mitchell estate "is   notoriously litigious." Place moonlights as a   poet/artist. Days, she does appellate work in behalf of indigent   sex   offenders.   Unlike   Goldsmith's Brown performance, her targeting of Mitchell's book is subtle and   complex; it's not   thoughtless, and perhaps not without empathy. "By   isolating   the appearance of blackness in the first [Gone With the Wind] book," she has insisted, she "invited [the estate] to sue to recover the 'darkies' she claimed ownership of[.]"

In other words, Place's self-defense is a socio-legal explication. "[B]y reproducing the entire book," she adds,

> I invited suit for wholesale theft of intellectual property. The question was whether the State would uphold Mitchell's right to profit from her appropriation against my appropriation of her.

310

I have always been careful to state that these works are not parodies i.e., not protected by fair use or other copyright exceptions. I am stealing the material from Mitchell because I believe she stole it first. Neither of us has any right to the matter (as in the lives) therein: the only difference between Mitchell and me is that I already know I am guilty. [….] I am very familiar with representing the guilty, and with being the white body that serves as both the defense against the State and as its emblem.[8]

To equate Place with Goldsmith is to be glib, at best. She recognizes Twitter as "a visual and textual platform" in which, she maintains (in this same Artist's Statement), she's "literalized the blackface of the original by substituting the image of Mammy for the more familiar

iconography of Rhett and Scarlett as my profile picture extending this association through use of a similar image from sheet music for 'Jemima's Wedding Day', a coon song from 1899."

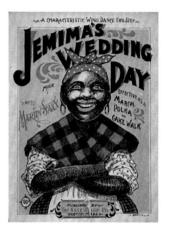

Place also points out that "White women were one of the most popular performers of coon songs." They were "particularly praised for their ability to deliver a convincing performance of genuine blackness: in the song, Jemima is praised as 'just the babe for me'. Both babe and Mammy are examples of what I call radical mimesis, direct representation of the thing itself."

What Place then adds takes us to the heart of the American tragedy: "These works are cruel. It is a cruelty to display these images." Even so, she continues,

> [i]t is also a cruelty to insist that only people of color be responsible for the articulation or the embodiment of race, to bear the burden of my history as well as the history of that oppression. Blackface is white face. I cannot speak of the pain of having the image put upon me, but I can speak to the culpability of its imposition. [....] I embody the perpetrator, historically and currently. That is my condition, and its effects are my responsibility. I am not interested in maintaining a position of rhetorical silence that would permit me to preserve either the precepts of individual property or the conceit of white Integrity. I have been fed the same poison as the rest of my kind, and I vomit it up for forensic analysis and the dog's dinner. It may also get on your shoes.[9]

Part 5 — A Brief Non-Conclusion

When the AWP removed Place from its planning committee for its 2016 conference in LA—after dis-invitations from such cultural institutions as NYC's MoMA—I was casting a vote at the national AAUP convention in DC over whether or not the University of Illinois should be censured for rescinding its offer to hire Steven Salaita with tenure.

Salaita had made a slew of incendiary, anti-Israel comments on Twitter. Many people got up to speak. All were in favor of censure, including a number of Jews and scholars of Judaic 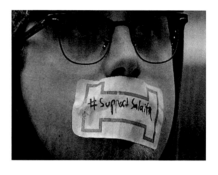 Studies. The vote was unanimous (but for one ballot cast by a member of that university).

Notes

1. Paul Stephens, *The Poetics of Information Overload: From Gertrude Stein to Conceptual Writing* (U of Minnesota P, 2015).

2. According to Michael Lally, in conversation with me in 2015.

3. The essay has appeared more than once, including on the Harriet blog, but perhaps the earliest iteration is on Archambeau's *Samizdat* blog (9 April 2011). Available online.

4. "A Critique of Conceptual Poetry." *The Argotist* (2016). Burt Kimmelman, "Untitled [Answers to Questions Posed by Geoffrey Side on Conceptual Poetry]," *The Argotist* (March 2016). Available Online.

5. "Why Are So Many People Invested in Kenneth Goldsmith? Or, Is Colonialist Poetry Easy?" (*VIDA": Women in Literary Arts*, 18 March 2015). Available online.

6. Aminah Shakhur, "Why a White Poet Should Not Be Attempting to Reclaim the 'N-Word'" (*Hyperallergic*, 22 May 2015). Available online.

7. Vanessa Place, "Untitled [Answers to Questions Posed by Geoffrey Side on Conceptual Poetry]," *The Argotist* (March 2016). Available Online.

8. "Notes to 'Miss Scarlett by Vanessa Place'." *The Poetry Foundation* (July/August 2009). Available online.

9. Vanessa Place, "Artist's Statement: Gone with the Wind @Vanessa Place," *Genius* (n.d.). Available online.

GEORGE OPPEN & MARTIN HEIDEGGER: THE PHILOSOPHY & POETRY OF *GELLASENHEIT* AND THE LANGUAGE OF FAITH

George Oppen's rendezvous with the work of Martin Heidegger in about 1950 (Nicholls 30),[1] and his progressively deepening relationship with this philosopher's ideas and language nurtured his development as a poet, allowing Oppen to establish working principles that honored his fellow Objectivist poets yet set him apart from them, thus freeing him to lend definition to the rather nebulous concept of Objectivist poetics. Oppen's third collection of poems, *This In Which*, fully establishes him not only as an Objectivist but also as a Heideggerian, and ushers in his subsequent prize-winning volume, *Of Being Numerous*. The great stature of this book notwithstanding, *This In Which* is Oppen's landmark book—or if not that then it is at least a rosetta stone allowing us to grasp his entire project. To account for his reading of Heidegger allows for a deep understanding of what Oppen was up to at this point in his career, especially in this volume.

Oppen thought of *This In Which* (1965) as the middle book within a triadic statement[2] made up of *The Materials* (1962) and the later volume, *Of Being Numerous* (1968) (Nicholls 65). Most commentary sees *Of Being Numerous* as Oppen's masterpiece,[3] and the worth of his subsequent poetry has been widely celebrated. Yet the mantle of greatness should go to the prior book, which is emblematic of Oppen's work. It made the later collections possible, insofar as Oppen came to understand what poetry could be. Heidegger was the crucial influence in this evolution—and I think Oppen believed this.

In passing, it's worth noting that Oppen's politics could not have been more diametrically opposed to Heidegger's. At least for a period in his life (when he first read Heidegger's work, during a politically enforced exile from the United States in Mexico), Oppen, a Jew, was what in America would have been called, at that time, a radical leftist,[4] while Heidegger, at least from the moment of Hitler's ascendancy and then throughout World War Two (arguably thereafter), was an unapologetic Nazi.[5] It's possible to understand Oppen as being capable of holding as separate questions of art, poetry, and aesthetics on the one hand, and on the other questions of politics, and one might find some significance in the fact that the period of Oppen's deepest, and most engaged, political activity coincides with his silence as a poet, after having published his first volume, *Discrete Series*, in 1934.

Alfred Kazin once quipped, when asked why he'd written so often about certain American authors who were anti-semites, "If I were to refrain from writing about anti-semitic writers then I would be out of a job as a literary critic" ("Talk"). Needing to be added here is what's now known of Heidegger's life, especially as concerns his participation in the Nazi program, likely was not to Oppen when he began to read Heidegger's writings, and thereafter.[6] In Heidegger, Oppen found a rich working-out of his instinctive ideas, proclivities, and perhaps even vocabulary.

Oppen once proclaimed his life and Heidegger's as being parallel, in a 1969 interview with L.S. Dembo, remarking that "[i]deas like Heidegger's have been important to me for a long time, as early as the first poem in *Discrete Series* [1934]" (169). Oppen suggested that it derives "from Heidegger's Acceptance Speech [i.e., his speech accepting the Chair of Philosophy at Freiburg University] made in 1929, the year I was writing the poem [i.e., the first poem of the collection, which was written in 1929]. [...] So I feel I have a natural sympathy with Heidegger [...]." To be sure, Oppen says that the two men's "statements are identical" ("George Oppen" 169). Since he'd not read Heidegger until much later, Oppen is somewhat mystical about what he sees as their lives' sympathetic trajectories.

And, make no mistake about it, Heidegger was a poet, and a kind of theologian—and his writing *does* comport with Oppen's —Oppen the quintessential poet able to articulate a poetics, mostly implied in his poetry, which understood the world in spiritual terms. Oppen the Objectivist—this is something I find extraordinary—shows us how the empirical, specific and precise (such as was epitomized in *Discrete Series*), invites into his poems the depth and grandeur of the religious. Consider the title poem of *This in Which*, "Psalm," which communicates a sense of astonishment, awe, perhaps a gratitude Heidegger shares:

> Psalm
> *Veritas sequitur . . .*
>
> In the small beauty of the forest
> The wild deer bedding down —
> That they are there!

Their eyes
Effortless, the soft lips
Nuzzle and the alien small teeth
Tear at the grass

The roots of it
Dangle from their mouths
Scattering earth in the strange woods.
They who are there.

Their paths
Nibbled thru the fields, the leaves that shade them
Hang in the distances
Of sun

The small nouns
Crying faith
In this in which the wild deer
Startle, and stare out.
(NCP 99)

Astonishment is not a word that comes up in Oppen's poetry, but the meaning of this word pervades it (cf. Nicholls 68-69). Oppen could easily have encountered it in Heidegger's book *What Is Philosophy*, which Oppen read by 1963 (Nicholls 194-95). In it, philosophy is conceived of as follows. "In astonishment we restrain ourselves (*être en arrêt*). We step back, as it were, from being, from the fact that it is as it is and not otherwise. And astonishment is not used up in this retreating from the Being of being, but, as this retreating and self-restraining, it is at the same time forcibly drawn to and, as it were, held fast by that from which it retreats. Thus astonishment is [a] disposition in which and for which the Being of being unfolds" (85).

What has to be understood is that the way in which Heidegger philosophized, the way in which he *did* philosophy, is not unlike the way in which Oppen *did* poetry. Looking back on his own method, Oppen comments, in that 1969 interview, "I set myself again and again . . . just to record the fact, to saying that I enjoy life very much and defining my feeling by the word 'curious' or, as at the end of [the poem] 'The Narrative' [from *This In Which*], 'joy', joy in the fact that one confronts a thing so large, that one is a part of it. The sense of awe, I suppose [...] ("George Oppen" 172-73; Chilton 102). Quoting this passage, Randolph Chilton (probably the first person critically to link Oppen to Heidegger) writes that "[a]we in the face of the real and a willingness merely to confront the pure, absolute, *inexplicable* sense of realized existence without moving beyond to any philosophical conception of its meaning tie Oppen directly to the Heidegger who pursues [Being]" (102; my emphasis).

Now, what Chilton says is quite right, but it needs some qualification. While Oppen acknowledges mystery in the world, it is not an inexplicability—as if the world should be deciphered; rather, before it, he experiences the sheer sense of wonder, one might even say the impulse to worship (cf. Nicholls 67). He engages the depth of the world's authenticity, and beauty—which take the form of a tension between concealment and disclosure. The marvelous play of this tension installs Oppen as the philosophical poet and Heidegger as the poetic philosopher.

Oppen does not have to confront or explain experience, or for that matter philosophy, specifically the philosophy of *Dasein* or Being; instead, he practices poetry in the Heideggerian sense of that act, not unlike the way in which Heidegger practices philosophy, so that what Heidegger calls *gelassenheit* or *releasement* takes place, a condition explained succinctly in the acceptance speech when Heidegger maintains that "Releasement toward things and openness to the mystery belong together. They grant us the possibility of dwelling in the world in a totally different way. They promise us a new ground and foundation upon which we can stand and endure in the world of technology without being imperiled by it" (*Discourse on Thinking* 55).

Reading this passage, the ultimate lines from *This In Which* spring to mind, in the poem titled "World, World": "The self is no mystery, the mystery is / That there is something for us to stand on. // We want to be here. // The act of being, the act of being / More than oneself" (NCP 159). In *What Is Philosophy* Heidegger says, "When we ask, 'What is philosophy?' then we are speaking about philosophy. By asking in this way we are obviously taking a stand above and, therefore, outside of philosophy. But the aim of our question is to enter *into* philosophy, to tarry in it, to conduct ourselves in a manner, that is, to 'philosophize'. [... .] Philosophy seeks what being is, insofar as it is. Philosophy is *en route* to the Being of being" (21, 55). Heidegger, in other words, wants to stand within philosophy and within being.

If we were to perform a liberal reading of "Psalm," which can be understood as an implicit statement of poetics, we would find what we may need to know about Oppen's comprehension and practice. I take it as a poem about poetry, or at least about Oppen's poetry, and I think it's the central text in his *oeuvre*. That the poem is an act of worship of the natural world is significant. It's no accident that the first poem in *This In Which*, titled "Technologies," follows immediately upon the book's opening epigraphs— the last one of which is from Heidegger, who writes of "the arduous path of appearance." Oppen ends the poem with the cleverly sweet epithet "Twig technologies"—

> From a hawk's
> Nest as they say
> The nest of such a bird
>
> Must be, and continue
> Therefore to talk about
> Twig technologies"
> (NCP 94)

—as if the world could be united in its natural impulse that incorporates humanity's drive toward technological knowledge containing the idea that humanity imposes its will upon the environment. The epigraph comes from *An Introduction to Metaphysics* (a book Oppen read carefully) where Heidegger explains the phrase as meaning "to take upon oneself being-there as a de-cision between being, nonbeing, and appearance" (113; Nicholls 64). In this book, and elsewhere too, Heidegger draws a basic distinction between the shaped world and the world simply before us, and thereby between knowledge and Knowledge. In the opening of his late essay "The Thing," which Oppen owned (Nicholls 182, 190-93), Heidegger talks about how technologies (he mentions the radio, time-lapse photography in film, and jet planes) have collapsed all distances, and yet humankind may be further from the possibility of living life genuinely. "Man puts the longest distances behind him in the shortest time," Heidegger notes.

> He puts the greatest distances behind himself and thus puts everything before himself at the shortest range.

> Yet the frantic abolition of all distances brings no nearness; for nearness does not consist in shortness of distance. (165)

Making reference to the atomic bomb, Heidegger then asks, "[i]s not this merging of everything into the distanceless more unearthly than everything bursting apart?" (166). It's as if, for Heidegger, there might no longer be the possibility of dimension. In his essay "The Origin of the Work of Art" (which was bound with "The Thing") there is a clear distinction being made between a piece of "equipment" (i.e., a tool) and a "work" of art, the former determined by a sense of usefulness, the latter free of such a restriction (29, 39-40, 46) and holding the promise of a world of dimensions and thus the fullness of being.

In his introduction to Heidegger's book *Existence and Being* (which Oppen had to have read [cf. Nicholls 194]), Werner Brock summarizes, while analyzing Heidegger's 1927 book *Being and Time*. He explains how "Heidegger realized that 'Dasein' [...] differed ontologically from all the things which are not 'Dasein' in essential respects. These things, when they are there by nature, are termed 'vorhanden' ('existent' in the usual sense of the word, literally: before one's hand, at hand, present); and when they are made by men, such as utensils, they are termed 'zuhanden' close at hand, in readiness, at one's disposal) [...]" (14).[7] The essence of the ancient Greek term *technē*, which could signify technology, craft or art, resides within the image of the tool in the hand, or basically the environment being shaped by the human hand, and Heidegger acknowledges this fact in a number of his works, thereby joining tool and artwork.[8]

Here we confront the problem of technology for Heidegger, which can be seen as emblematic of our larger sense of alienation, even if out of necessity, from the world in which we live. In a poem like "Psalm" Oppen seeks to restore a sense of nearness in the world. The poem's scene is one in which there is no technological intervention. The natural world is "vorhanden" (before one's hand), which is made possible by the sponsorship of Being or *Dasein*, and disclosed to the poem's speaker by his ability to suspend his will, to refrain from turning the scene in his mind into a technological artifact, into a perception that is "zuhanden" (in readiness, such as a tool), as if the deer, leaves, and sun detailed in the poem might exist for some purpose.

For all their analytical prowess, however, Heidegger's works are inconclusive as they actively search for nearness and being. One way to translate Heidegger's basic term *Dasein* is as "there-being." And it is this sense of the world before us, the world "there," in which we are capable of investing "faith"—a key word in "Psalm"—that poetry inherits, for

Oppen, its basic gesture or impulse. Paul Naylor has noted that Oppen's *modus operandi* in *Of Being Numerous* is the deictic pronoun (100-01 ff.). The world is *there* before one (cf. Nicholls 74). I would add that Oppen and Heidegger depend on tautological thinking, literally the contemplation of what is self-evident, and so for Oppen the things within the realized world become supremely relevant.

Oppen tells Dembo, "I'm really concerned with the substantive, with the subject of the sentence, with what we are talking about, and not rushing over the subject-matter in order to make a comment about it. It is still the principle with me, of more than poetry, to notice, to state, to lay down the substantive for its own sake" ("George Oppen" 161). When Dembo asks Oppen about "Psalm"— quoting lines that end with the exclamation "That they are there!"—Dembo is suggesting that the poem's persona is not responding to the manifest world "intellectually or discursively, but only to the physical tangibility or reality of the object he views" (162).

Oppen replies with an important and subtle distinction: "Yes, if one knows what 'physical' means or what it contrasts with. But responds by faith, as I admitted somewhere, and to his own experience" (162). And when Dembo asks him, "What exactly is the faith?" Oppen says, "Well, that the nouns do refer to something; that it's there, that it's true, the whole implication of these nouns; that appearances represent reality, whether or not they misrepresent it: that this in which the thing takes place, this thing is here, and that these things do take place" (163).[9] Oppen is not being coy when he highlights the notion of physicality.

The concept of the Greek term *physis* is taken up at length by Heidegger in *Introduction to Metaphysics*. Oppen's copy of this book contains the handwritten note "'This in which' all truth is contained—the universe contains all truth — [*illegible*]" (in Nicholls 64). *Introduction to Metaphysics* begins with the most fundamental philosophical question: "Why are there essents [i.e., 'existents, things that are'] rather than nothing?" (1). As Oppen must have been well aware, the term *physis* for Heidegger comprehended much more than it does now in our normal parlance: For the ancient Greeks, Heidegger writes, "the essent was called *physics*" (13). Yet, Heidegger continues, "The realm of being as such and as a whole is *physis* — i.e. its essence and character are defined as that which emerges and endures" (16). Ultimately *physis* "signifies the being of the essent" (17).

Heidegger then equates *physis* with the idea of *shining light* and by implication *appearance*. Following his discussion of *physis* in *Introduction to Metaphysics*, Heidegger equates *being* and *appearing*: "for the Greeks standing-in-itself was nothing other than standing-there, standing-in-the-light. Being means appearing. Appearing is not something subsequent that sometimes happens to being. Appearing is the very essence of being" (101).

Heidegger then returns to this question of *physis* when he argues that

> [t]he essence of being is *physis*. Appearing is the power that emerges. Appearing makes manifest. Already we know then that being, appearing,

causes to emerge from concealment. Since the
essent as such *is*, it places itself in and stands
in *unconcealment, alētheia*. We translate, and
at the same time thoughtlessly misinterpret,
this word as 'truth'. [... .] For the Greek
essence of truth is possible only in one with
the Greek essence of being as *physis*. On the
strength of the unique and essential relationship
between *physis* and *alētheia* the Greeks would have
said: The essent is true insofar as it is. (102)[10]

Likewise in "Psalm." And, in a reprise of this poem
published in 1978, titled "If It All Went Up in Smoke,"
light serves a key dramatic function. It is the light that
allows the poem's persona to realize the "beauty" of the
deer, leaves, and so on:

If It All Went Up in Smoke

that smoke
would remain

the forever
savage country poem's light borrowed

light of the landscape and one's footprints praise

from distance
in the close
crowd all

that is strange the sources

the wells the poem begins

neither in word
nor meaning but the small
selves haunting

us in stones and is less

always than that help me I am
of that people the grass

blades touch

and touch in their small

distances the poem
begins[.]
(NCP 274)

Heidegger sets out for Oppen the basis for an Objectivist poetry that presumes the physical world, that which the poet details, is anything but inert. Hence the tension, in Oppen's poetry, between concealment and disclosure is palpable.

Both Heidegger and Oppen left behind them their respective testaments of their strivings in writing to be authentic and to invoke a world of authenticity. In this sense, neither body of work explains anything. Rather, in their respective works, they imagine a redolent world, one that coalesces, gathering itself in a fulfillment. It is art, poetry, that makes this possible. Their writings are aware of themselves as such. In a letter to a student, which is appended to his essay "The Thing," Heidegger writes as follows. "In thinking of Being, it is never the case that only something actual is represented in our minds and then given out as that which alone is true. To think 'Being' means: to respond to the appeal of its presencing. The response stems from the appeal and releases itself toward that appeal" (183).

Notes

1. Peter Nicholls reports that "Oppen told Charles Tomlinson that he 'was startled on encountering Heidegger some time ago, 1950' (UCSD [Oppen Papers at the University of California San Diego] 16, 34, 4) and whether or not this date is precise we might conclude that he had read the first of Heidegger's volumes to be translated, *Existence and Being* (1949), at some point during the Mexico years" (30). A number of works cover George and Mary Oppen's sojourn in Mexico, not least among them Nicholls' recent book (20-29).

2. Nicholls cites "Conversation with George Oppen," conducted by Amirkhanian and Gitlin, 24.

3. Henry Weinfield, in his new book *The Music of Thought in the Poetry of George Oppen and William Bronk*, is the latest critic to do so, though he uses the term "masterpiece" to refer specifically to the volume's title poem "Of Being Numerous" (6).

4. A recent, well documented article by Eric Hoffman makes the question of Oppen's participation in espionage activities in behalf of the Soviet Union plausible (see Works Cited).

5. Cf. Anthony Stephens' quite unflattering portrait of Heidegger as the good Nazi and Stephens' speculation as concerns Heidegger's efforts to reconcile his philosophy with the received Nazi dogma, which includes, among other things, strikingly, a reproduction of an address by Heidegger to students (inserted in par. 2), in which

he advances the Nazi agenda in 1933, thus speaking of "the present and future German reality and law" (trans. Stephens; see citation in Works Cited). But of course there are a number of publications about and lots of documentation of Heidegger's extreme right-wing politics.

6. Cf. among many sources Alex Steiner (see Works Cited) who reports that Heidegger never really made public his Nazi past or attempted to repudiate it and who speaks of a general "myopia" among intellectuals until recent times about Heidegger's Nazism. The breakthrough book on Heidegger's Nazi past, Victor Farias' *Heidegger and Nazism*, appeared in 1989, five years after Oppen's death.

7. Consider in this context Heidegger's grouping of *equipment* and the *work of art* as having "an affinity [...] insofar as it [i.e., the artwork] is something produced by the human hand" ("The Origin of the Work of Art" 29). All the same, the artwork possesses a "self-sufficient presence" (29).

8. For example in the definitive essay "The Question Concerning Technology" Heidegger writes that "[w]e must observe two things with respect to the meaning of this word [i.e., *technē*]. One is that *technē* is the name not only for the activities and skills of the craftsman, but also for the arts of the mind and the fine arts" (12-13).

9. As Nicholls writes, Oppen had a "fondness," for instance in a poem like "'Psalm', [...] for the 'small nouns' [NCP 99], which seem to register a simple 'faith' in the world's existence rather than a desire to act upon it in any

way. Here [...] Oppen is close to Heidegger who saw it as the essential task of the philosopher to 'preserve the *force of the most elemental words* in which Dasein expresses itself'" (Nicholls 65; Heidegger *Being and Time* 262, emphases in the original).

10. Cf., in "The Origin of the Work of Art," The word *technē* denotes [...] a mode of knowing. To know means to have seen, in the widest sense of seeing, which means to apprehend what is present, as such. For Greek thought the nature of knowing consists in *aletheia*, that is, in the uncovering of beings. It supports and guides all comportment toward beings. *Technē*, as knowledge experienced in the Greek manner, is a bringing forth of beings *out* of concealedness and specifically *into* the unconcealedness of their appearance; *Technē* never signifies the action of making" (59). In his later essay "Building Dwelling Thinking" Heidegger explains that "[t]he Greek for 'to bring forth or to produce' is *tikto*. The word *technē*, technique, belongs to the verb's root *tec*. To the Greeks *technē* means neither art nor handicraft but rather: to make something appear, within what is present, as this or that, in this way or that way. The Greeks conceive of *technē*, producing, in terms of letting appear" (159).

Works Cited

Brock, Werner. "Introduction." Martin Heidegger. *Existence and Being*. Chicago: Henry Regnery, 1949.

Chilton, Randolph. "The Place of Being in the Poetry of George Oppen." *George Oppen: Man and Poet*. Ed. Burton Hatlen. Orono, ME: National Poetry Foundation, 1981. 89-112.

Farias, Victor. *Heidegger and Nazism*. Eds. and For. Joseph Margolis and Tom Rockmore. Trs. Paul Burrell and Dominic Di Bernardi, and Gabriel R. Ricci. Philadelphia, PA: Temple University Press, 1989.

Heidegger, Martin. *Being and Time*. Trs. John Macquarrie and Edward Robinson. Oxford, UK: Blackwell, 1962.

_____ . "Building Dwelling Thinking." *Poetry, Language, Thought*. Intr. and Tr. Albert Hofstadter. New York: Harper & Row, 1971. 143-62.

_____ .*Discourse on Thinking* [a Translation of *Gelassehheit*]. Trs. John M. Anderson and E. Hans Freund. Intr. John M. Anderson. New York: Harper & Row, 1966.

_____ . *Existence and Being*. Chicago: Henry Regnery, 1949.

_____ . *An Introduction to Metaphysics*. Tr. Ralph Manheim. New Haven, Yale UP, 1959.

_____ . "The Origin of the Work of Art." *Poetry, Language, Thought*. Intr. and Tr. Albert Hofstadter. New York: Harper & Row, 1971. 15-88.

_____ . "The Question Concerning Technology." *The Question Concerning Technology and Other Essays*.

Intr. and Tr. William Lovitt. New York: Harper & Row, 1977. 3-35.

———. "The Thing," *Poetry, Language, Thought*. Intr. and Tr. Albert Hofstadter. New York: Harper & Row, 1971. 163-86.

———. *What Is Philosophy?* Trs. and Intr. Jean T. Wilde and William Kluback. New York: Rowman and Littlefield, 1956.

Hoffman, Eric. "A Poetry of Action: George Oppen and Communism." *American Communist History* 6.1 (June 2007): 1-28.

Kazin, Alred. "Talk at the Graduate Center, City University of New York." New York City. October 1986.

Naylor, Paul. "The Pre-Position 'Of': Being, Seeing and Knowing in George Oppen's Poetry." *Contemporary Literature* 32.1 (1991): 100-15.

Nicholls, Peter. *George Oppen and the Fate of Modernism*. Oxford, UK: Oxford UP, 2007.

Oppen, George. "A Conversation with George Oppen [conducted by Charles Amirkhanian and David Gitlin]." *Ironwood* 5 (1975): 21-24.

———. *Discrete Series*. Intr. Ezra Pound. New York: Objectivist P, 1934.

———. "George Oppen [Interiew with George Oppen conducted by L. S. Dembo on 25 April 1968]" in "The 'Objectivist' Poet: Four Interviews." *Contemporary Literature* 10 (1969): 159-77.

———. "If It All Went Up in Smoke." *Primitive*. Santa Barbara: Black Sparrow P, 1978. *New Collected*

Poems. Ed. Michael Davidson. Pref. Eliot Weinberger. New York: New Directions, 2002. 274.

_____ . *The Materials*. New York: New Directions, 1962.

_____ . *New Collected Poems*. Ed. Michael Davidson. Pref. Eliot Weinberger. New York: New Directions, 2002.

_____ . *Of Being Numerous*. New York: New Directions, 1968.

_____ . *This in Which*. New York: New Directions, 1965.

Steiner, Alex. "The Case of Martin Heidegger, Philosopher and Nazi." (3 April 2000). World Socialist Website. 19 March 2009.

Stephens, Anthony. "Cutting Poets to Size — Heidegger, Hölderlin, Rilke." *Jacket* 32 (April 2007). Accessed 19 March 2009.

Weinfield, Henry. *The Music of Thought in the Poetry of George Oppen and William Bronk*. Iowa City: U of Iowa P, 2009.

PRAGUE AND MEMORY

Part I

Palác Lucerna

You enter the Lantern Palace from either of two streets. The entrances are about fifty paces from Wenceslas Square. Vodičkova and Štěpánská, the two streets, traverse the square at its midpoint. The Lantern Palace (Palác Lucerna), in its art nouveau design and softly glowing interiors, recalls the past. Now it's surrounded by the bustle of commerce.

Prague's burghers must have gotten the idea to imbue the open stretch of land that became Wenceslas Square with beauty and dignity. The "square" is actually a long rectangle, which had been the city's horse market. Horses could be ridden up its length, as a kind of test drive, before they were purchased. Now the majestic *Národní Muzeum* (The National Museum) rises across an avenue at one end. At the other end of the square there's a glitzy shopping promenade. But if you stroll just a block further you'll reach Rytířská where there's an array of theaters, an opera house, a cathedral, a huge tower and gate, among other architectural works that are now considered historical treasures.

In the center of Prague, an old-world of "culture" swaddles a new world of hypercapitalism that, in its dazzling way, draws shoppers, drinkers and diners seven days a week without let-up. Wenceslas Square is also filled with large department stores, some smaller shops, a hotel or two, with restaurants and cafés strung along walkways on either side of a long grassy island. It's interrupted by cars and trams crossing through.

The Lantern Palace, whose aesthetics evoke a period preceding the present-day commercial buzz on the square and its surrounding area, nevertheless was Prague's first multi-purpose arcade; in this sense it looks ahead to the modern city. The beautiful Lucerna's sheer existence holds time in suspension, juxtaposing the hallowed and throwaway. Its arcade is a place of golden light and calm. Not unlike the larger Wenceslas Square of which in effect it's a part, the Lantern Palace is bound by busy thoroughfares.

The arcade's two portals invite in a perpetual crowd of shoppers and tourists, especially from Vodičkova where trams stop one after the other. People climb on or step off to disappear into the throng. They flood the entire street and its corner on the square where some of them gather at a café, whose chairs and tables spill out nearly to the curb. The greater crowd on the square absorbs them.

* * * *

If you exit the Lucerna onto the other side street, Štěpánská, you'll be a block closer to the statue of St. Wenceslas, the patron saint of Bohemia, which was put up at the end of the square bordered by Wilsonova (named after Woodrow Wilson.) Across the avenue there's the sprawling National Museum. Wenceslas was a tenth-century duke. He sits triumphantly on his horse, rider and horse facing the length of the square (their backs to the museum). He's dressed in armor; an unfurled banner's attached to the point of his upraised lance.

The statue's the square's major landmark. People on dates rendezvous there—"under the horse's tail," as they say. Before the likeness of Bohemia's patron saint, people also gather for organized protest—public dissent. Diane and I were there for a large protest against the newly reelected Czech leadership, in January 2018, and later that winter for a much smaller protest against NATO. There were lots of speeches, signs and some music, in both protests.

In the minds of the people of Prague, the Square is the closest this city truly has to a town center. There's also *Náměstí Republiky* (The Square of the Republic), a more handsome shopping mecca. And there's the famous, and more beautiful, Old Town Square with its immense statue of Jan Hus and nearby its six-hundred-year-old astronomical clock high above the crowd, in its tower. Tourists always go there. But Wenceslas Square—now, really, a wide mall —is taken as the place where political struggle is to be performed.

The ornate Lucerna—its atrium of delicately articulated glass panels and metalwork, its marble floors and arches, its sweeping stairway—is more the hidden gem. Even so, its presence—while unnoticed by some people, situated as it is off the square—can be subtly felt when walking by. People may first wander into it, then remember to return. It includes a theater, a concert hall, high-end retail shops, restaurants and cafés, as well as a cinema.

The lantern is the architectural motif throughout. The light in the kino, before the film begins, is golden. People enter the kino by way of an upstairs *kavárna* (café). It, too, is bathed in a golden light. This glow is the light of the past, a light imagined in the Lucerna's creation during the last days, after centuries, of Austro-Hungarian rule.

The Kavárna Lucerna is both sumptuous and elegant. On one side of its teardrop bar you find the entrance to the kino. You enter the Kino Lucerna from the café, walking up some stairs into a softly lit theater with plush seats. When the movie ends, everyone stays in their seats until all the credits have been shown. This seems less a formality than the custom. After the film, the café fills with people who drink and talk into the night.

Newly arrived in the depths of a Prague winter, Diane and I settled into the café for some coffee and smoked fish. We happened upon its entrance, which was hidden behind heavy curtains at the top of a grand stairway ascending from the arcade below. It was hard to know what, exactly, to make of a sculpture we couldn't help but gawk at, on the way up those stairs.

The sculpture was of a large horse hanging

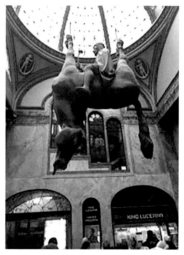

David Černý, "Saint Wenceslas" (1999)

upside-down from a high ceiling. An armored rider was sitting astride its belly. The horse's protruding tongue, and its tail, were pointing downward. Once seated at our table, we considered rider and horse at eye-level, through our picture window.

The Havels

From a balcony, in 1989, Václav Havel addressed the aspirations of a hundred thousand Czechs who, at risk to themselves, had gathered below. This was a heady moment in the Velvet Revolution. It was late November. Before the year was out, Havel would become the first President of modern Czechoslovakia, by dint of a popular vote. The Czechs were free once again, but this was fifty years since the Nazis had paraded the length of the Square to dramatize their vanquishing of the Czechs.

The streets where you enter the Lucerna run into the square near that balcony. The Palace's old-world, softly glowing interiors were the invention of Havel's grandfather, Vácslav. He began work on it in 1907, completing it in 1921. Conceived in the last years of Austro-Hungarian Imperial rule, after three centuries of Czech subjugation, *Palác Lucerna* came into being at the dawn of Czechoslovakia's "First Republic" that was inaugurated in 1918.

The First Republic was a vibrant, democratic society. It lasted two decades. It had been authorized by the League of Nations after the Great War. The Lucerna's design reflects these two periods. It would later come to stand in contradistinction to the drab contours of Communist life, following the Nazis' defeat and, following the

Velvet Revolution, the glitzy capitalism of present-day Prague.

The Havel family was wealthy. It was also integral to the community of Prague's intellectuals and artists. When the Czech Communists officially took power in 1948, the Havels were divested of all their property. The grandson Ivan, Václav's brother and a writer, was allowed to live in an upper-floor apartment of a building also built by Vácslav, which overlooks the Vltava River and its promenade. The building had been appropriated along with the rest of the Havels' possessions. The Lucerna's now managed by Ivan's widow.

As a child, Václav was not allowed to attend school since he, too, was a member of the bourgeoisie. He grew up to be a famous playwright. He'd discover the theater during his time in the army. At home his upbringing may have predisposed him not only toward the theater but, in a way, toward the inherent drama of political dissent. He came to prominence as part of Charter 77, which was a group of free-thinking artists, musicians and writers who ran afoul of the government's social strictures. It was named after a document the group had put together in January 1977, meant to call out the government's failure to adhere to its constitutional duties and to agreements it had made internationally, with respect to implementing and safeguarding human rights protections.

Havel's is a theater of the absurd. His plays, as well as his samizdat essays, which were surreptitiously and eagerly shared by readers during the forty years of totalitarianism after the war, are highly critical of Czech Communist society. There were several stints in prison in store for Havel and these other people who made up the dissident group. The harsh treatment may also have prepared him for his particular role in bringing about the Communists' downfall.

Václav's uncle Miloš is also a part of this story. Almost single-handedly, Miloš Havel created the Czech film industry after the First World War. As the Nazis marched onto Wenceslas Square, in 1939, the Lucerna was being taken over for their future planning meetings. They also forced Miloš to relinquish his holdings in the movie studios he'd established. They let him continue to run them, though; and after the war the Communists tried him for collaboration. He was acquitted but banned from the movie industry, the one he'd created. His second attempt to get out of the country was successful, and his life came to an end in Munich.

* * * *

Thirty years after Nazi tanks and troops filled Wenceslas Square in their bravura show of dominance over the Czechs, it was occupied once again by foreigners. This time the tanks belonged to the Warsaw Pact armies, led by the Soviets. They simply showed up one morning, to the Czechs' complete surprise. They meant to put an end to the Czechs' notion of "Socialism with a human face." The Soviets feared that Czechoslovakia was spinning out of their control, which may very well have been the case, albeit the Czechs themselves may not have fully realized what the reforms they were initiating would mean.

Plaques now to be seen on the square, surrounded by candles and flowers on any given day, remember Jan Palach and Jan Zajíc, two high school boys who, on separate occasions during the occupation, set themselves aflame, burning to death there on the square, as a public protest. The plaques can be found on the grassy middle island. They're quite close to the balcony where Havel, the grandson, would rouse a massive crowd to action. The revolution broke out two decades after the Prague Spring of 1968. In snapshots of Havel giving that speech, which were taken from over his shoulder, the vast throng on the Square below has filled every bit of ground. The center island of grass had been designed by the Communists to hinder large crowds from assembling as one.

The nearby Lucerna, on the winter afternoon Diane and I first discovered it, was hosting an exhibit of photos showing invasions of cities behind the Iron Curtain. We noticed them on our way out. The pictures were arrayed along the café's walls. Fabulous and disturbing, at times quietly tragic, they were quintessential scenes of Soviet armed interventions. Appropriately edgy, understated captions informed viewers about which satellite country was being invaded and when. Incongruously large tanks rolled onto plazas or squatted in small streets. Some pictures showed heads and shoulders of leather-helmeted soldiers who peered around them from their portholes in the tanks' armor. They seemed a bit bewildered, as they eyed civilians on foot who might, obliquely, dare to eye them back.

Weeks later we returned to the Lucerna. The photos were gone. A whole new display had been mounted. It was a collection of movie posters.

* * * *

There are many theaters in Prague. Their architecture varies from baroque opulence to a modern, all-sleek-lines sharpness that's very much the Czech condition today and reveals something of the Czech wit, its edge. The differences, old and new, reflect Czech eras, political and economic conditions. Prague, most of all, is in the midst of vivid change.

The image of Václav Havel—how he's remembered in the present, or by some young adults forgotten—is indicative of this change. When Havel's treated with humor, perhaps irreverently, there's also an underlying respect. In the dénouement of a recent broadly satiric Czech film we saw that winter, a number of people end up running around Prague, the film having turned madcap; they're all wearing masks—in Havel's likeness. His presence is the air people breathe, so he can be taken for granted.

Everyone on our side of the pond knows Havel as the playwright who was a principal in the Velvet Revolution. Some of us may also know he was part of Charter 77 and associated with the psychedelic musical group The Plastic People of the Universe. He's remembered as having been the Czech President, of course. Highly revered across Czech society by many, Havel's a great deal more so in Prague—including by many younger people. I imagine the stories about world leaders having to make the two-hour trek to his country cottage in Hrádeček (where he felt most at home) is a source of Czech pride.

He wasn't especially equipped to lead a country. He brought hardship to many, lacking understanding of economics, for instance, possibly due to being manipulated by Václav Klaus, his Prime Minister. Yet he was no doubt a great statesman and is widely acknowledged as that. Sometimes he's adored.

A number of the younger generation, however, such as some students from blue-collar families, who are not enrolled in an elite university, don't pay as much attention—not only to his memory but also to politics. These kids are separating themselves from the Havel mythos. They're more fatalistic. If asked to compare Havel with the present Czech Republic's demagogic leaders, these students shrug. No matter what, they say, they'll simply "endure"—for them it doesn't much matter who's in power. Some of them complain about the Prague airport being named for him.

Yet Havel is viewed more than ever in popular culture as the great hero. We attended a musical, *Velvet Havel*, which was performed in one of the newer, sleek theatres. As a musical, and simply as pure theater, it was wonderfully raucous—an unvarnished and absurdist retrospective on him, done in a theatrics he'd have loved.

After the performance we met Miloš Orson Štědroň, who wrote the musical's score and libretto. His wife joined us for drinks. She was singing the following week in two satirical productions of unfinished comic operas by Shostakovich. He'd hidden the manuscripts of these two operas in the back of a closet where his housekeeper discovered them after his death. They'd been staged only twice before.

We attended those performances too. They were surrealist and viciously anti-Stalin, and seemed forerunners, in their satirical verve, of Štědroň's *Velvet Havel* that, nonetheless, treated the Czech leader with affection.

Štědroň cited Ionesco and Beckett as having been formative for him, when I asked about the roots of his dramaturgy. Thinking some more, he added that Jaroslav Hašek's subversive, comically bitter, anti-war novel, *The Good Soldier Schweik*, was the start of it all for him. The book's illustrations by Josef Lada are on permanent display at the Prague National Gallery.

* * * *

Absurdism and subversion are endemic here. They make up the fabric of Czech life at a signal moment in Czech cultural-political history. They merge to become a third, exquisitely sharp, subtle, element in the Czech psyche: hilarity. It threatens the release of chaos into the Bohemian bloodstream.

Shortly before Miloš Zeman was first elected President (to the dismay of a great many), David Černý sculpted a huge, bright purple hand, with its extremely long middle finger sticking straight up, and placed it on a barge he anchored in the Vltava River, just below Prague Castle. This outrageous work of public art set off a political scandal. It was also a sheer thrill. The aesthetics of the sculpture met with wide approval.

Černý knows how to play the role of provocateur (but that's not all his work's about). For reasons I can't fathom, he was the artist representing the Czech Republic in Brussels, when the President was to serve

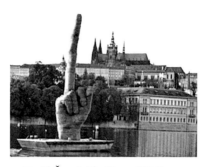

David Černý, *The Finger* (2013)

his six-month term as head of the EU. Černý created *Entropa*—a colorful, huge, and amorphous installation—a most geographically inaccurate map of Europe. Every country is represented by satiric, sometimes bawdy, iconography.

The Italian portion of the " map" is made up of soccer players, each masturbating with a soccer ball. The Belgian portion consists of half-eaten chocolates in the shape of waffles. Luxembourg is depicted as a piece of gold with a "For Sale" sign. Nowadays, *Entropa* is on display at Techmania, a science and technology museum in Pilsen, maybe to keep it where no one will find it.

Černý's sculptures transform buildings and plazas, streetscapes, or an indoor space like the arcade of the Lucerna. One favorite of strollers in Prague is *Man Hanging Out*—a seven foot-high sculpture of Freud. (Freud was born in Moravia. Einstein, Kepler, Brahe and Copernicus all spent time in Prague. Kafka was a Prague native.) *Man Hanging Out* has Freud dressed in a suit. He's holding onto a pole that juts out from a building four stories above the

347

street (reminiscent of Hitchcock films like *Vertigo* and *Spellbound*). His other arm's at his side, the hand tucked in his pants pocket. He's simply holding on. In another part of town there's a figure also poised above a street (by some other artist). It's a sculpture of a young woman with a parasol, which hangs from a wire between two buildings.

Černý's huge, brass, naked crawling babies populate the park in front of the Museum Kampa (which features Modernist artists banned by the Communists). The babies' bodies are fleshy but their faces are machine-like (not quite

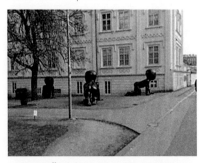

David Černý, *Brown-nosers* (2003)

resembling a Lego construction). They'd first been affixed along the vertical struts of Prague's Žižkov Television Tower, crawling toward the pinnacle. The needle sticking into the sky is visible from all points.

* * * *

Another internationally known Czech artist, Daniel Pešta, represented the Czech Republic at the Venice Biennale on three occasions. He's a conceptualist. He started out as a painter but now works in many modes and mediums. He returns again and again to two objects; red string, meant to evoke blood, genetic coding, fatalism, and endlessness; and the mask that in itself says a lot about Czech history and culture, and about Pešta's life.

348

He was born in 1959. Under Communism he laid low, making graphic art on consignment. By the later eighties, however, he'd sensed something like what became the Velvet Revolution was imminent (like Havel he became involved with rock groups). In 1998, he made his first trip to New York, where he saw the possibilities of working in multimedia and turned to conceptual art.

In his 1978 essay "The Power of the Powerless," Havel talked about the Czechs' daily "acts of acquiescence," which led to "spiritual suffocation" in life under Communism. Czech society was "permeated with hypocrisy and lies." A mask can signify this duplicity, can

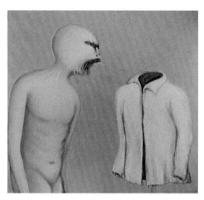

Daniel Pešta, *Scream III* (2015-2016), acrylic on canvas

stand for covering up, and a lot more. *Separation (Triptych)*, a Pešta installation that was shown at the DOX Centre for

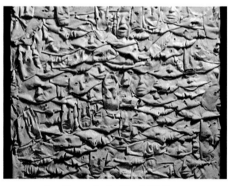

Acrylic masks by Daniel Pešta

Contemporary Art, in our Prague neighborhood, is made of masks compressed into three large rubber cubes, each in a different pastel color.

They're a chilling vision of anonymous, now lifeless, faces. In a review, then, I wrote in *Hyperallergic* that his "greatness derive[d] from his synthesis of empathy and formal concerns, organized in order to interrogate hypocrisy." Whatever Pešta does is intent on pushing the conversation out of complacency, so that Czech society may realize itself once again, post 1989.

Emerging from the Darkness

Everyone in the Lucerna Café was our age, the first time we were there. That was in the afternoon. We returned to see a film one evening. There was a much younger crowd. Prague's younger generation is fundamentally different from both its parents' and grandparents'. Prague's young Czechs are engaging, open, friendly, tending to be optimistic. Their grandparents long for the good old days. This much could be said about grandparents and grandchildren anywhere. The Czech parents, though, are unusual. They continue to feel the pain of deprivation, having come of age under communism.

Czechs don't see things like Westerners, even in Prague. Lives were distorted by their government. An impersonal bureaucracy forced adolescents to study metallurgy, for example, when what they wanted was to study philosophy or history. There are remnants of that bureaucracy. During the Communist years, a friend of ours was sent to Leningrad to earn a doctorate in Russian literature. Because she'd left the country, she was placed on a list that still prevents her from getting work. She's not been able to get her name removed. The parents of today's young Czechs struggled through their training, abhorring it.

After the Revolution, lives had to be restarted. Czechoslovakian Communism pictured itself as dreamy, high minded. The belief was that a new day had dawned. People would be happy in their work and life. This idealized life was depicted in the public art then. A huge bust of a stolid-looking Stalin was erected on a high point in the city, in a park whose rampart overlooks the Vltava River. (Having sculpted the Stalin head, its artist committed suicide before it was unveiled.) Shortly after it appeared, Stalin was denounced by Kruschev. Eventually a metronome, equally huge, took the bust's place. It's still there.

Living under Czech Communism, there were obvious incongruities. Someone told us of the dismay she felt as a child when first visiting her playmate's apartment. It was exactly the same as hers, the furniture included. The government's experiments with community sometimes meant kids grew up in a housing complex far from where their parents worked. People in the housing complex ate in a communal dining room, instead of a family cooking and eating at home. After the Velvet Revolution, Communist housing, the prefabicrated *panelacky* rushed into production to cope with a housing shortage, would be modified with various colors of paint, balconies and other additions, in attempts to create difference.

Prague remained gray and dingy for most of the Havel presidency. The glaring exception in its first decade was

The Dancing House—designed in 1992, finished four years later, an influence on the city's physical and cultural renewal that truly was underway after the millennium. Now the colorful city is bursting with vitality as well as idiosyncrasy. New buildings, constructed in the last years, are wildly innovative —a strong counterpoint to the old, yet deeply beautiful, classic constructions with their spires, delicate stonework and statuary, which preceded Communism. Some statues still stand from the Communist era; the difference is striking. The new buildings are swervy, jazzy, a bit kooky—joyfully so.

Part II

To Forget

We're sitting around the table in our friends' backyard, in a small town near Pardubice University where they teach (it's an hour's train ride from Prague). Over lunch, our talk drifts into the uncertain moment. Our friends are Czech citizens. She's from this part of Bohemia. Her husband's half Silesian, half Slovak. Czechoslovakia dissolved well over two decades ago, in an amicable divorce, Slovakia now a nation of its own. Our friends were students then. They both had Fulbright fellowships taking them, at different times, to different parts of America.

The present Czech Republic's led by two demagogues— Zeman the President, and Andrej Babiš, his Prime Minister. Diane and I are old enough to remember violence and turmoil in our youths—bombings, civilians shot dead by our own soldiers. Now we see firsthand what it's like to have an American President who, like Zeman and Babiš, is a demagogue.

In Prague, political demonstrations usually start on Wenceslas Square, below the statue. People then make their way across the Charles Bridge to the monumental Prague Castle. The largest ancient castle in the world, it was begun in 870. President Zeman is commonly referred to as "the Castle." Babiš, the Prime Minister, in the depth of his corruption, is more like Trump (except that Zeman is the coarser of the two Czech politicians). Babiš is a businessman and thief who's referred to as "the Government."

The two of them were narrowly reinstated in office by popular vote (but they've not won parliamentary consent so the nation looks away). The election was a shock to many, our friends included.

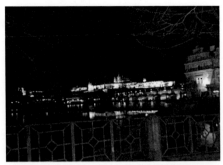

Prague Castle across the Vltava River

Older voters, remembering Communism with some fondness, helped to put these two Putin-adorers over the top. The Czechs are as bitterly divided here as we are in America.

Diane presses this fact upon our hosts, over our lovely outdoor lunch, emphasizing that the present moment is crucial, when a coalition of liberal democracies must hold together. This is especially so as the US and UK are obsessively self-involved, fixated inward. Both nations are caught up in follies they've created for themselves, crippled by them. They seem to be acting as if on cue, in trying to emulate "illiberal democracies" (Victor Orban's coinage). The tensions in the EU are palpable.

So we're puzzled by our friends' vehement objections. Along with other Czechs, they feel frustrated by the German behemoth. Germany draws off their excess wealth, Czechs complain. Still, Diane and I are struck by how bitterly our friends talk about, of all people, Emmanuel Macron. It's in the news that he's just called the Czechs "traitors" (referring to the recent Czech election). But is *traitor* a mistranslation into Czech, or at lunch into English?

354

I point out the greater need for solidarity with someone like Macron, who'll hold steady in the coalition against Putin. Our friends' resentment, however, which derives from the near chaos in the daily news, has to do with France's role in crafting the Munich Agreement. *Huh? What was that? What did she say!? The Munich Agreement? Wasn't that eighty years ago?*

Great Britain, Italy, and France, three of the four signatories to the Munich Pact, sold out the Czechs in 1938, trying to appease Germany. Of course, between then and now, the worst conflagration humanity has ever known has taken place. And in Bohemia, Moravia and Slovakia there's been one, then another foreign occupation. In Europe, it's all about history. In Europe, one is always confronted by the past—an ancient castle, a world war cemetery, a death camp.

* * * *

Prague Castle was begun to be built well over a thousand years ago. Charles University, named after the great Bohemian king, was founded two and a half centuries before Jamestown was settled in what's now Virginia. Prague's ancient history has its own magnetism. It co-exists with what may be a willful lack of attention to the complexities of Czech history, especially since the demise of the First Republic with the Nazis' takeover, a fact we've found striking, given the outsized changes in Czech lives over this span of time. The past is not a fading specter here, a disappearance into the mists of time.

If there's an absence of recent Czech history, for a new Czech generation, which constitutes a kind of tacit silence, that's still of quite another order from, let's say, the disappearance of the recent past in Vienna (Austria seems to be the one glaring exception to Europe's wider embrace of its past). As taught in Austrian schools, the twentieth and twenty-first centuries have seemingly been removed, especially in this city. School children may not get beyond 1916, which was the sunsetting of the Hapsburgs.

The determined ignorance of history in Prague and Vienna, respectively, is worth the comparison above all because of the two capital cities' cultural and economic ties and rivalries over centuries, including during Austro-Hungarian rule. Vienna, just over the Czech border, the quintessential European metropolis that lies at the heart of Europe is stopped-time. The Viennese amnesia is extraordinary.

What may be unique about Vienna is that forgetting has become a national, tribal act, and this is precisely because of Austria's past. It's a past that has a power for Vienna, which has nothing to do with the force of history. The Austrian motivation to let go of the past has little to do with the post-war order. A city lying outside the Soviet perimeter, a city of the West, Vienna nevertheless became time-out-of-mind and -memory both. Once back on its feet after the Second World War, the city laid down a bet on tourism This decision was a symptom of something deeper. Vienna capitalizes on Austrian amnesia, and its stopped-time is this city's most lucrative commodity.

Here, then, post-Nazi, is a city, an entire nation, standing in diametrical opposition to today's Germany, Berlin most of all. Germany made a necessary choice for its future. Berlin remembers, wants to remember. Vienna, on the other hand, is like Disney World. It's the theme park's ever-present faux real. Disney World evokes an ersatz elegance and purity, like *The Sound of Music*. It's the cheap version of a hollowed out aristocratic grandeur.

Vienna's quite a comfortable city to be in, from the tourist's perspective. Its sights are hypnotizing. A great many of them have precisely to do with its past aristocracy, and its empire. That aristocracy was magnificence as show.

* * * *

The Vienna Opera House never puts on the same opera twice in succession, even when there's a matinée. There's no such thing as *Tosca* enjoying a week's run. Equipment trucks proceed to and from that magnificent building, transporting old and new stage sets, in a constant loop.

This perpetual cycle of opera productions happens to be a legacy of the Hapsburgs, whose practice was to demolish all surrounding buildings within the area now referred to as the Ring, then to rebuild them. The cycle ran every third or fourth generation. In this manner—this planned, recurrent, destruction and rebuilding—the Hapsburgs let the world know how wealthy they were, therefore how powerful. Vienna's Ringstrasse was once a wall circling the great palaces and other like splendors. What's left inside the Ring today are the uncommon artifacts, along with the stories they tell, of the Imperial household. The objects show how the family lived and ruled.

The Sisi museum tells the tale of the last Empress. The tale's a tragic one—operatic, actually. It goes like this: From age sixteen, she found herself trapped playing the role of a living relic. An outsider to the family, she was left powerless, not even allowed to raise her own children; decisions were made by their grandmother, her mother-in-law. Sisi turned to writing poetry, in gilded isolation. The maudlin tease, as her life is presented at each stop along a winding route in what was the household, is whether the poetry being replicated in the exhibition discloses her descent not merely into grief but madness as well.

The Jewish Museum, located in another part of town, is a bit of a contrast—its Annex, in yet another neighborhood, which has been sequestered within the large city, although the siting of it was dictated by the fact that the Annex is mostly about displaying and explaining recently discovered ruins of Vienna's Jewish ghetto. (You examine them first by descending some stairs.) The Annex building is so completely non-descript as to be unrecognizable. It's not easy to find, even when standing in the Judenplatz, looking all around. Inside, an armed guard in civilian garb, wearing a yarmulke, is positioned near the ticket desk.

There's but one memorial to the Holocaust in Vienna (again, in stark contrast to Berlin). It's in another plaza. Enigmatic but fine-looking, powerful, it yields its secret slowly. At the core of the monument is a sculpture of an elderly Jewish man on his knees, scrubbing the street with a brush. The figure is dwarfed within a complex of monolithic slabs of stone.

Nazism was alive and well in Austria. Nazi ideology was robustly nurtured in Vienna. Children were enrolled in youth corps and remained zealous Nazis for their entire lives as members of various ideological organizations. Nazi party membership was proportionately quite sizeable. In post-war occupation Mark Clark, the presiding American General, once he realized how deeply rooted and widespread Nazism had been there, scaled back his denazification program simply to be able to govern.

Arriving in Vienna, you find yourself in a gleaming, finely tuned, modern city. Its confection of high-tech glamour and old-world reliquary sells forgetfulness, while depending on the historical to supply context, as a predicate for the city's bad faith. Any museum frames the past, holding it in a stasis. Vienna's museums, however, the past seemingly alive, keep it in confinement.

To Remember

Yet the rest of Europe is contrary to Austria, as well as to the United States. Caught in the throes of its past Europe, in large, draws strength from it, perhaps Germany most of all. The European Union's raison d'etre is European history. Its mandate to reengineer European economies, hence Europe's politics, is an attempt to avoid further internecine war. But the EU, the greatest experiment of all, is unavoidably and stupendously clumsy in its administration from Brussels—so its half-billion inhabitants come to feel, perhaps fatally, distant and detached from it. The design of the Union is meant to overcome this. The Union may not.

Germany, meanwhile, is doing exceedingly well within the EU, as the largest of the Union's economies. Germany faces challenges invented by the Germans themselves, on the other hand. What could Merkel, have done but welcome so many refugees since 2015, given Germany's Nazi past? The Czech Republic, in comparison, let in eleven people. It simply ignores EU rules! Some countries— Hungary, spectacularly, fenced its borders—pointedly defy the EU on immigration.

Austria took in refugees in number equivalent to one percent of its population, and filed for an exemption. The new Austrian Prime Minister pushed for external borders in Europe—regardless of any problems that might arise for countries like Italy and Greece—in his striving to appease anti-immigrant hardliners but also people like Merkel who embrace tolerance and an open society. The difference between Austria and Germany—between Vienna and Berlin, two cities on opposite trajectories—is stark.

* * * *

Diane and I could not avoid comparing Berlin, when we were there, with both Prague and New York. Berlin offers a very different kind of life than what's to be had in Prague. I was seated on a Prague tram one late afternoon—across from me was a woman who was being a man. Dressed in bomber jacket, jeans and heavy leather boots, she reached into her canvas courier bag to pull out, of all things, a book of George Perec's poems, which had been translated into Czech. What a rare delight!

We came to a stop in the busier commercial part of town; it was the rush hour. Lots of people got on, business types who were tired and eager to get home. A woman in a business suit, seeing my companion dressed in what the woman must have felt was a man's clothes, openly glared at her. I was taken aback—especially because people in Prague, at least in public, maintain a cordiality—but I'd come to realize that gay people in Prague keep almost entirely undercover. It's rare to see a gay couple strolling along as "gay" on a Prague street.

Arriving in Berlin's Hautbanhof, we sensed the city's élan. We made our way to the station's information office where we sorted through various pamphlets and guides. There was a listing of the upcoming week's "queer" happenings. Berlin is inspiring. It's a big cosmopolitan city.

Unlike New York, it's very green; a third of its area is parkland. It's geographically much larger than Prague and has three times Prague's population of a million. The trees, grass and birds have a calming effect. Everything works in Berlin (everything works in Prague too, and in Vienna), and the sense of order—regardless of the fact that most of the city was rebuilt after the war—is part of the city's experience. Visually, though, Berlin lacks the beauty and imagination of Prague.

I don't think the Germans are capable of designing beautiful cityscapes, at least not the mindedly *built* structures. I wonder if they ever were. But what a city! Berlin's alive—reminding us of New York but without New York's massive, unrelenting energy and density. London seems more like

New York, yet in another way (Paris, Rome, other cities don't, can't). London's a broad mix of people, which gives it its vitality. It's reminiscent of New York, most of all, because of a sense that the city's out of control.

Berlin's definitely not that, and this is a reason to fall in love with it. Order, I now think, can preclude soaring beauty. Prague is coherent, orderly—but the Bohemians' exquisite aesthetics are magic (even now as much of Prague's infrastructure is in the process of change). Regardless of the great German painting and forward-looking architectural movements in times past, is it really true that Berlin is now the center of the art world? Does Berlin's reputation depend on the work of breakthrough artists who were part of the German generation growing up in the war, such as Gerhard Richter?

Berlin does welcome art and architecture great in imagination and sympathy, for instance Daniel Liebeskind's design of the Jewish Museum there. In simply being in it, for any length of time, the museum becomes a sacred space. This is in great measure because of Liebeskind's architectural genius—the look and feel, the dimensions of the rooms, the means of getting around within the building. The curation is to be admired too. Photos and artifacts are presented elegantly, everyday objects and letters, informational texts, and art works—but they've been kept to a minimum, and presented within rooms and passages of various arrangements.

The consequent elegance of memory foregrounds the

Holocaust. Its history is of course powerful. Beauty and loss suffuse everything and everyone there, inside the building and in the garden beyond it. Such a museum, in Berlin, was what was needed.

Memorials to the Holocaust are ubiquitous in Berlin. In Prague, we'd discovered brass plaques embedded in sidewalks meant to keep alive the memory of people who were taken from their homes, ultimately to their deaths, during the Nazi years and thereafter. These people lived where the plaques have been set. We noticed these plaques in Berlin too. They're of the same size and composition, and also embedded in sidewalks.

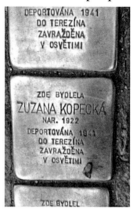

Memorials to the Nazi victims in Prague

Many of them remember people who attempted escape from the eastern part of the city, most after the Berlin Wall was constructed. A plaque's location marks the place of escape, at the precise crossing point. The plaques document both the failed and successful escapes from East Berlin. They provide, when known, a name, otherwise a description ("ein Mann" wearing a tan overcoat and hat), and the date of attempt.

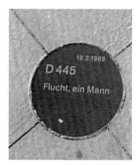

Memorial to an anonymous escape from East Berlin

* * * *

The Berlin Wall itself still stands in some parts of Berlin —in order to remember. At the East Side Gallery, an open-air affair, the murals and graffiti on the Wall left standing, in that part of the city, are a contrast to the plain slabs left up near where The Wall Museum has been sited. Further along the avenue, steel struts of the Wall have been left up. In one spot they border a grassy field containing photos and captions.

The Wall Museum proper houses compelling, sweeping presentations, an abundance of them in a variety of mediums. Many stories of individual people are told, meant to make plain the lives of everyone caught in the divided city as the greater Cold War developed. There are historical films and photos, along with audio or video recordings, in more recent times by survivors, and other historical artifacts, prominent among them newspaper accounts—in stunning clarity the story of the Wall, how the idea of it took shape, the circumstances leading up to its construction.

We hadn't grasped the depth of government insinuation into every facet and moment of people's lives, until we visited the Stasi Museum. East Germany, as a surveillance state, surpassed all other nations. What was achieved there is shocking up close. We began to feel what was at stake for the Berliners. In East Germany everyone spied on everyone else.

One bit of especially revealing footage, at the Wall Museum, shows an ordinary moment that turned weird in seconds. At the same time it was completely understandable. An East German soldier was standing guard as laborers were first building the Wall. They were troweling cement, the wall rising in small increments. You see West Berlin achingly within reach for these people, only feet away. People were going about their lives there, right before the East Germans' eyes.

The difference in quality of living between East and West Berlin was already plain. In a split second, as a tram was coming along on the Western side, stopping to pick up passengers, the soldier guarding the workers made his break, his bayonetted rifle in hand, hurtling over the concrete blocks and drying cement. He didn't have far to run. The tram driver waited until he got inside before pulling away.

Our apartment in Berlin was a block from the dividing line. On Sunday, we strolled through Mauer Park (*mauer*, wall). People have come to Berlin from all over the world; most of them visit the park, now living there.

* * * *

Like everywhere in Europe, Berlin's wars, its holocausts, are never far off. Germany's devoted itself to memory and bearing responsibility. (German school children make the journey to Auschwitz.) In return, the city's diverse, alive. There's a warmth the people in Prague normally extend to others, which I didn't find in either Vienna or Berlin. Yet in Berlin there's a lifting spirit of laissez-faire, which is so very necessary right now.

Berlin's at a crossroads. I don't think New York is, while it should be. Dear Praha's found its new direction. The city's filled with the offices of multinational corporations. English is everywhere, to be seen and heard. That includes lots of mixed Czech and English phrasing, or sometimes just straight-ahead English. Scrawled on a wall near the entrance to a Prague metro station: "Graffiti saved my life."

The English graffiti is an artifact of American cultural hegemony. I make this stipulation while sitting in a restaurant named Hamburg, a block from our apartment in Holešovice, a Prague neighborhood recently turned artsy and gentrified. Michael Jackson is being pumped through the bars' sound system.

It seemed like everyone in Berlin spoke idiomatic English. German and English are similar, of course, while Czech and English have nothing to do with one another. Czech attempts at the American idiom are sometimes strange, disturbingly funny. But this may have as much or more to do with cultural miscues.

In a small Czech town, a ten-year old's baseball cap displayed the phrase "extreme obscene." In Pilsen, kitty corner to the main square, there's a big sneaker store named "Snow Bitch," which earned a second turn of our heads. We asked one of Diane's students, who lives in Pilsen, about it. She simply said people didn't really know what was wrong with it, but anyway that wasn't the point.

The Czech Republic is an old-world society that was paved

paved over by Communist historical, architectural, and artistic revisionism—all to be supplanted by post Cold-War capitalism, and now by the multinational and high-tech version of it. I've had the thought more than once that, with Brexit, Prague might attract some of London's financial services and otherwise digitally sophisticated economy, challenging Paris and Frankfurt.

There's more English in the center of Prague to be heard and seen than German, Russian, Ukrainian and Polish combined (as well as Roma and Vietnamese, their language-flows weaving through Prague on their own). But in Berlin everyone speaks really good English. It's difficult to avoid marveling at how World War II, then the Cold War, made Germany what it's become.

Berlin's truly an international city, on a par with a city like New York in a number of ways, or London, both larger in population. In the liberal democracies' present struggle for survival, along with Paris, Berlin is key. It's earned its seat at the big table for many reasons.

I suppose Berlin's geo-political cachet may call for, in some people's minds, the city's emotionless buildings. Even the remnants outlasting the war's saturated aerial bombardments, such as the remaining portion of the Brandenburg Gate, seem to me beset by gravity. No one is as efficient as the Germans. But for my money the Germans don't have it in them to create visual beauty anything like Czech brilliance and verve.

I can't help but think that some of Prague's cultural authority, in times past having been felt abroad, such in Vienna, has to do with the city's utter beauty, certainly as the Austrian capitol's rival. Not just the old Prague, now—what city, other than Prague, displays postmodern architecture as undulation, in comparison with the elegant, graceful older buildings and streetscapes? Most of the new, snazzy high rises are far enough from the old city to avoid such association. The Dancing House is another matter. It rose on the site of a mistaken aerial bombing during the war (Prague didn't suffer other such attacks). The bombsite spurred an architectural reconception that, unexpectedly, while radically different, is genuinely Czech in nature. The building is a conscious amalgam of old and new, one or the other creating its motif, depending on where you stand, from where you look, both swervy and understatedly straight up.

The Dancing House, the product of Bohemian wit, may have planted the seed that's led to recently constructed high rises in other parts of town. The newer—they could be called irreverent—tall buildings (such as in the Holešovice and Karlín districts) are now the consequence of the multinational, corporate order that looks to be absorbing

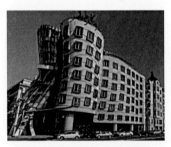

the city, while allowing "classical," the older, urbanscapes to hold onto memory. It's an intact history preserved with an eye to the tourist trade, yet it's more than this.

The Dancing House, Prague

Major infrastructure projects, on the grand scale, are

underway—paid for by EU "catch-up" money dispensed to its newer members. The Czechs seem to be using it well. Although people in Prague have mentioned a level of corruption that prolongs time-to-completion of these projects, there's a new water tunnel being constructed —visibly progressing, and new highways.

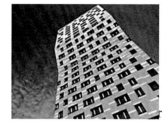

Berlin is really cosmopolitan, though. Prague is visually stunning in a way neither New York nor London can ever hope to be. Maybe Berlin's architecture could, in theory, have been so, a city more on a scale with Prague. In any case, the German city is open and free in ways other cities should be. Rich, at the same time comfortable, and welcoming, city's human embrace is astonishing.

Freedom, in Prague, is often expressed only through codes of body language and speech bred during the totalitarian half-century preceding the First Republic (if not earlier too). People in Prague are heartfelt but watchful. Tentative, simultaneously full of hope, they look for the right signals.

No city can stand comparison with Prague. Some of that has to do with the geography—the meandering Vltava River and the hills rising up sharply from it. Berlin, nevertheless, so very green—trees and birds ever present, enveloping you—has its rivers. They too create an urban ambiance.

* * * *

Then there's Russia. On the morning the news broke, in Berlin, that Trump had refused to sign the G7 joint statement, Diane and I were breakfasting at an outdoor café a block from Mauer Park. I noticed a German couple at the next table. They were grimly smiling at the widely circulated photo of Merkel with her fists on a table as she confronted the American President, leaning into his face, as he sat across from her and the other G7 leaders, arms folded in front of him. The photo was featured on the front page of the German newspapers. (People in Berlin still read newspapers.) These Berliners were proud of their leader. And they were waiting to see what would come of both Germany—as Merkel faced a challenge from the right —and liberal democracy.

At our garden lunch near Pardubice with our Czech friends, they well understood what the Poles were thinking. Poland shares a border with Russia. No one at lunch wished to offer a fig leaf for the burgeoning fascism in today's Poland or for that matter the naked fascism in Hungary (and as could develop in Austria and Italy)—except for Tomáš's rejoinder that the Poles suffered terribly under the Nazis.

As for the Czech Republic—will it continue to veer rightward? It's a prosperous country, with very low unemployment, the highest per capita car ownership in Europe, the lowest infant mortality rate in the world. Children in Prague are being parented well, their fathers intimately engaged in the kids' lives.

Prague's businessman-prime minister realizes how important the EU is. It's just that the Czech Republic is merely along for the ride. With a total aggregate of ten million people (the Poles are four times as many), the Czech Republic is a bit player.

Part III

History

Living in Bohemia, we come to realize we're in a different part of the world. If you look quickly it all seems familiar. But then you start noticing. When trying to comprehend contemporary Prague, two historical turning points must be kept in mind.

One is the Velvet Revolution in late 1989. The other is the formation of Czechoslovakia, seven decades before, its "First Republic" in 1918. Before Václav Havel became the nation's President, in 1989, the Czechs had been living under foreign rule for over three centuries. The twenty glorious years of the First Republic—once sovereignty had been granted collectively to Bohemia, Moravia and Slovakia—were a flowering of democracy, the creation of an open society.

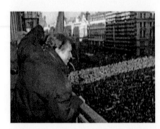

Václav Havel addresses the crowd, Wenceslas Square

Modeled on the US political system, the First Republic came into being because of the vision and drive of Tomáš Garrigue Masaryk, who was married to an American woman, Charlotte Garrigue (he took Garrigue as his middle name). American democracy was foremost in their minds. The Czechs and Slovaks had compelling geopolitical reasons to join together. The new nation of Czechoslovakia was formed at the end of the Great War, in return for Czech and Slovak support of the

Allies. Woodrow Wilson prevailed upon the League of Nations to sponsor the new sovereign state.

Different culturally, speaking somewhat different languages, Czechs and Slovaks share a singular experience in all of Eastern Europe—that of a robustly free, self-determining society. It's said that the new nation was the most democratic, functioning, thriving democracy on the continent. In 1938, the Nazis marched into the so-called Sudetenland, and the rest of Czechoslovakia the following year—the direct consequence of the Munich Agreement—what the Czechs, to this day, call the Mnichovská zrada (the Munich Betrayal); it comes up in conversations.

The Cold War had already begun by the conclusion of the hot war, coalescing before everyone's eyes. People watched it evolve. By pre-agreement, the Western forces stood back in order to allow the Soviets to liberate the Czech and Slovak territories. Two Czech factions vied for power (one had been headquartered in London, the other in Moscow). The Czech Communists—more ruthless, ignoring legal niceties—seized political control, officially winning the election of 1948. They invited the Soviet assistance. Life under the sway of the Soviet Union officially began y ɑsuch an outcome had been imagined by the time the Germans were being rounded up for imprisonment.

The Czechs' unique role in the Cold War is not merely incidental. Czechoslovakia officially, having embraced the Soviets, suffered less deprivation than all other citizens living behind the Iron Curtain. Communism was sinister, often cruel and cynical, yet Czechoslovakia's material standard of living was better than even Russia's.

The Czechs were handled from Moscow, to borrow Havel's phrase, with the "gloves on." (Charter 77 dissidents received the bare-knuckles treatment.) The Czechoslovakian version of Communist control was terrible in its own way, to be sure. Beyond any physical abuse or impoverishment, it was truly Orwellian. The story of Pilsen makes this point emphatically.

Pilsen

Pilsen became a prime example of totalitarianism. The city and its vicinity were liberated by Patton's forces— unlike everywhere else in the country, and contrary to the allies' 1945 agreement with the Soviets. When the Communists officially took power in 1948, clergy and artists, intelligentsia and all known dissidents were imprisoned or executed. There were show trials.

All of Czechoslovakia would eventually become part of the Warsaw Pact configuration, the Soviet Union and its satellite nations. During the Communist years, the people in Pilsen and the small towns around it, freed of the Nazis by the Americans, acknowledged to each other and to their children what really happened— Patton's army had saved them from the Nazis' further depredations. (Only in 1990, a year after Communism's fall, did the memorializing of the city's liberation by American soldiers, which took the form of a festival right after the war, commence again.)

Publicly, until the Velvet Revolution, the Czechs parroted what became the Communist official history, which held that Russian soldiers had removed the German forces. It was even claimed, as part of official Communist historiography, that some Russians had been wearing American uniforms in those early May days in 1945, seen to have uprooted the German forces, and setting the Czechs free. This story was meant as a retort to a common, rash exclamation among the Czechs: "But I remember the American soldiers in their uniforms!" The question to be asked about this official lie, now, is whether the doubleness was the intention.

* * * *

Pilsen is the fourth largest city in the Czech Republic, the home of pilsener beer and the Patton Museum. Patton is fanatically worshipped here, his life and deeds a hagiography. That he's often viewed by Americans with a gimlet eye is a surprise to the Czechs. Once that point of view is shared, it's quickly let drop.

Patton's army liberated Pilsen on May 6, 1945, first engaging the enemy there two days earlier. The annual liberation celebration begins on May 4th. We attended the opening ceremony. Locals and press filled the opera house, to hear from surviving American and Belgian vets. High school students were there. As solemn as this event was, over three days some eccentric version of Mardi Gras unfolded. Probably a thousand people, among more than ninety-thousand taking part in this bacchanale, were dressed in World War II American uniforms or 1940s civilian garb and makeup, and stayed that way for the festival's three days.

Pilsen's streets and squares were clogged by strollers along with hundreds of vintage US jeeps, armored cars, tanks and trucks, which were part of an hours-long parade, driven by American-uniformed celebrants. Surviving veterans sat

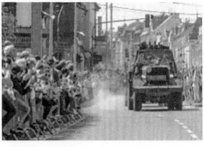

or stood to wave, one to a jeep, the crowd lined either side of a long avenue. Patton's grandson was the honored guest, who came by, waving at us from his passing jeep. Two American fighter

The Liberation Festival parade in Pilsen, 2018

jets flew over, wagging their wings in salute. Then came two vintage fighter planes, single engines buzzing, flying back and forth.

The Count Basie Orchestra was the featured event in the town's main square, one evening. A couple of thousand people danced, drank beer, ate a variety of foods, milling about on all sides of a church with a tall steeple. There was

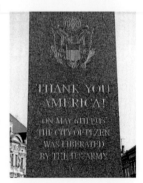

some ecstatic jitterbugging. The best of the bands we heard, the next evening, was a fabulous Blue Grass ensemble, the lyrics in Czech.

On the sixth of May, 1945, the commanding German officer along with ten thousand soldiers surrendered. Czech collaborators were arrested with the aid of the Czech resistance. After signing the capitulation document, the German commandant shot

Pilsen's War Memorial in English (it stands next to an otherwise identical memorial in Czech)

376

himself. Meanwhile, American soldiers were, methodically, firing back at German snipers to pick them off from a bell tower and some upper-story windows—the skirmishing vividly on display in archival footage shown in an endless loop, at the Patton Museum.

The closing ceremony was held at the Czech-American War Memorial that features two towers, one inscribed in Czech, the other English ("THANK YOU AMERICA!"). The Czechs in Pilsen, deeply grateful to America for freeing them from the Nazis, also remember liberation after communism. The festival's an expression of great relief for having gotten out of the Soviet Union's grasp. Each year there's a full-blown mock-up of the American war— not fake battles as you'd see in the States, but replicated bivouacs and the like. People celebrate with a vengeance, making up for lost time.

East-West

Before we left for Prague in January, 2018, we attended a staging of a play, *The Visiting Experts*, by Egon Bondy (who was a theatrical rival of Havel), at the Bohemian National Hall in Manhattan. The deeply disturbing drama was written and performed in Slovak (English supertitles). After the Czechoslovakian schism, in 1993, Bondy chose Slovakian citizenship.

The storyline disappears within a phantasmagorical surrealism. The plot is simple. Two experts visit two other experts in another country to study their methods of state-sponsored torture. Torture is random. Only Russia is mentioned, its secret-police methods compared with the other two countries' not as gruesome.

On our flight to Prague, I read an article by Masha Gessen about some brave Russians who'd located, marked, and were publicly honoring a killing field and burial ground (Gessen covered the event). Aside from the now well-documented Katyn Forest exterminations, thousands of executions of Poles at this new site had gone unacknowledged. The mass burial ground contains their bodies. The Russian citizens who created the memorial did so at risk to themselves.

I began to grasp why, in Eastern Europe, the West is considered soft, weak, and decadent. No American could really have rendered any of Bondy's four dramatic roles. In frigid Prague, our 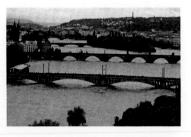 first evening, we consumed delicious, restorative, hot soup in a restaurant near our apartment. At that moment I adopted the mantra I'd hold to throughout our time there: *Soup and Murder.* The Vltava River meanders northward through the city, nearly looping back on itself at one point. Ten degrees Fahrenheit felt especially cold. Prague is based on that river. Life in Prague is conditioned by it.

This is why the city evolved into the thing of utter beauty it is. This is why Czechs have soup twice a day in the winter months. The French military campaign of 1812 ground to a halt in the snows of Russia.

So did the German invasion—which was the turn in the Second World War. What do beauty and endurance have to do with one another? The Czechs endured for half a millennium (officially they became subjects of the Austro-Hungarian Empire the year the Pilgrims landed at Plymouth Rock). On the other hand, the Czechs, along with the Slovaks, have inside them an experience they share with the West, which is beyond the scope of the rest of Eastern Europe. It makes me think about what it means to be civilized. For all their great art, architecture, literature, music, philosophy, food, drink, and so on, the peoples of the East have never really known democracy—but for the Czechs and Slovaks. A Czech friend once remarked, "it takes time to learn to think democratically, to harbor expectations of what a democracy implicitly promises, and what it demands—to insist on one's rights."

* * * *

Prague's grand castle was at times the seat of Holy Roman Emperors. During the Austrian rule of more recent times, the Czechs would learn which streets in Prague, which hotels, restaurants, cafés, theatres and opera were off limits. The boundaries, at times unspoken, were inviolable.

Given that the language of power was German, it's striking how little of this language has made its way into Czech, even allowing for the difference between Germanic and Slavic language groups. The difference is cultural. In some respects, whatever else might have been in play during the centuries of subjugation, Czechs could not ignore the history of Bohemian relations with France and and Italy (as well as

with Austria and Poland, which share a common border—
the Czechs and Poles said to be two peoples standing
back to back). So much is the same, so much different.
During the Cold War, dissidents from the two countries
would meet secretly at the border.

The Czechs, like the Poles and Germans, are beer drinkers.
The Czechs consume more beer per capita than any other
nation. It's said that all things are really discussed over beer.
The Poles also consume vodka, like the Russians. The
French and Italians drink wine, as do the Germans and
Austrians.

* * * *

Slavonice is a story of German and Czech. It's known for
its Renaissance sgraffiti on the sides of some of its buildings,
and for frescoes within them. An enlightened Czech ruler
had invited in Italian and French artisans. Some of the
sgraffiti is still being uncovered and restored. It's a small
town lying a mere kilometer from Austria. And it's not far
from the Slovak border, closer still to Brno, the Czech
Republic's second city, and Vienna. The town's character
is the result of complex cultural, geopolitical, and
linguistic mixings over extended periods of time—also
marked by sudden upheavals.

The border with Austria runs along a hill at the town's
outskirts. During the Cold War, the hill featured a 3,000-
volt electrified fence, within eyeshot. A low-lying stone
wall behind some houses leads one's sight off to it in the
distance. It was weird, people told us, to live on the Czech
side of that hill, knowing the fence was lethal.

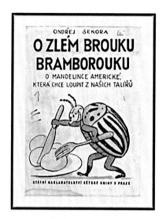

Czech children's book
by Ondřej Sekora

The pages of what had once been a popular children's book during the Cold War are filled with lovely illustrations. It's about a bug infestation that ruined the American potato crop one year. The bugs are quite cute. The book was on display in a Slavonice gallery. The town's community arts center was constructed by the Soviets as a commons, a leisure center for Communist elite who were allowed to live in the town or its periphery. Slavonice was part of a restricted zone—no one in or out without intense vetting.

Slavonice was a major stopover along a trade route, in ancient times, much later a stop on a postal route connecting Prague and Vienna. Later a rail line closely connected the two cities. Slavonice's Jewish merchants produced textiles for Viennese buyers.

The town survived under various regimes as part Czech and part German. In 1938, it was occupied by the Nazis (as part of their claim upon the Sudetenland). Many of the Czechs were removed then, as were all of the town's Jews to concentration camps. At the end of the war, Slavonice's German families were uprooted in a single night, after having lived there for four hundred years. Seven families were allowed to stay because they proved they were anti-Nazi—in the circumstances this was nearly impossible to do; six of them were of mixed marriages.

The Germans being expelled were allowed to take no more than thirty-eight kilograms of belongings; they were given a half hour to pack. Elsewhere, Germans and Austrians suffered a similar fate. In Brno, twenty thousand Germans were marched fifty kilometers out of the city, two thousand of them dying along the way.

After the expulsions, Slavonice was repopulated entirely by Czechs. In more recent times, the grandchildren of those expelled in 1945 were welcomed into the town by the Czechs now living there, many of them born since then.

As much or more German is spoken in Slavonice, today, as Czech. The town's a major arts destination. But many tourists show up just to eat and drink in the cafés on the town square, where they admire Slavonice's beautiful buildings, towers and fountains. These exist both in and out of time.

* * * *

Czech was always an underground language. The first Czech dictionary was created at the turn of the twentieth century, derived from a 1870 translation of the King James Bible. Czech literature didn't start to be written until the mid-nineteenth century (Kafka, of course, wrote in German— what I remember Aharon Appelfeld once referring to as "a Jewish German"). Czech, more to the point Bohemian, humor is similar to that of all Eastern European cultures be they Slavic or not. It's nonetheless unique. It's quite different from what's to be found in German or, generally, Western European cultures.

Czech humor is quirky and uniquely dark. It's not that the Czechs don't also possess a drollery—as do the Russians, Lithuanians, Poles, and Romanians. Rather, it's the Czech, especially the Bohemian, viewpoint, an insight into the ways in which power and grace may coexist. Hence it's a delicate humor—one that takes irony for granted—extremely incisive, wickedly hilarious. The Czechs' history helps to account for this.

In another article Gessen tries to explain the Russian mindset, recalling a remark by a friend, Slavenka Drakulić (a Croatian): Being able to laugh was, she says, "the ultimate personal triumph over the daily humiliations of life under Communist rule," including in Russia. Gessen then shares a current Russian joke. It goes like this: Putin opens his refrigerator and the "jellied meat begins to quake, but he reassures it by saying he is getting the yogurt."

The joke is blunt. It expresses unmitigated power, as if that could be the entirety of the human experience and without consequence. Gessen's purchase on America's political paralysis these days is, in our cultural dilemma, required reading. But it's Russian. It's different—slightly, yes—in certain key ways.

Russians have, in their history, often discovered themselves in the role of overlord. Russian has always been a dominant language. Czech, also a Slavic language, has been a language of abjection for half a millennium, spoken by people forced to live under the rule of others.

Epilogue

On Easter Monday, Diane and I set out to visit Terezín. We had no idea that everything in Prague, including most buses leaving the city, were to be in brief hibernation that day. The Easter Sunday was a bustling, big, festive day, the holiday mostly a good time out for families who shopped and dined. (The Czechs are, for the most part, atheists.) Prague was abuzz. Monday was silent. There was no notice anywhere, online or at the bus stations, that the bus from Prague to Terezín would not be running.

The Nazis renamed it Theresienstadt. Terezín is an hour's drive from Prague. We did manage

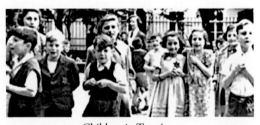
Children in Terezín

to get there a month later. Like the Czech Roma, who were collected in the Lety concentration camp near Prague, nearly all of the Terezín inmates, in both ghetto and prison (comprised of Jews and non-Jews, many of them Czechs), were shipped to their deaths in Auschwitz. Many didn't live long enough to make that last journey.

Once the Communists took control, after the war, anyone deemed to be potential trouble was imprisoned in a far-flung facility in Vojna and put to work nearby in a uranium mine. Among these prisoners were former Nazis. The prison administration soon recognized that these people had a particular talent, so they were elevated to serve as something like the Auschwitz capos. What these Czech Communists saw in their Nazi charges was a likeness. They were soulmates.

* * * *

The first of May, called Labor Day in the Czech Republic, is a major holiday. Yet Prague was empty and silent. I sat alone in a café, reading and writing over coffee. My waiter, with little to do, hung around to talk. I commented on how deserted not only his café but also the whole neighborhood was. He said, simply, that yes, everyone had gone to their country houses for the long weekend.

The custom of retreating from the city to the family's country cottage had become all the more cherished once the Communists took control. Alone in your house in the country, with your family, you were free of surveillance. You could relax, talk as you wished. The Czechs who were children under the Communists tell about how, as kids, they knew full well to adhere to a different story of family life and conversation, once stepping out the door of their home, into society.

* * * *

The good old days of Communism are still fondly recollected in Prague and elsewhere by senior citizens. It seems to be a malaise that lingers, but when these people have passed on, hopefully a subsequent election will choose a stronger alliance with the West. Nostalgia is a powerful force that may, in the Czech Republic, be indistinguishable from profound psychological trauma I see young people struggling to transcend in creative, exciting ways.

I think for instance of the Vnitroblok Café that was also a sneaker store (there's an innumerable variety of sneakers worn in Prague), an art gallery, dance studio, and in its courtyard a cheeseburger and pulled-pork restaurant whose kitchen, equipped with its own soundtrack, was set up inside an American school bus. The bus was shipped from Cobb County, Georgia, license plate and all. You see this sort of innovation everywhere in Prague—in the cafés, on the streets, in the way the young people dress, in their guarded insouciance I hope never to forget.

* * * *

Life in the New York metropolitan area, as I look back on what was another world, a life in Prague, can seem a puzzle. We live in a leafy suburb, less than an hour from midtown Manhattan. We know the drill. Flying back into Newark-Liberty airport, the massive controlled frenzy of reentering America, then a car ride to our leafy, pretty neighborhood, I felt grateful for the quiet. The calm nights are a reprieve from my having to compensate at every turn for what had been normal. The night is a salve. In daylight I try to make sense of the disjunct between the there and the here.

Everything, now, in the United States, has become uncertain—in a way I'd come to feel was integral to life in Eastern Europe not that long ago, and now is, increasingly, in Western Europe. Diane and I spend our free time working to win back the US Congress for the Democratic party, in what we see is an unqualified national emergency. We don't have time to indulge ourselves in the niceties of adjusting to being back. Yet it all sinks in.

386

Aside from the soaring beauty of Prague—the visual grace of its architecture, the often subliminally disruptive nature of its art, which I found to be so very compelling, and the grandeur of its symphonic music we got to hear at the Rudolfinum, surely the most sumptuous, gorgeous, elegant concert hall anywhere—the history of Europe, all its self-inflicted tragedies, is helping us, what we know of it now, in America's fight for its soul.

FILM NOIR

for Charles Borkhuis

Each hoping to escape a loveless marriage, my mother and father met in the Army and married at the end of the Second World War. They were children of the Depression who were swept up in the great cataclysm that followed. I was born in 1947. Four years later, when my brother was born, I was given a brightly colored, toy gas station made of metal. In my earliest years there were things like that—solid, palpable. I had my parents' kisses, and the touch of their hands. A television set became a part of our home, when I was six—which may have been timed with my parents' divorce.

The split was long coming. On Fire Island, one summer, they tried to reconcile. There was a hurricane. My brother was sponging water from a bucket, squeezing it onto the kitchen floor—still too young to understand we were bailing ourselves out—my father giggling at his mistake. My mother was standing apart, sullen, quiet. When the storm passed, I went outside. The island was flooded. Rowboats floated along the sidewalks, people getting themselves from somewhere to somewhere else. I dove into the water, flopping around in it. My clothes and hair were drenched. I was happy. I'd found an oblivion I was already shaped to seek.

My mother and father were locked in a passion of near-mythic stature. Whether or not they mistook it for love, in 1945, they'd seized it, a buoy floating by. Now the waters had receded. Still stricken by the vehemence of their battles, I watched my father take his final exit. All the better in some orderly world—there were happy families on TV, the dad coming home from work, the mom vacuuming and cooking (in high heels and a dress). My parents' travails were the birth of my sorrow that was infused with a greater, deeper anguish.

I suppose everyone was confused, in having to stand down from the war. Much of this involved latent grief. As a boy, the only place I felt was real was my grandmother's home, her street and apartment in the Brownsville section of Brooklyn. I see now the irony in this. Brownsville was a shtetl and the Holocaust was still unfolding. I was thirteen when Eichmann was kidnapped in Buenos Aires. A week later photos in *Life* magazine crossed over from their black-and-white narratives on the magazine's glossy pages, to the end point of my childhood.

The palpable, there in these pages, was now inside me. A man came to visit my Israeli companion when we were camping in Colorado Springs; we were among tens of thousands who were there to celebrate the Boy Scouts' fiftieth annual Jamboree, having traveled as members of a "Brooklyn" scout troop across the country. The man, a friend of Schmuel's family, brought the issue of *Life* with him. Speaking mostly in Hebrew, blue numbers tattooed on his forearm, he laid the magazine open for us, slowly turning its pages. There stood Eichmann, handlers either side of him, answering questions put to him by a plain-clothes official seated at a folding card table in a small room (bare but for an Israeli flag tacked to the wall behind him).

In my grandmother's home, away from my parents' battles, there was a solidity I craved. There was also a misery that thickened the air, along with the aroma of her boiled chicken on the stove. As a young and lost adult, unemployed, decades later, I'd borrow books from a Manhattan library. I happened upon Yukio Mishima's great novel, *Spring Snow*. So much time since the breach in my life, I discovered a fated sadness I recognized. Mishima made real another kind of unhappiness—a Japanese desolation after atomic bombing and national, cultural defeat. Nevertheless, I sensed something akin to my feelings of loss and estrangement.

The novel begins with a memory of the Russo-Japanese War. A torchlight parade passes before the front gate of the home where Kiyoki Mastugae, Mishima's boy protagonist, lives with his family. His grandmother, who lost two sons in the war, never opens the envelopes the government sends her, which contain a monthly pension, instead leaving them on the ledge of the household shrine. Inside the house there's a photograph of soldiers who are gathered to honor the war dead.

Kiyoki will succumb to a pure, impossible love for a girl of another family with whom he's been raised, and this will destroy him. His second-hand experience of the war, starting when he was still quite young, presages his own death. The photograph becomes a memory for Kiyoki—a memory he's never had. Titled "Vicinity of Tokuri Temple: Memorial Services for the War Dead," the photograph bears the weight of a collective melancholy. It was "composed with an artist's eye for structure," Mishima writes.

The "thousands of soldiers" in it have their backs to the camera; they're bowing to a wooden, unpainted cenotaph. They seem to have been purposely arranged, and their uniforms have the allure of "figures in a painting." In the foreground there's a number of "very tall trees," which have been placed "at graceful intervals" so as to "complement the overall harmony of the landscape." Upper branches of these trees appear "to bend in the wind with a tragic grandeur."

In innocence, a boy observes the scene, unconsciously taken in by its composition. The soldiers are "bathed in a strange half-light" that has the effect of accentuating "the curves of bent shoulders and the napes of necks," thus imbuing "the entire picture with an indescribable sense of grief" (trans. Michael Gallagher). I, too, was living in the second-hand loss of an uncle. He was someone I never knew, who had been killed in Normandy.

On Friday evenings, lighting the *Shabbos* candle, my grandmother sobbed, thinking of her boy who'd been shot by a German sniper. I carry this hurt in me, more than a half-century since my nights with her. I remember the photo of my uncle *Yussel*—my middle name in English, Joseph—in his uniform. He resembles my mother, her younger sister and older brother. I could locate my own image in his (much the same lips, cheek bones). All my uncles saw combat. The war was made vivid through them. They'd brought home their uniforms and military gear, some of which I used as a scout.

Growing up in the fifties, I transferred my pain to the black and white stories on television, and to the films I saw in theatres (some portraying the war), especially the foreign films that had not yet been tainted with the technicolor, then, of nearly every Hollywood feature. There were exceptions—a film on a serious subject, or one in the tradition of film noir. These were, for me, to borrow from McLuhan, a cool medium. They became what was most important. By thirteen, high as a kite on marijuana, the TV shows and films became, even more, a saturation for me—both a great pleasure and respite. Yes, Hitchcock's *The Birds* was spectacular (*Psycho* had been shot in black and white), especially watching it when high. But the comfort I savored was to be found in the older films.

The emergence of American film noir, its sheer compulsion, was a consequence of the Depression and the War. Yes, I know—German Expressionism (to which Hollywood's debt is enormous). Yet the films on constrained budgets, their low lighting, new insights into the play of shadows, and other happy accidents that led to American B movies—for all these, there was also an American trauma that was being acted out in the underworld. This was what most drew me in. I realize all this now. Yet I did have a sense of it—seeing on the screen the plight of people in whom I gladly invested myself as corollary to the plight of everyone around me.

The world of film noir hearkens to its own morality. That I was a Red Diaper baby during the McCarthy years and later, who was living in a part of Brooklyn quite different from Brownsville, with few Jews and plenty of American patriots after the Korean War, a mob-run neighborhood in which flare-ups of violence were not unusual (the sympathies of the hoods, if they had any, were in line with right-wing ideology)—these all shunted me off into my own country, where I lived according to my own rules.

Film noir is the most American form. We may never get enough of it. Recent "neo-noir," often entertaining, perhaps suspense-filled, though, lacks a certain something. The problem is that, whatever recent "noir" films are or are not, something has been filled in: color. What is memory in black and white? I might better ask: Why do I wish my memories to be in black and white? Why must the world I think is essential be in black and white?

Laura (1944) has been called the quintessential noir film. For me, however, the fact that it's set in New York City—requiring the sinister elements of its plot be ensconced within the milieu of high society (maybe this was a holdover from Depression-era films that featured the posh life)—is a disqualification. Laura needed to exude a whiff of the old world. And as much as this "noir" project tried for some exoticism—which I maintain is a requisite element in American noir—it had to settle for the Dana Andrews role of detective Mark McPherson.

This is a cop who can't conceal his longing, a loneliness. It burdens him, in his investigation of Laura's murder. He's in love with the woman who's been killed. Later in the story he falls asleep in her apartment, on an evening, below a painting of her hanging on the wall. When he awakens, she's alive and well, in the flesh; she's let herself in to get a few things. McPherson's search for the murderer will go on (now the question is who the dead woman was).

The image of Laura, played by a compelling Gene Tierney, is a double entendre. It works both through memory and the painting. The device was also employed in another film, made the same year, *The Woman in the Window*. In this film, the double entendre has the effect of shifting the story's focus to the flight of the killer (the question of who is pursuing him is secondary). What's different, in this other film, is that the female lead's image is crucial to the structure of the plot. The setup for this film is the man who's gazing at a painting of the woman, which has been placed in a store window. Just then, he hears her voice coming from a dark alley—she speaks to him from the shadows, then emerges to take him to her apartment. There, he unwittingly kills her jealous boyfriend.

His subsequent attempts to hide the body, in the rest of this tale, are a bad dream—but it's no dream. In Laura, on the other hand, the dream is McPherson's need for love, his longing for Laura. In *The Woman in the Window*, the waking nightmare has to do with the killer's panicked flight to avoid his destiny. The longing McPherson suffers is for an image: he's fallen for Laura before he meets her, as his investigation takes him into the "picture" of her life, the day-to-day details of it adumbrated by others in her circle. In its material form, his desire leads to him solving the case. Along the way, Andrews has to exhibit a disquiet in each of his scenes; his moods are meant to complement Laura's magnetism.

This dramatic arrangement is why the film can't work as film noir—that is to say, why it can't locate its element of danger. Laura is lovely to watch, and herein lies its strength. But its fascination is how it can't shuck a devotion to wealth and power that belong to New York. Preceding *Laura*, *The Maltese Falcon* (1941), given this film's parameters, is free of such struggle; John Huston, its director, must have had an easier time of it. Was *Laura*, based on a 1943 novel by Very Caspary, intended to distinguish itself apart from the whole Hammett-Chandler tradition? Who is powerful, wealthy, refined in the earlier film? That would be Sidney Greenstreet's jaded Kasper Gutman (bathetically referred to as "the fat man" out of his earshot). He is exotic. And he is dangerous—more so than he may first appear. (His frown, when someone says something he doesn't like, tells us how scary he can be.)

He wields power without lifting a pinky. Gutman *is* powerful. He emerges unscathed from the tangle of vipers he's playing off each other. The members of this demimonde are harassed by the police at every turn. As the hard-nosed cops close in, Gutman leaves the rest of them to pick up the pieces. He dons his hat, politely says goodbye, and departs on his own terms—without the falcon he so desires. In this world of people beset by their circumstances, however, he can afford to be an optimist. Even so, Gutman could never gain acceptance into the Manhattan soirees of *Laura's* world. He's an interloper, though of a different order than that of the later film's McPherson. Neither will ever quit.

Gutman looks to another day when he *will* get his hands on that statuette. In the earlier film, the image, which is necessary to the double entendre, is this figure of a falcon —a likeness of something that causes a turnabout, when it's revealed that the sculpture the crooks are after is not the genuine article (this the cue for Gutman's exit). The one thing Gutman can't avoid is having to consort with down-and-out, desperate crazies. The private eye Sam Spade is the outlier, who's not crazy and who manages to hold on to his dignity—yet Spade, too, really, is just as down and out. This is a state of affairs that's signal in American film noir.

What else is important is that the story takes place in San Francisco, the west coast, the limit of the American migration. The people in *The Maltese Falcon* have failed—the Americans have, while the foreigners (Gutman and Joel Cairo—even the name is a give-away) represent another kind of hard luck, and in their peculiar way their craziness is the most disturbing. But the others, including the cops and Spade's diligent secretary—all of them have come up empty in some other kind of venture, that being their quest for the American Dream. Film Noir—American Film Noir, which, to my mind, is film noir's greatest cinematic burgeoning—belongs in California, is inherent there. The characters in *Laura*, which is set in New York, are dry, witty and delightful. But there's no tragic element to any of their witticisms. There's nothing *really* funny in any of these people.

In *The Maltese Falcon*, there's comedy. Nevertheless, the world inhabited by this film's characters is inherently tragic. The film pivots in Spade's apartment when the two plainclothes cops show up unexpectedly. They try to face Spade down in his doorway. It's the middle of the night. Lieutenant Dundy, a big guy, is acting especially overbearing—because that's who he is and because that's how he gets his way. (He's not the suave, sensitive McPherson of *Laura*.) The cops don't have a warrant. They want to get inside, knowing perfectly well that what's going on in there isn't kosher. The scene is, actually, hilarious:

Spade (Humphrey Bogart): "You guys pick swell hours to do your visiting in. What now?"

Lieutenant Dundy (Barton MacLane): "We want to talk to you."

Spade: "Go ahead and talk."

Sergeant Polhaus (Ward Bond), whining: "Do we have to do it out in the hall?"

Spade: "You can't come in."

Polhaus: "Come off it now, Sam."

Spade: "You aren't tryin' to strongarm me, are you?"

Polhaus: "Why don't you be reasonable?"

Dundy: "It would pay you to play along with us. You got away with this and that, but you can't keep it up forever."

Spade: "Stop me when you can."

Dundy: "That's what I intend to do."

Spade: "Haven't you anything better to do than pop in here early every morning asking fool questions?"

Dundy: "And gettin' a lot of lyin' answers."

Spade: "Take it easy."

Dundy: "If you say there's nothin' between you and Archer's wife, you're a liar." (Archer was Spade's recently murdered partner.)

Spade: "Is that the hot tip that brought you up here at this ungodly hour?"

Dundy: "That's one of 'em."

A commotion ensues inside the apartment—a spat between Cairo (Peter Lorre) and the *femme fatale* Brigid O'Shaughnessy (Mary Astor). To say they don't get along is for sure an understatement. (Unlike in *Laura*, in this film no one gets along with anyone.) The cops rush in.

More fruitless Q&A follows. Dundy grows increasingly impatient, finally is fed up. He decides to arrest them all:

Dundy: "Get your hats."

Spade: "Well, boys and girls, we put it over nicely!"

Dundy: "Go on, get your hats!"

Spade: Don't you know when you're bein' kidded?

Dundy: "No, but that can wait till we get to the Hall."

Spade: "Wake up, Dundy, you're being kidded! When I heard the buzzer, I said: There's the police again. They're getting to be a nuisance! When you hear them, scream. Then we'll see how far we can string 'em till they tumble."

Polhaus: "Stop it, Sam!"

But Spade won't let go. And Dundy's now really worked up a head of steam—he socks Spade in the jaw. Spade's smile totally vanishes; the look on his face says plenty, as he screws up his body to hit back.

Polhaus: "No, Sam! No!"

Spade (in a half growl, loudly): "Then get him out of here!"

Dundy, perfunctorily, thwarted: "Get their names and addresses."

This scene is perfectly paced. It's taut; the actors are nearly ahead of their lines. It's wonderful. And in a way the scene is all about how everyone's busy trying to put on everyone else.

On a subliminal level, everyone in this film feels out of place, uncomfortable where they are. They're living in what I'll call a wrong world. In such a world, people don't really make choices. Here, too, we can compare them with the deracinated characters in *Laura*. Yes, there may have been some wrong-doing in that film, but its characters seem not only aloof. They're nice as well. (The exception is Andrews' McPherson, who seems to be trying in whatever way not to be duped.)

For example, there's no homicidal, mad, monotonal "gunsel." (He seems not to have a name in *The Maltese Falcon*, until Gutman refers to him in the third person as Wilmer, when offering to throw him to the cops as the fall guy for the murder that's the film's *MacGuffin*, as Hitchcock would say.) Yet this is not a matter of warding off depravity. The world of *Laura* is crowded with the genteel of a higher society (again, the exception is McPherson, who realizes he's trespassing). Nothing is really wrong in their world—whereas the people in *The Maltese Falcon* are, essentially, responding to a wrongness that plays itself out in a number of ways.

A few years ago, my wife and I were living in Prague. I'd be up late at night while she slept. (She was teaching at the University of Pardubice, so she'd turn in early to make a long commute to her morning class.) We'd rented a highrise apartment in a hip, artsy neighborhood away from the incessant flood of tourists to Prague's "Old Town," in this most beautiful of cities. Not thinking what I was doing, I started watching old black-and-white crime movies. The city's lights, through the apartment's picture windows, were the perfect backdrop. One evening, I left off my film before I'd finished it, went to my desk, and started to compose a metrically complicated, long poem I titled "Film Noir."

Only after returning to America, my poem completed, did I start to consider why I must have written it. What about film noir sustained me in my life there—in an endlessly fascinating society? Everyone was reeling from their recent, tragic past—the Czechs having staggered out of a totalitarian darkness, in which they'd suffered mightily (to say nothing of preceding centuries when they were subjects in the Austro-Hungarian Empire). They're a people whose history goes back to the founding of Prague Castle in 870 CE. The castle is a great presence. Now the people of Prague are trying to find a way in their hyper-capitalist, edgy city. Hence, the question of poetry—of art—had to arise in my poem. I was creating it while living in this gorgeous metropolis whose architecture and art stop you in your tracks. My experience there became the lens through which I was seeing more than just the Bohemian world.

The wrongness of the world is healed by poetry. Yet poetry transcends it. Like defying gravity, poetry will always be ignorant of it—because of this, it will never be pulled down into it. What the characters in *The Maltese Falcon* lack is the salvation of art, of poetry. Likewise, in my narrative poem (based on the plot of *The Woman in the Window*), a professor who teaches poetry is set loose in the big city, and lured into committing an unintentional homicide. The world is far from perfect. He works at a leafy college to the north, where he reads Keats's "Ode to Autumn" to his students. This is a poem of sublime beauty. And it's a poem about sublime beauty. It is, let's say, a perfect poem.

Keats comes along in 1820 to insist that such perfection is possible. The world of "Ode to Autumn" is a *locus amoenus* (literally, a "pleasing place"—in medieval literature often depicted as a garden). The world that becomes the subject and substance of film noir, however, is the world of the fallen, of exiles from the Garden of Eden. Different from Milton's *Paradise Lost*, in "Ode to Autumn" there's no *felix culpa* ("fortunate fall" in which, only *because* of suffering through sin, one comes to the salvation of Christ). The people of film noir are doomed forever. As such, they exist without the possibility of true repose. In Keats's poem, though, the harvest has been brought in. It's a time of satisfaction, plenitude, beauty, rest. In the fallen world, people are perennially restless.

The thing is, they may not be fully conscious of this. When you're in the world of *film noir*, you're sleepwalking your way through life. That's the existential situation, arguably, for us all. Or rather, the promise of film noir is that it wants to tell us this. But there's something else about film noir, certainly as the genre emerged in America: American film noir is aware of itself. Such a film—and this enhances its *frisson*, making the film so very compelling in a campy way—subtly breaks the fourth wall. I don't mean a character starts to address us, such as Woody Allen plays up through the Jeff Daniels character in *The Purple Rose of Cairo* (1985), who first just starts talking to the Mia Farrow character in the audience. She's watching the film in the darkness. She acknowledges him. He sees her, so he steps off the screen, having found his opportunity. The two of them run off for a fantastical adventure.

In *The Maltese Falcon*, Spade, who has a perverse compulsion to needle Dundy, asks him the question: "Don't you know when you're bein' kidded?" That's the wink. That's the film acknowledging our watching of it. And *that's* film noir, or at least American film noir. That's the script writer, director, and actors subtly sharing their giddy fun with you. So are we, the audience, being kidded? Yes, we're watching the movie and we're in the movie. The darker the life in the movie—in which, when you get right down to it, that is to say when the hammer of criminal justice comes down on its steel stamp to impose a permanent imprint (like at the end of the fifties police procedural *Dragnet*)—the more of a romp the noir film is. I watched *Dragnet* on TV every week as a boy—a black-and-white, LA, half-hour of drollery. (There's a world of crime out there, and Sgt Joe Friday keeps the lid on it.) It was all in the way Friday, played by Jack Webb, delivered his lines—in monotone. Just so, in monochrome, homicide is simple. Thus my poem's concluding lines:

> Homicide is simple, people simple — poetry
> not so simple, as it bestows a story we need
> in which no one's in trouble — like in a movie when
> the world's good and it makes sense, but then it all
>   goes wrong.

It's all *too* simple, in fact. It's the same damn tawdry story each damn week. But what will this cop do when he retires? Go fishing? Gimme a break! People—fallible, imperfect people (always the plot's attraction)—are simple in that they're predictable. They get into trouble.

German Expressionist films of the 1930s were sincere— the darkness was *really* dark. But, if anything is meant to be a romp, it's American Film Noir. The poet Charles Borkhuis declaims, "darkness is never dark enough." Why is that? In film noir there's an inherent paradox. German Expressionism was *eerie* and *tragic*. Not so American film noir. In France, after the Second World War, Jean-Pierre Melville's films constitute a significant chapter in "dark" cinema. An important French precursor to his work was *Touchez pas au grisbi* ("Don't Touch the Loot"), directed by Jacques Becker as an aging Parisian gangster, which was released in 1954. It's impeccably paced and suave in a way no American film, even Laura, can ever achieve. It was a big influence on Melville.

Melville's towering achievement, *Army of Shadows* (1969), his one film without gangsters, is not meant to be a homage to noir nor does it follow the noir playbook—although it's a very dark film, while it relates the story of heroic figures in the French underground (Melville was one of them). His earlier noir films look ahead to Dassin, Truffaut, Chabrol and others. And yet a near-contemporary of *Army of Shadows* is meant to be, and for sure is, a classic noir masterpiece. *Le Samourai* (1967), which introduced Alain Delon, is completely indebted to American forties film noir (as were other films Melville made). Then again, the Delon protagonist elicits a bit too much sympathy and is purely sexy, thus without the flaws we see in someone like Bogart or Robert Mitchum, who are sexy after all, while an actor like Edward G. Robinson (the protagonist in the film my poem is based on) is not. Delon is pretty.

The Woman in the Window (which I mined for most of the plot in my poem) features a deadly back-stabbing that was an accident (yeah, right). That scene is funny. The beautiful woman (Joan Bennett) stands over her newly dead boyfriend and tells his killer (Robinson), the professor for whom the entire universe has suddenly been turned inside out, "he was never much of a lover." Her remark unavoidably reveals a weariness. Shit happens.

"Tired anyway," I write, "I turn off the movie." The film's dark seriousness, like my poem, is meant to be darkly humorous. Yet it's *sympatico*. The killer in the film, too, grows more weary in his flight from justice. It's out of ennui, the humdrum nature of his life, that he stopped at that storefront on his way from dinner to his hotel, meaning consciously to head there, yet unconsciously—what? To escape, he gazes through the plate glass window at the image of the woman in a framed painting (*framed*—get it?), and falls in love with the painting and the woman inside the frame. Only then does her voice emanate from the adjacent, shadowy alley. Later, in her apartment, where the two were having drinks, the dead man lying at her feet, she confides in him —in her delicious, subtly incongruous, and perfectly timed way. Her comment, within the plot, is now irrelevant.

So, why is poetry not so simple? I based my poem on that 1944 film classic, but Keats's "Ode to Autumn" is not part of the film's plot. The poem contrasts to the film and to film noir as a genre. Destiny, for the people in the fallen world of film noir, may not be pretty—what we should not forget, though, is that the plot and all else in American film noir is tongue-in-cheek. In watching it, our subliminal awareness of it—for the most part not our consciousness of it—senses the fact that it's film, a fiction. Film noir is funny —the most droll form of comedy but, yes, it's comedy. American film noir, to be sure, from within our subconscious, tells us to lighten up.

Even *The Postman Always Rings Twice* (1946)—how sinister can you get?—winks at its viewers. We're in the audience, in the dark. If John Garfield and Lana Turner had really cut up, had really bloodied her husband Cecil

Kellaway, the older actor playing the *senex amans* (the "loving old man"—this medieval trope required that the young woman be kept within a walled garden) who is the film's sap of a besotted husband, then the spell would have been broken. The 1981 remake of the film, with Jessica Lange and Jack Nicholson, missed the point. It mistakenly gravitated toward hot sex, which was now allowed by the censors, right after the murder. But we all know these lovers in the earlier film will get caught, and that's not because we've accommodated ourselves to the Hollywood censorship of that earlier period.

Is it ourselves who yearn to be bad, not without real consequences? Film noir is an exquisite confection that nevertheless resonates modern life. What's obvious are the burdened lives of the film's characters. What's complicated is the way the plot twists and turns, twists and turns *them*, as we watch. Are we voyeurs, then? I don't think so. Indeed, we're in sympathy with the film as a production—one in which people's fallibility is on display—yet we're really not in sympathy with such people. Rather, we're enjoying the tale. It's not *schadenfreude*. It's something more like what I imagine the Elizabethan audience came to the Globe theatre to see. The spectacle of tragedy is gorgeous in how inevitably the story leads to the fall, and ironically so. Sophisticated Londoners knew full well that, after the sword fight, the actors would get up to take their bows. We want to be strung along, like Spade and O'Shaughnessy and the other crooks string along the detectives. And we want to be bad. But we don't want to face the consequences of that.

At the end of *The Maltese Falcon*, Sergeant Polhaus picks up the fake statuette of the bird—it's fake, and it's been the cause of double dealing as well as murder. "It's heavy," he remarks, in his utter banality. "What is it?" Flatly, Spade says to him after a brief yet 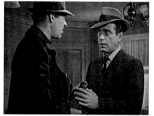 contemplative pause, "It's the stuff dreams are made of." *Exeunt.*

In the perfectly foggy, misty, San Francisco night, *The Maltese Falcon* constantly asks us to think and rethink about who the good guys are. The beautiful Brigid O'Shaughnessy is finally, unequivocally, revealed as the viper *par excellence*. She will take the fall for the rest of them, but not willingly. "I've no earthly reason to think I can trust you," Spade tells her. "If I do this and get away with it, you'll have something on me that you can use whenever you want to. Since I've got something on you I couldn't be sure that you wouldn't put a hole in me someday. . . . All we've got is that maybe you love me and maybe I love you." (This is a scene, a plot, I imagine, Melville adored.) "You know whether you love me or not," O'Shaughnessy says. And Spade answers, "Maybe I do. I'll have some rotten nights after I've sent you over, but that'll pass. If all I've said doesn't mean anything to you then forget it and we'll make it just this: I won't, because all of me wants to regardless of consequences and because you've counted on it the same as you counted on it with all the others." Maybe.

Brigid O'Shaughnessy is the *femme fatale* in my poem —that is to say, in that 1944 Edward G. Robinson vehicle, *The Woman in the Window.* She's Joan Bennett, the woman in the painting, who lures the professor to her apartment, the woman who, as it happens, has left her scissors lying beside her sewing box where Robinson, 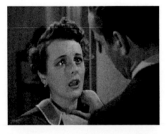 in his tenacious struggle with her boyfriend who's found them out, can take hold of it to stab him in the back. Will she get away with it? Did she plan it? In *The Maltese Falcon* I don't think she does, at least as far as I know.

Spade: "If you get a good break, you'll be out of Tehachapi in twenty years and you can come back to me then. I hope they don't hang you, precious, by that sweet neck."

O'Shaughnessy: "You're not. . . ."

Spade: "Yes, angel, I'm gonna send you over. The chances are you'll get off with life. If you're a good girl, you'll be out in twenty years. I'll be waiting for you. If they hang you, I'll always remember you."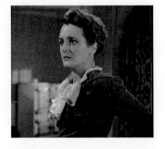

By the time Susan Hayward gives her bravura, haunting performance in *I Want to Live* (1958), recounting the actual arrest of Barbara Graham and ultimately her execution in California's gas chamber—a black-and-white film when color was *de rigeur*, the film's texture honoring its subject—film noir has essentially become passé. Subsequent noir movies will just be an invitation to indulge in nostalgia, maybe to think about how the earlier, truly noir, noir film was the real thing.

And yet it was never *real!* Rather, it's that sly, ephemeral wink at the audience, which a viewer might detect in America's classic noir cinema. Weary, sleepy, I turned off *The Woman in the Window* and went to bed, that night in Prague. Did I know what would happen, in the movie's plot? Well, yes, in a way I did.

The restless world continues on. I think of George Oppen's poem, "The Little Hole":

> The little hole in the eye
> Williams called it, the little hole
>
> Has exposed us naked
> To the world
>
> And will not close.
>
> Blankly the world
> Looks in

And we compose
Colors

And the sense

Of home
And there are those

In it so violent
And so alone

They cannot rest.

About the Author

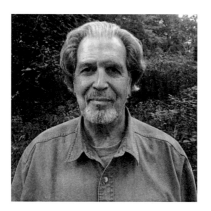

BURT KIMMELMAN is a distinguished professor of Humanities at New Jersey Institute of Technology. He has published ten collections of poetry, seven volumes of criticism, and more than a hundred articles mostly on literature, some on architecture, art, as well as memoir. He lives in New Jersey with his wife, the writer Diane Simmons.

Author photograph by Jane Kimmelman

411

Other books by Bur t Kimmelman
published by Dos Madres Press

There Ar e Words (2007)
The Way We Live (2011)
Wings Ap art (2019)

He is also included in:
Realms of the Mothers:
The First Decade of Dos Madres Press - 2016

For the full Dos Madres Press cat alog:
www.dosmadres.com